365 Ways to Wok

Other books in this series are:

365 Ways to Wok

Linda Drachman

A JOHN BOSWELL ASSOCIATES BOOK

HarperCollins*Publishers*

Dear Reader:

We welcome your recommendations for future 365 Ways books. Send your suggestions and a recipe, if you'd like, to Cookbook Editor, HarperCollins Publishers, 10 East 53rd Street, New York, NY 10022. If we choose your title suggestion or your recipe we will acknowledge you in the book and send you a free copy.

Thank you for your support.

Sincerely yours,
The Editor

Series Editor: Susan Wyler
Design: Nigel Rollings
Index: Maro Riofrancos

LIBRARY OF CONGRESS CATALOG CARD NUMBER 92-53371

ISBN 0-06-016643-6

93 94 95 96 97 HC 10 9 8 7 6 5 4 3

Contents

1   **Wok Appetizers, Snacks, and Starters**   5

The wok makes it easy to simmer, sauté, and fry up a savory assortment of appetizers and snacks. Let Hot 'n' Snappy Chicken Wings, Meatballs in Molasses Lime Sauce, and Almond Chicken Nuggets with Honey Mustard Dipping Sauce lead off your next party.

2   **One-Wok Soups and Chowders**   19

It's big and it's round, and it makes a great soup pot. From the wok come savory spoonables like Every Bean Imaginable Bean Soup, Zucchini Tomato Soup with Corn and Basil, Creamy Cod Chowder, and Spinach Tortellini Soup. You'll find all the recipes you need to start a dinner or provide a meal in a bowl.

3   **Stir-Frying American Style**   39

Stir-frying makes all kinds of cooking quick and easy. Here is a collection of American flavors tossed up in a flash. Shrimp Drenched in Buttered Bread Crumbs, Pork in Chunky Chile Tomato Sauce, and Garlicky Salsa Chicken are just a few of the offerings.

4   **Chinese Stir-Fry Classics**   61

You'll throw away your take-out menus when you see what you can whip up in your wok. Tasty recipes like Sticky Spareribs with Black Beans, Chinese Pepper Steak, Stir-Fried Chicken with Broccoli and Peanuts, and Stir-Fried Shrimp with Water Chestnuts and Peas will send you running for your chopsticks.

5   **Wokking Around the Mediterranean**   83

Many French, Italian, and Middle Eastern dishes lend themselves beautifully to the convenience of wok cookery. Find out how versatile your wok is with Spiced Chicken Marrakesh, Cheesy Chicken Marinara, Veal Scaloppine with Mushrooms and White Wine, Pork Loin Normandy Style, with Apples and Prunes in Apple Cider, and Shrimp Scampi.

6   **Wokking to Applause**   103

Show off with one-pot wok spectaculars such as Fresh Tuna with Artichokes and Mushrooms in Madeira Cream Sauce, Chicken Paillards with Port Wine Sauce, Chicken with Raspberry Glaze, Veal and Macadamia Nuts in Pineapple-Lime Sauce, even Sauerbraten.

Introduction

The wok is one of the oldest cooking utensils known to man. In chinese the word *wok* means "pot," and certainly, the wok has served as the basic kitchen tool in such diverse countries as China, India, Japan, Thailand, the Philippines, and Indonesia. In fact, it is so functional and versatile that once you start using it regularly, you may never go back to your everyday pots and pans.

Cooking in a wok is a timesaver. Less effort and energy are expended. Cost is another factor. A wok is inexpensive to purchase, and as you will see in *365 Ways to Wok*, it literally replaces almost all your other pots and pans.

The best woks—in the sense of most practical though they are the least expensive—are made of spun steel, which is a very good conductor of heat and responds rapidly to temperature changes. Many people mistake this for iron, but while it has the weight and heat-conducting properties associated with iron, it is less brittle and will not react with acidic foods or wine when you cook. While they are slightly less practical for all-purpose cooking, stainless steel woks, carbon steel woks, aluminum woks, iron woks, woks with nonstick finishes, and electric woks are also available.

Because of its wide sloping sides, the wok has more surface area than a standard, flat-bottomed frying pan or skillet. The entire wok can be heated to very high temperatures, and that is one of its greatest assets. Stir-frying, which means cooking food over high heat while moving it around constantly, seals in flavor and preserves textures—and it is just about the fastest method of cooking there is.

Most woks have round bottoms, which also facilitate stir-frying. They are usually sold with rings to help them balance on the burner. If you are cooking on an electric stove, though, you may find a flat-bottomed wok more suitable. You will want as large a wok as possible, and a 14-inch diameter is the most practical size for home cooking. It is also the perfect size in which to prepare a meal for four to six people. Just to be sure, it's a good idea to measure the diameter of your largest burner before going to the store to buy the wok and ring.

While the wok is the best possible pot for stir-frying, it is also excellent for sautéing, steaming, stewing, poaching, and braising. You can boil in it, fry in it, even "bake" in it. *365 Ways to Wok* features recipes that use the wok for every possible kind of dish.

To use your wok to its fullest, a few inexpensive accessories are highly recommended:

DOMED LID—This fits right over the wok like a cover, but it has raised sides, which allows plenty of room for steaming and ensures that the lid will not touch the food.

STIR-FRY SPATULA—Flat with shallow sides, like a child's shovel, this spatula-spoon is ideal for stirring and tossing food continuously while stir-frying. It is usually made of iron or stainless steel. Look for one with a wooden or bamboo handle to prevent burning your hands.

STRAINER—A round, flat wire or net mesh, sometimes called a skimmer. This facilitates removing poached or fried foods from their liquid cooking medium. Again, a wooden or bamboo handle is recommended.

RACK—For steaming, you will need a round wire or bamboo rack that will fit inside the wok. I also found it quite useful for a number of "baked" recipes, such as Chile Cheese and Corn Custards, Carrot Cake, and Vanilla and Chocolate Custards. It is not necessary to purchase a separate bamboo steamer for any of the recipes in *365 Ways to Wok.*

Before you use your new wok, it should be thoroughly cleaned with soap, hot water, and a nonabrasive scouring pad to remove the sticky store film. After this initial cleaning, it is recommended that you rinse the wok out with hot water and a bamboo brush or sponge to remove any food residue left after cooking. Dry thoroughly before putting the wok away.

Your wok must be oiled or "seasoned" before cooking for the first time, to prevent food from sticking. Here's how to do it. Wipe the inside with a light coating of flavorless vegetable oil. Set the wok over low heat and heat until it is very hot but not smoking. Turn off the heat and let the wok cool. Wipe out any excess oil with a paper towel. Repeat the procedure until the inside surface feels smooth. Now you are ready to cook.

Anything that you can cook stovetop can be successfully prepared in your wok—anything! When I stopped thinking of my wok as an Asian stir-fryer and steamer exclusively, and visualized it instead as a large saucepan and skillet, I realized that the possibilities were limitless. The wok could literally be used to cook everything, and it became quite a creative endeavor to see what would be next.

Wok-Steamed Turkey, Stuffed Rolled Flank Steak, Jelly Donuts, and the incredibly popular (with my family) Cocoa Fudge Pudding Cake were some of the recipes that inspired an "I don't believe you made this in a wok!" (as stated by any number of surprised dinner guests, who discovered that the entire dinner was wok-made, and they were guinea pigs).

365 Ways to Wok covers the techniques of stir-frying, sautéing, pan-frying, steaming, stewing, poaching, braising, and "baking." It features recipes from all over the world, including America, China, Italy, and the Middle East. It runs the gamut from appetizers to desserts. Some of the recipes are traditional; others are innovative adaptations or new creations.

Almost all of the ingredients in 365 Ways to Wok are found in supermarkets. Some of the recipes call for ingredients that are acidic, such as tomatoes, and for wine. Using the seasoned iron wok did not produce any problems in the resulting dishes, as reactive pans sometimes do, and the "seasoned" finish of the wok remained intact.

I'd like the wok to become as essential and natural to your style and method of cooking as your old familiar frying pan, pasta pot, soup kettle, and saucepan. I hope you reach for it naturally next time you are ready to cook. For that reason, and for ease in storage, I have my woks hanging above the stove on secure hooks where I can easily see and reach them. Finally, I want you to have fun using your wok, the way I do with mine. Hopefully, these recipes will show you how.

Chapter 1

Wok Appetizers, Snacks, and Starters

Appetizers are the tease, the little tidbits that whet your appetite for what is to come. In many parts of the country, hors d'oeuvres and dessert buffets have become an alternative to traditional menus. Smaller portions are welcome in these days of lighter eating, and it is so much fun to sample a number of different dishes. So choose one of the tempting starters in this chapter to snack on, or make a menu out of several.

I've designed the recipes that follow to be easy on the cook. Many of the appetizers and snacks can be assembled in advance, frozen until the day they will be served, and then cooked or just reheated before being served.

There are a number of fried dishes in this section, but give them a chance; they are much lighter than you'd think. The wide surface area of the wok makes frying simple and less messy. Some of the possibilities are Baby Brie in Puff Pastry, Spinach and Roquefort Turnovers, Fried Mozzarella Sticks, and Easy Mini Reuben Appetizers. Heat the required amount of oil to 350°F. Carefully lower the food into the wok. The generous surface area allows several items to cook at once without crowding and lowering the oil temperature. Fried foods emerge golden brown and crispy on the outside and moist inside—and less greasy. Remove with a strainer or slotted spoon and drain well on several thicknesses of paper towels to remove as much excess oil as possible before serving.

Two to two and a half cups of oil is generally sufficient, and often it can be reused. If the oil is not burned and has not picked up an odor from the food cooked in it, let it cool completely; then strain through a double layer of cheesecloth into a clean jar with a lid.

Using the wok as a saucepan offers many other appetizing possibilities. You can cook up batches of assorted meatballs in a flash—Sweet and Sour Meatballs, Salsa Meatballs, Turkish Meatballs, and Swedish Meatballs are fabulous. It's a good idea to prepare enough for two meals or parties and stash them in containers in the freezer. Then just take them out the day you'll be needing them, thaw and reheat.

1 SHRIMP BOILED IN BEER WITH COCKTAIL SAUCE

Prep: 20 minutes   Cook: 3 minutes   Serves: 4

For extra flavor and juiciness, these shrimp are not shelled until after they're cooked, so be sure to serve with plenty of napkins. This recipe doubles easily. For a crowd, double the beer mixture and cook the shrimp in batches, removing them with a skimmer as they are done.

1 12-ounce bottle beer
2 bay leaves
1 teaspoon whole black peppercorns
1 pound medium shrimp
⅔ cup ketchup
¼ cup prepared white horseradish

Juice of 1 lemon
Few drops of hot pepper sauce
Few drops of Worcestershire sauce

1. In a wok, combine beer, bay leaves, peppercorns, and 1½ cups water. Bring to a boil. Add shrimp. Return liquid to a boil, reduce heat to medium, and cook until shrimp are pink, about 3 minutes; drain. As soon as shrimp are cool enough to handle, shell and devein. Refrigerate until ready to serve.

2. Meanwhile, prepare cocktail sauce. In a medium bowl, combine ketchup, horseradish, lemon juice, hot pepper sauce, and Worcestershire sauce. Whisk to blend well. Arrange shrimp on a platter with cocktail sauce for dipping.

2 ALMOND CHICKEN NUGGETS WITH HONEY MUSTARD DIPPING SAUCE

Prep: 15 minutes   Marinate: 1 hour   Cook: 15 to 20 minutes
Serves: 4 to 6

2 tablespoons vegetable oil
2 tablespoons lemon juice
2 tablespoons soy sauce
1½ pounds skinless, boneless chicken breasts, cut into 1-inch cubes
1 cup finely ground almonds

1 (1¼-ounce) package Oriental Seasoning mix
¼ cup honey mustard
2 tablespoons honey
2 tablespoons orange juice
Peanut oil, for frying

1. In a shallow dish, mix together vegetable oil, lemon juice, and soy sauce. Add chicken and toss to coat. Marinate 1 hour, stirring occasionally.

2. Place ground nuts and seasoning mix in a plastic bag. Remove chicken from marinade. Add several pieces at a time to bag and shake to coat well. Remove to a plate.

3. In a small bowl, combine mustard, honey, and orange juice. Stir to blend well. Set dipping sauce aside.

4. In a wok, heat 2 inches peanut oil over medium-high heat until temperature measures 350°F on a deep-frying thermometer. Add coated chicken and fry in batches, turning, until crisp and golden outside and cooked through, about 5 minutes. Remove with slotted spoon or skimmer and drain on paper towels. As chicken is cooked, place on a baking sheet in a preheated 300°F oven to keep warm. Serve on toothpicks with dipping sauce on the side.

3 SALMON, ASPARAGUS, AND POTATO FRITTATA

Prep: 10 minutes   Cook: 11 to 15 minutes   Serves: 4 to 6

Frittatas are usually started on top of the stove and finished under the broiler, where the cheese melts evenly and the top emerges puffed and golden. You can accomplish these same results using your wok, without heating up the oven. This recipe can serve two as a main course.

5 eggs
½ teaspoon salt
¼ teaspoon pepper
3 tablespoons vegetable oil
¼ pound fresh asparagus, cut diagonally into ½-inch slices

3 scallions, chopped
1 medium potato, cooked, peeled, and thinly sliced
1 (7½-ounce) can sockeye salmon, bones removed, drained, and flaked
½ cup grated Jarlsberg cheese

1. In a medium bowl, beat eggs with salt and pepper until blended. Set aside.

2. In a wok, heat oil over medium-high heat until hot, swirling to coat sides of pan. Add asparagus and scallions and cook, stirring, until crisp-tender, 3 to 4 minutes. Add potato and cook, turning, until browned, 4 to 6 minutes. Add salmon and cook, stirring gently, 1 minute.

3. Add beaten eggs. Cook, lifting up edges of frittata and tilting wok to allow uncooked portion of eggs to run under, 2 to 3 minutes. Reduce heat to low.

4. Sprinkle cheese over eggs. Cook, covered, until cheese melts and frittata is puffed, 1 to 2 minutes.

4   HOT 'N' SNAPPY CHICKEN WINGS

Prep: 5 minutes   Marinate: 1 hour   Cook: 26 to 28 minutes
Serves: 4

3 tablespoons vegetable oil
2 tablespoons balsamic
   vinegar
3 garlic cloves, crushed
2 teaspoons ground cumin
1 teaspoon paprika
1 teaspoon chili powder

¼ teaspoon crushed hot red
   pepper
2 pounds chicken wings, tips
   discarded
½ cup chicken broth
¼ cup vodka

1. In a large bowl, combine 1 tablespoon oil with balsamic vinegar, garlic, cumin, paprika, chili powder, and hot pepper. Mix well. Add chicken wings and toss to coat. Marinate at room temperature for 1 hour. Remove chicken; reserve marinade.

2. In a wok, heat remaining 2 tablespoons oil over medium-high heat until hot, swirling to coat sides of pan. Add chicken wings extending up sides of pan in one layer, and cook, turning, until browned all over, 6 to 8 minutes. Pour off fat.

3. Add reserved marinade, chicken broth, and vodka. Reduce heat to medium-low, cover, and cook until wings are tender, about 20 minutes.

5   POTATO-SCALLION SILVER DOLLARS

Prep: 10 minutes   Cook: 15 to 18 minutes   Serves: 4 to 6

2 tablespoons butter
4 scallions, chopped
½ small red bell pepper,
   minced
2 garlic cloves, minced
2 pounds russet potatoes
   (about 6), boiled and
   mashed

3 eggs, beaten
¼ cup sour cream
¾ teaspoon salt
½ teaspoon dried rosemary
¼ teaspoon pepper
   About ½ cup vegetable oil

1. In a wok, melt butter over medium heat. Add scallions, bell pepper, and garlic and cook, stirring, until soft, 3 to 5 minutes. Remove to a large bowl and let cool slightly. (Wipe out wok but do not rinse.)

2. Add mashed potatoes, eggs, sour cream, salt, rosemary, and pepper to scallion mixture. Blend well.

3. In wok, heat 3 tablespoons oil over medium-high heat until hot, swirling to coat sides of pan. Drop in about one-third of mixture by tablespoons. Fry until golden on bottom, 3 to 4 minutes. Turn and cook until brown on other side, 1 to 2 minutes. Remove from wok and drain on paper towels. Repeat procedure 2 times with remaining potato mixture and more oil as needed.

6 MEATBALLS IN MOLASSES LIME SAUCE

Prep: 15 minutes   Cook: 1 hour   Serves: 6

3 tablespoons vegetable oil
4 scallions, finely chopped
2 celery ribs, chopped
1 large onion, chopped
1 (28-ounce) can tomato puree
¼ cup blackstrap molasses
3 tablespoons fresh lime juice
1 teaspoon grated lime zest

¼ cup raisins
1½ pounds ground chuck
   (80% lean)
1 egg, beaten
⅓ cup dry bread crumbs
½ teaspoon cumin
½ teaspoon salt
¼ teaspoon pepper

1. In a wok, heat 1 tablespoon oil over medium-high heat until hot, swirling to coat sides of pan. Add scallions and cook, stirring, until soft, 3 to 4 minutes. Remove to a large bowl and let cool.

2. In same wok, heat remaining 2 tablespoons oil over medium-high heat until hot. Add celery and onion and cook, stirring, until softened, 3 to 5 minutes. Add tomato puree, molasses, lime juice, lime zest, and raisins. Cover and cook 10 minutes.

3. Meanwhile, add ground chuck, egg, bread crumbs, cumin, salt, and pepper to cooked scallions in bowl. Mix thoroughly, preferably with your hands, to blend well. Shape into balls 1 inch in diameter.

4. Add meatballs to sauce in wok. Reduce heat to low. Cover and cook 45 minutes.

7 SALSA MEATBALLS

Prep: 10 minutes   Cook: 48 to 49 minutes   Serves: 6

2 tablespoons olive oil
1 medium green bell pepper,
   chopped
1 medium onion, chopped
1 garlic clove, minced
1½ pounds ground chuck
   (80% lean)
½ cup dry bread crumbs

½ cup tomato juice
½ teaspoon salt
¼ teaspoon pepper
1 (12-ounce) bottle mild thick
   and chunky salsa
1 (7-ounce) bottle beer
2 teaspoons Worcestershire
   sauce

1. In a wok, heat olive oil over high heat until hot, swirling to coat sides of pan. Add bell pepper, onion, and garlic and cook, stirring, until softened, 3 to 4 minutes.

2. Meanwhile, in a large bowl, combine ground chuck, bread crumbs, tomato juice, salt, and pepper. Mix until well blended. Shape into 1-inch balls.

3. Add salsa, beer, and Worcestershire sauce to wok. Bring to a boil, then reduce to a simmer. Add meatballs, cover, and cook 45 minutes.

8   SWEET AND SOUR MEATBALLS

Prep: 15 minutes   Cook: 53 to 57 minutes   Serves: 6

3 tablespoons vegetable oil
1 medium leek (white part only), finely chopped
1½ pounds ground chuck (80% lean)
½ cup dried bread crumbs
½ cup tomato sauce
¼ cup chopped parsley
1 beaten egg
1 teaspoon salt

¼ teaspoon pepper
2 medium onions, chopped
2 celery ribs, chopped
1 garlic clove, minced
1 (32-ounce) bottle ketchup
2 cups unsweetened pineapple juice
¼ cup firmly packed brown sugar

1. In a wok, heat 1 tablespoon oil over medium-high heat until hot. Add leek and cook, stirring, until softened, 5 to 7 minutes. Remove leek to a large bowl and let cool completely.

2. Add ground chuck to cooked leek along with bread crumbs, tomato sauce, parsley, egg, salt, and pepper. Mix thoroughly and shape into balls 1 inch in diameter.

3. In same wok, heat remaining 2 tablespoons oil over medium-high heat, swirling to coat sides of pan. Add onions, celery, and garlic and cook until softened, 3 to 5 minutes. Add ketchup, pineapple juice, and brown sugar and mix well. Raise heat and bring to a boil.

4. Place meatballs in sauce. Reduce heat to medium-low, cover, and cook 45 minutes.

9   SWEDISH MEATBALLS

Prep: 10 minutes   Cook: 29 to 36 minutes   Serves: 4 to 6

This is a popular party dish that doubles easily. Serve from a chafing dish with toothpicks or small plates and cocktail forks. If you can find a jar of lingonberry sauce, it makes a wonderful condiment to spoon alongside the meatballs.

6½ tablespoons butter
1 medium onion, finely chopped
¼ cup bread crumbs
½ cup heavy cream
1 pound ground chuck (80% lean)

1 tablespoon minced fresh dill or 1½ teaspoons dried
½ teaspoon salt
¼ teaspoon pepper
¼ teaspoon ground cloves
½ cup beef broth

1. In a wok, heat 2 tablespoons butter over medium heat until hot. Add onion and cook, stirring, until soft, 4 to 6 minutes. Remove to a bowl. (Wipe out wok but do not rinse.)

2. Add bread crumbs and cream to onion in bowl. Stir to mix. Add ground chuck, dill, salt, pepper, and cloves. Mix, preferably with your hands, until well blended. Shape into 1-inch balls.

3. In wok, melt 1½ tablespoons butter over medium heat until hot, swirling to coat sides of pan. Add one-third of meatballs in a single layer and cook, turning, until browned all over, 5 to 7 minutes. Remove meatballs to a plate and drain off fat. Repeat twice with remaining butter and meatballs. Remove to plate with other meatballs.

4. Pour beef broth into wok. Cook over medium-high heat, scraping up browned bits from bottom of wok, 2 minutes. Reduce heat to medium. Return meatballs to wok. Cook until heated through, 2 to 3 minutes.

---

10   TURKISH MEATBALLS
Prep: 10 minutes   Cook: 40 to 42 minutes   Serves: 4

The pairing of cumin, turmeric, and cinnamon with meat is typical of Turkish cooking. I like to serve this with a big salad and plenty of steamed rice to soak up the sauce.

1 pound ground round (85% lean)	½ teaspoon cinnamon
1 egg, beaten	½ teaspoon salt
2 slices of white bread, soaked in water and squeezed	¼ teaspoon pepper
1 medium onion, grated	½ cup flour
2 garlic cloves, crushed	2 tablespoons olive oil
½ cup chopped parsley	1 small onion, chopped
½ teaspoon ground cumin	¾ cup crushed tomatoes
½ teaspoon turmeric	2 tablespoons Asian sesame oil
	½ cup dry red wine

1. In a large bowl, combine ground round, egg, bread, onion, garlic, parsley, cumin, turmeric, cinnamon, salt, and pepper. Mix, preferably with your hands, until well blended. Shape mixture into meatballs 1½ inches in diameter.

2. Place flour in a shallow dish. Dredge meatballs, rolling to coat; shake off excess.

3. In a wok, heat olive oil over medium-high heat until hot, swirling to coat sides of pan. Add meatballs in one layer and cook, turning, until meatballs are browned all over, 5 to 7 minutes. Remove to a plate. Drain off fat from wok; wipe dry.

4. Combine chopped onion, crushed tomatoes, sesame oil, and wine in wok. Bring to a boil. Reduce heat to low. Return meatballs to wok. Cover and cook 35 minutes.

11   SPINACH AND ROQUEFORT TURNOVERS
Prep: 20 minutes   Cook: 10 to 14 minutes   Serves: 8

Even the most elegant appetizers are simple to prepare with frozen or refrigerated pastry doughs.

1 cup ricotta cheese	1 egg
½ cup crumbled roquefort or	¼ teaspoon pepper
bleu cheese	2 sheets frozen prepared puff
1 (10-ounce) package frozen	pastry (17¼-ounce
chopped spinach, thawed	package), thawed
and drained	1 egg, beaten
2 tablespoons chopped	About 2 cups vegetable oil,
pimiento	for frying

1. In a medium bowl, combine ricotta, roquefort, spinach, pimiento, egg, and pepper. Blend well.

2. On a lightly floured board, roll out 1 sheet of puff pastry to a 16-inch square. Cut into 4 (4-inch) squares. Repeat with second sheet. Brush edges with beaten egg.

3. Spoon spinach-cheese filling onto pastry squares, dividing evenly. Bring dough ends together envelope fashion on top and sides and pinch to seal, snugly enclosing filling.

4. In a wok, heat 4 inches of oil over medium-high heat until temperature reaches 350°F on a deep-frying thermometer. Fry 4 turnovers until golden brown on bottom, 3 to 4 minutes. Turn and fry until golden and crispy on second side, 2 to 3 minutes. Remove with a slotted spoon or skimmer from wok and drain on paper towels. Add oil to maintain 4-inch level, if necessary, and repeat with remaining 4 turnovers. Serve hot or at room temperature.

12   HOT AND SPICY NUTS
Prep: 5 minutes   Cook: 3 to 4 minutes   Serves: 4 to 6

2 cups shelled peanuts	½ teaspoon paprika
2 cups shelled walnuts	½ teaspoon garlic powder
¼ cup peanut oil	¼ teaspoon crushed hot red
1 teaspoon chili powder	pepper
½ teaspoon ground cumin	

1. Place peanuts and walnuts in a bowl. Toss to mix.

2. In a small bowl, combine oil, chili powder, cumin, paprika, garlic powder, and hot pepper. Whisk to blend well. Pour over nuts and toss until evenly coated.

3. Heat wok over medium heat until hot. Add coated nuts and cook, stirring, until nuts are lightly toasted and fragrant, 3 to 4 minutes.

13   CHILE CHEESE AND CORN CUSTARD
Prep: 10 minutes   Cook: 45 to 50 minutes   Serves: 4

3 eggs
¾ cup sour cream
4 tablespoons butter, melted and cooled
1 (8-ounce) can cream-style corn

1 (4-ounce) can diced green chiles
1 cup grated Monterey Jack cheese (4 ounces)
⅓ cup yellow cornmeal
½ teaspoon garlic powder

1. In a large bowl, beat eggs, sour cream, and melted butter until light and well blended. Add corn, chiles, cheese, cornmeal, and garlic powder. Spoon mixture into 4 greased 4-ounce custard cups.

2. Place a small wire cake rack in a wok. Put filled custard cups on rack. Pour enough boiling water into wok to come halfway up sides of custard cups. Simmer, covered, until custard is firm in center, 45 to 50 minutes. Serve custards in their cups warm or at room temperature.

14   BABY BRIE IN PUFF PASTRY
Prep: 20 minutes   Cook: 11 to 15 minutes   Serves: 4

This elegant first course can be assembled in advance and refrigerated several hours before frying.

3 tablespoons butter
2 medium leeks (white part only), chopped
½ teaspoon dried thyme
2 sheets frozen prepared puff pastry (17¼-ounce package), thawed

1 egg, beaten
¼ cup Dijon mustard
4 (4-ounce) mini-wheels of Brie cheese, rind removed
Vegetable oil, for frying

1. In a wok, melt butter over medium heat until hot, swirling to coat sides of pan. Add leeks and thyme and cook, stirring, until soft, 6 to 8 minutes. Remove to a plate. Rinse and dry wok.

2. On a lightly floured board, roll out 1 sheet of puff pastry to a 9 x 18-inch rectangle. Cut in half crosswise to form 2 (9-inch) squares. Repeat with second sheet. Brush edges with beaten egg.

3. Brush Dijon mustard over pastry squares leaving about ½-inch margins around edges. Spread one-quarter of leeks over each piece of pastry. Top each section with a wheel of Brie. Bring pastry ends together envelope fashion on top and sides and pinch to snugly enclose cheese.

4. In wok, heat 4 inches of oil over medium-high heat until temperature reaches 350°F on a deep-frying thermometer. Add puff pastries and fry until golden brown on bottom, 3 to 4 minutes. Turn and fry until golden and crispy on second side, 2 to 3 minutes. Remove from wok with a slotted spoon or skimmer and drain on paper towels.

15   EASY MINI-REUBEN APPETIZERS

Prep: 20 minutes   Cook: 12 to 20 minutes   Serves: 6 to 8

Here is an easy hot hors d'oeuvre version of the classic deli sandwich.

2 (8-ounce) cans refrigerated crescent rolls
½ cup Russian or Thousand Island salad dressing
½ pound thinly sliced corned beef, cut into ¼-inch strips

2 (8-ounce) cans sauerkraut, drained
2 cups shredded Swiss cheese (8 ounces)
1 egg, beaten
Vegetable oil, for frying

1. Separate crescent rolls into a total of 16 triangles. Brush each one lightly with Russian dressing. Top with corned beef and sauerkraut, dividing evenly. Sprinkle cheese over all. Roll up filled crescents, starting at wide end. Brush tops with beaten egg and seal firmly, crimping edges with a fork.

2. In a wok, heat 3 inches of oil over medium-high heat until temperature reaches 350°F on a deep-frying thermometer. Fry 4 Reubens at a time until golden on bottom, 2 to 3 minutes. Turn and fry until golden on second side, 1 to 2 minutes. Remove with a skimmer and drain on paper towels. Repeat procedure 3 times, adding additional oil if needed. Serve hot.

16   NEPTUNE PACKETS

Prep: 15 minutes   Cook: 10 to 14 minutes   Serves: 4 to 6

4 ounces cream cheese, softened
2 scallions, chopped
2 tablespoons chili sauce
1 tablespoon mayonnaise
½ teaspoon Worcestershire sauce

½ medium cucumber, peeled, seeded, and chopped
¼ pound imitation crabmeat, chopped
1 (8-ounce) package refrigerated crescent rolls
Vegetable oil, for frying

1. In a medium bowl, combine cream cheese, scallions, chili sauce, mayonnaise, and Worcestershire sauce. Mix until well blended. Stir in cucumber and crabmeat.

2. Separate crescent rolls and unroll into triangles. Place 1 tablespoon filling in center of each piece of dough. Starting with long end, roll up dough, enclosing filing.

3. In a wok, heat 4 inches oil over medium-high heat until temperature reaches 350°F on a deep-frying thermometer. Add 4 filled rolls and fry until golden brown on bottom, 3 to 4 minutes. Turn and fry until golden and crispy on second side, 2 to 3 minutes. Remove from wok with a skimmer and drain on paper towels. Add oil to maintain 4-inch level, if necessary, and repeat with remaining 4 turnovers.

17 CRISP MEDITERRANEAN MINI CHEESE SANDWICHES

Prep: 10 minutes   Cook: 5 to 7 minutes   Serves: 4

A marriage of two great cuisines—French and Italian—produces this tasty little nibble. Leftover bread works fine!

1½ cups Italian-seasoned bread crumbs
2 eggs
½ cup shredded mozzarella cheese
2 tablespoons grated Parmesan cheese

½ teaspoon dried oregano
16 slices of narrow French bread (baguette), cut ⅛ inch thick
½ cup vegetable oil

1. Place bread crumbs in a shallow dish. In a bowl, beat eggs until blended.

2. In a small bowl, combine mozzarella, Parmesan cheese, and oregano. Pack some of mixture on top of a baguette slice. Top with another baguette slice, pressing top slice on firmly. Repeat with remaining bread pieces and cheese mixture to make 8 sandwiches.

3. Dip sandwiches in beaten egg and then in crumbs to coat. Shake off excess crumbs.

4. In a wok, heat oil over medium-high heat until hot. Add sandwiches and cook until golden brown on bottom, 3 to 4 minutes. Turn and cook until brown on other side, 2 to 3 minutes. Drain briefly on paper towels and serve while hot.

18 FRIED MOZZARELLA STICKS

Prep: 10 minutes   Cook: 3 to 4 minutes per batch   Serves: 4

1 (12-ounce) package part-skim-milk mozzarella cheese
2 eggs, beaten
2 tablespoons grated Parmesan cheese

1½ cups Italian-seasoned bread crumbs
2½ cups vegetable oil
1 cup prepared spaghetti or marinara sauce, heated

1. Cut mozzarella into 3½ x ½-inch strips. In a bowl, combine eggs and Parmesan cheese. Beat until blended. Place bread crumbs in a shallow dish. Dip mozzarella sticks into egg mixture and then in bread crumbs to coat.

2. In a wok, heat oil over medium-high heat until temperature measures 350°F on a deep-frying thermometer. Fry mozzarella sticks in batches without crowding, turning, until golden brown, 3 to 4 minutes. Remove with a slotted spoon or skimmer and drain on paper towels. Serve with spaghetti sauce on the side for dipping.

19   CANDIED POPCORN
Prep: 5 minutes   Cook: 12 minutes   Serves: 4

6 tablespoons vegetable oil
⅓ cup popcorn kernels
⅓ cup packed brown sugar
2 tablespoons orange juice
1 teaspoon vanilla extract

1 teaspoon cinnamon
½ teaspoon grated nutmeg
2 teaspoons grated orange zest
   (optional)

1. Preheat oven to 375°F. In a wok, heat 3 tablespoons oil over medium-high heat until hot. Add popcorn. Cover and cook, shaking wok, until kernels have popped, about 4 minutes. Remove from heat.

2. In a medium bowl, whisk together remaining 3 tablespoons oil, brown sugar, juice, vanilla, cinnamon, nutmeg, and orange zest. Pour over popcorn and toss to combine.

3. Turn popcorn out onto a greased baking sheet, spreading kernels into a single layer. Bake until sugar melts and is syrupy, about 3 minutes. Immediately transfer popcorn to a bowl. When cool, break into clumps.

20   FARMER'S EGGS
Prep: 10 minutes   Cook: 14 to 21 minutes   Serves: 4 to 6

5 slices of thick-cut bacon,
   diced
2 tablespoons vegetable oil
1 medium red bell pepper,
   finely diced
1 medium green bell pepper,
   finely diced
1 medium onion, chopped

1 medium potato, cooked,
   peeled, and thinly sliced
5 eggs
½ teaspoon salt
¼ teaspoon pepper
½ cup grated sharp Cheddar
   cheese

1. In a wok, cook bacon over medium-high heat until crisp, 3 to 4 minutes. Remove bacon to paper towels. Drain off fat.

2. In same wok, heat oil over medium-high heat. Add red and green bell peppers and onion and cook, stirring, until softened, 4 to 6 minutes. Add potato and cook, turning, until browned, 4 to 6 minutes. Return bacon to wok.

3. Beat eggs with salt and pepper. Add to wok and cook, lifting edges and tilting wok to allow uncooked portion of eggs to run under, 2 to 3 minutes. Reduce heat to low.

4. Sprinkle cheese over eggs. Cook, covered, until cheese melts and omelet is puffed, 1 to 2 minutes.

21 FRANKS IN TIPSY SAUCE

Prep: 5 minutes   Cook: 5 to 8 minutes   Serves: 8 to 10

Here's an easy no-fuss hors d'oeuvre that's perfect for a cocktail party or buffet. Keep warm in a fondue pot or chafing dish if you like.

3 tablespoons vegetable oil
2 medium onions, minced
1 medium green bell pepper, minced
3 cups ketchup
½ cup bourbon
½ cup packed brown sugar

2 tablespoons Dijon mustard
½ teaspoon Worcestershire sauce
2 (12-ounce) packages beef franks, cut into 1-inch pieces

1. In a wok, heat oil over medium-high heat. Add onions and bell pepper and cook, stirring often, until soft, 3 to 5 minutes. Add ketchup, bourbon, brown sugar, Dijon mustard, and Worcestershire sauce and stir to combine. Bring to a boil. Reduce heat to medium-low.

2. Add franks and cook until heated through, 2 to 3 minutes. Serve hot, with toothpicks or small plates and cocktail forks.

22 SAVORY POPCORN

Prep: 5 minutes   Cook: 12 minutes   Serves: 4

6 tablespoons olive oil
⅓ cup popcorn kernels
3 tablespoons grated Parmesan cheese

1 teaspoon dried oregano
½ teaspoon dried basil
⅛ teaspoon crushed hot red pepper

1. Preheat oven to 375°F. In a wok, heat 3 tablespoons olive oil over medium-high heat until hot. Add popcorn. Cover and cook, shaking wok, until kernels have popped, about 4 minutes. Remove from heat.

2. In a medium bowl, whisk together remaining 3 tablespoons oil, cheese, oregano, basil, and hot pepper. Pour over popcorn and toss to coat.

3. Arrange popcorn in a single layer on a large greased baking sheet. Bake until hot and crusty, about 8 minutes.

Chapter 2

One-Wok Soups and Chowders

Soups can be served as a first course at an elegant dinner party or at a family supper. It can form the main component of a meal. Soups may be light broths or hearty chowders. They can be paired with sandwiches or salads for lunch or supper. They can be served hot or cold. Their versatility is stunning.

Here are a few things to keep in mind: Vegetables are usually diced into equal-sized pieces to cook evenly. They sometimes go through a short initial cooking period in a small amount of oil over medium-high heat to soften them before a liquid is added.

Soups with meat are prepared in a few different ways. Either the meat is browned separately and then combined with precooked vegetables, as in Chunky Vegetable, Beef, and Orzo Soup; Steak, Potato, and Mushroom Soup; and Hungarian Beef Soup—or uncooked meat, such as top rib, and water are combined in the wok, brought to a boil, skimmed when necessary, seasoned, and left to simmer. Grains are added toward the end, when the meat is tender, as are vegetables, in recipes like Easy Vegetable, Beef, and Barley Soup and Beef and Barley Vegetable Soup.

A third variation is the quickest. Cooked meat or poultry is added at the end of the cooking time, eliminating the initial browning, as in Quick Vegetable Soup with Roast Beef and Elbows and Smoked Turkey and Two-Bean Soup.

In recipes like Clam Bisque, Creamy Cod Chowder, and Shrimp Gumbo, the vegetables are cooked first, then the liquid and seasonings are added. Only at the end are the fish or shellfish put into the wok, with just enough time to cook to melting tenderness.

23   BARLEY SOUP WITH SHERRY AND ROSEMARY

Prep: 5 minutes   Cook: 39 to 45 minutes   Serves: 4 to 6

2 tablespoons olive oil
1 medium onion, chopped
1 medium carrot, chopped
1 garlic clove, minced
¾ cup quick-cooking barley
½ cup dry sherry

1 teaspoon dried rosemary
1 teaspoon salt
¼ teaspoon pepper
¼ teaspoon Worcestershire sauce

1. In a wok, heat olive oil over medium-high heat, swirling to coat sides of pan. Add onion, carrot, and garlic and cook, stirring, until softened, 3 to 5 minutes. Add barley and cook, stirring to coat, 1 minute.

2. Add sherry, rosemary, salt, pepper, Worcestershire sauce, and 6 cups water. Bring to a boil. Reduce heat to low, cover, and cook until barley is tender, 35 to 40 minutes.

24   SPINACH BEAN SOUP

Prep: 10 minutes   Cook: 25 to 30 minutes   Serves: 4

3 tablespoons olive oil
1 medium onion, chopped
1 medium carrot, chopped
1 celery rib, chopped
1 garlic clove, minced
1 (10-ounce) package frozen chopped spinach, thawed and squeezed dry
1 (28-ounce) can crushed tomatoes

1 (14½-ounce) can chicken broth
1 (19-ounce) can kidney beans, rinsed and drained
¼ cup chopped parsley
½ teaspoon salt
¼ teaspoon pepper

1. In a wok, heat olive oil over medium-high heat until hot, swirling to coat sides of pan. Add onion, carrot, celery, and garlic. Cook, stirring, until onion and celery are softened, 3 to 5 minutes. Add spinach. Cook, stirring, 2 minutes.

2. Add tomatoes and chicken broth. Bring to a boil. Add beans, parsley, salt, and pepper. Reduce heat to low. Cover and simmer 20 minutes.

25   BEET SOUP WITH DILL
Prep: 10 minutes   Cook: 16 to 20 minutes   Serves: 4 to 6

This Old World soup is sometimes referred to as borscht, and is traditionally topped with a generous spoonful of sour cream. It is good both hot and cold.

2 tablespoons vegetable oil
1 medium onion, chopped
1 medium carrot, grated
1 cup grated cabbage
1 garlic clove, minced
1 (16-ounce) can diced beets, undrained

1 (14-ounce) can beef broth
¼ cup lemon juice
2 tablespoons brown sugar
1 tablespoon chopped fresh dill or 1 teaspoon dried
1½ teaspoons salt
¼ teaspoon pepper

1. In a wok, heat oil over medium-high heat until hot, swirling to coat sides of pan. Add onion, carrot, cabbage, and garlic and cook, stirring, until crisp-tender, 4 to 5 minutes.

2. Add beets, beef broth, lemon juice, brown sugar, dill, salt, pepper, and 1½ cups water. Bring to a boil. Reduce heat to medium-low and cook, covered, until vegetables are soft, 12 to 15 minutes.

26   CURRIED BROCCOLI SOUP
Prep: 10 minutes   Cook: 19 to 22 minutes   Serves: 6

3 tablespoons butter
1 medium onion, chopped
2 tablespoons flour
2 teaspoons curry powder
½ teaspoon cumin
2 (14½-ounce) cans chicken broth

1 small head of broccoli, coarsely chopped
1 teaspoon salt
¼ teaspoon pepper
1 cup light cream or half-and-half

1. In a wok, melt butter over medium heat. Add onion and cook, stirring, until softened, 3 to 5 minutes. Add flour, curry powder, and cumin and cook, stirring, until fragrant, 1 minute.

2. Whisk in chicken broth and 1 cup water. Bring to a boil, whisking until smooth. Add broccoli, salt, and pepper. Reduce heat to medium-low, cover, and cook 15 minutes. With a slotted spoon, remove vegetables to a food processor or blender along with 1 cup liquid. Process until smooth. Return puree to wok.

3. Stir in cream. Cook until heated through, 1 to 2 minutes.

27   CHICKEN, BROWN RICE AND VEGETABLE SOUP

Prep: 10 minutes   Cook: 55 to 58 minutes   Serves: 6

2 tablespoons olive oil
1 medium onion, chopped
1 garlic clove, minced
1 medium zucchini, cut into
    ½-inch dice
1 medium tomato, seeded and
    cut into ½-inch dice
2 (14½-ounce) cans chicken
    broth
1 (8-ounce) can tomato sauce

1 teaspoon salt
¼ teaspoon pepper
¼ cup brown rice
1 pound skinless, boneless
    chicken breasts, cut into
    1-inch pieces
1 cup corn kernels, fresh,
    frozen, or canned
2 tablespoons chopped fresh
    basil or 1 teaspoon dried

1. In a wok, heat olive oil over medium-high heat, swirling to coat sides of pan. Add onion, garlic, and zucchini and cook, stirring, until softened, 3 to 4 minutes. Add tomato. Cook 2 minutes.

2. Add chicken broth, tomato sauce, salt, pepper, and 2 cups water. Bring to a boil. Reduce heat to medium-low.

3. Add brown rice, cover, and cook 35 minutes. Add chicken and cook until rice is tender and chicken is white throughout, 10 to 12 minutes, skimming as necessary. Stir in corn and basil. Simmer 5 minutes.

28   BACON CHICKEN CHOWDER

Prep: 10 minutes   Cook: 23 to 29 minutes   Serves: 4

6 slices of bacon, diced
1 tablespoon vegetable oil
1 medium onion, finely
    chopped
1 celery rib, finely chopped
2 (14½-ounce) cans chicken
    broth
1 (13-ounce) can evaporated
    skimmed milk

½ (20-ounce) bag frozen
    potatoes and carrots
2 cups cut-up cooked
    chicken
¼ cup chopped parsley
½ teaspoon salt
¼ teaspoon pepper

1. In a wok, cook bacon over medium-high heat until crisp, 3 to 4 minutes. Remove bacon to paper towels. Drain off fat from wok.

2. In same wok, heat oil over medium-high heat. Add onion and celery. Cook, stirring, until softened, 3 to 5 minutes.

3. Return bacon to wok. Add chicken broth, evaporated milk, potatoes and carrots, and 1 cup water. Bring to a boil. Reduce heat to medium-low and cook until potatoes and carrots are tender, 12 to 15 minutes.

4. Add chicken, parsley, salt, and pepper. Cook 5 minutes.

29 TOMATO, BEAN, AND PASTA SOUP
Prep: 10 minutes   Cook: 11 to 14 minutes   Serves: 6

2 tablespoons olive oil
1 onion, chopped
1 carrot, thinly sliced
1 garlic clove, crushed
1 (28-ounce) can crushed
    tomatoes
2 cups chicken broth
1½ cups elbow macaroni
1 (19½-ounce) can red kidney
    beans, rinsed and drained

¼ cup chopped Italian flat-leaf
    parsley
¼ cup chopped fresh basil or
    1 teaspoon dried
1 teaspoon salt
¼ teaspoon black pepper
¼ teaspoon crushed hot red
    pepper

1. In a wok, heat olive oil over medium-high heat until hot. Add onion, carrot, and garlic. Cook, stirring, until carrots are crisp-tender, 4 to 5 minutes.

2. Add tomatoes, chicken broth, and 1 cup water. Cook, stirring occasionally, 2 minutes. Add macaroni. Cook until pasta is tender but still firm, 6 to 8 minutes.

3. Add beans, parsley, basil, salt, black pepper, and hot pepper. Simmer 1 minute and serve hot.

30 SPANISH CHICKEN SOUP
Prep: 10 minutes   Cook: 70 to 72 minutes   Serves: 6

3 pounds chicken, cut up
2 medium potatoes, peeled
    and cut into cubes
1 medium onion, chopped
1 medium green bell pepper,
    chopped
2 mild chile peppers, seeded
    and chopped

2 garlic cloves, crushed
2 ounces vermicelli, broken
    into pieces (about 1 cup)
Salt and fresh ground black
    pepper
¼ cup chopped cilantro

1. In a wok, combine chicken, potatoes, onion, bell pepper, chile peppers, and garlic with 2 quarts cold water. Bring to a boil. Reduce heat to medium-low and cook, covered, 1 hour, skimming as necessary. Strain broth and reserve. Remove chicken and vegetables to a bowl. Wipe out wok.

2. Skin and bone the chicken and cut into pieces. Return strained broth, chicken, and potatoes to wok. Place remaining vegetables in a strainer. Mash with back of a wooden spoon and push vegetables through strainer into wok.

3. Bring broth to a boil. Add vermicelli, salt, and pepper and cook until pasta is tender but still firm, 8 to 10 minutes. Add cilantro and cook 2 minutes.

31 CLAM BISQUE

Prep: 10 minutes   Cook: 11 to 15 minutes   Serves: 4

A cross between Manhattan clam chowder and a creamy New England–style bisque, this tasty soup will please both camps of clam chowder lovers.

2 tablespoons olive oil
1 medium onion, finely diced
1 celery rib, finely diced
1 medium green bell pepper, finely diced
1 carrot, finely diced
1 garlic clove, minced
1 (16-ounce) can crushed tomatoes

1 cup dry white wine
1 cup heavy cream
2 (6½-ounce) cans chopped clams, with their juices
¼ cup chopped parsley
1 teaspoon dried thyme leaves
½ teaspoon salt
¼ teaspoon pepper

1. In a wok, heat olive oil over medium-high heat, swirling to coat sides of pan. Add onion and celery. Cook, stirring, until softened, 3 to 5 minutes. Add bell pepper, carrot, and garlic and cook 2 minutes longer.

2. Add tomatoes, wine, cream, clam juice, parsley, thyme, salt, pepper, and 1 cup water. Bring to a boil; reduce heat to medium-low. Simmer until vegetables are tender, 5 to 7 minutes. Add clams and cook 1 minute. Serve hot.

32 SMOKED TURKEY AND TWO-BEAN SOUP

Prep: 10 minutes   Cook: 18 minutes   Serves: 6

3 tablespoons olive oil
1 medium onion, chopped
1 celery rib, diced
2 medium carrots, diced
1 medium green bell pepper, diced
2 garlic cloves, minced
½ pound smoked turkey, cut into ½-inch chunks
2 (14½-ounce) cans chicken broth

1 (15-ounce) can white kidney beans (cannellini), undrained
1 (15-ounce) can red kidney beans, undrained
¼ cup chopped parsley
1 tablespoon chopped fresh rosemary or 1 teaspoon dried
Salt and freshly ground pepper

1. In a wok, heat olive oil over medium-high heat, swirling to coat sides of pan. Add onion and celery and cook until softened, about 3 minutes. Add carrots, bell pepper, and garlic and cook, stirring, 3 minutes longer. Add turkey and cook, stirring, 2 minutes.

2. Add chicken broth and 2 cups water. Bring to a boil. Reduce heat to medium-low. Add white and red beans with their liquid, parsley, rosemary, salt, and pepper. Cover and simmer 10 minutes.

33 GOLDEN CORN AND SWEET RED PEPPER SOUP

Prep: 5 minutes   Cook: 13 to 14 minutes   Serves: 4 to 5

2 tablespoons vegetable oil	3 cups light cream or
1 medium red bell pepper,	half-and-half
diced	1 cup chicken broth
1 small onion, minced	1 teaspoon salt
2 (16-ounce) cans golden	¼ teaspoon pepper
cream-style corn	1 tablespoon butter

1. In a wok, heat oil over medium-high heat, swirling to coat sides of pan. Add bell pepper and onion and cook, stirring, until onion is softened, 3 to 4 minutes.

2. Add cream-style corn, cream, chicken broth, salt, and pepper. Reduce heat to medium-low. Cover and cook 10 minutes. Stir in butter until melted. Serve hot.

34 CREAMY COD CHOWDER

Prep: 10 minutes   Cook: 21 to 27 minutes   Serves: 6

You'll remember how good down-home New England cooking is when you taste this substantial chowder. Serve as a first course or accompany with a tossed salad and crusty bread for a meal in a bowl.

6 slices of bacon, cut into	1 (13-ounce) can evaporated
½-inch squares	milk
3 tablespoons olive oil	3 medium russet potatoes,
1 medium onion, chopped	peeled and cut into
1 medium carrot, chopped	½-inch cubes
1 celery rib, chopped	1 pound cod, cut into ¾-inch
2 tablespoons flour	chunks
1 (10-ounce) can cream of	1 teaspoon salt
potato soup	¼ teaspoon pepper

1. In a wok, cook bacon over medium-high heat until crisp on both sides, 4 to 6 minutes. Remove bacon to paper towels. Drain off fat from wok.

2. In same wok, heat olive oil over medium-high heat, swirling to coat sides of pan. Add onion, carrot, and celery and cook, stirring often, until softened, 4 to 6 minutes. Stir in flour. Cook, stirring, 2 minutes.

3. Add cream of potato soup, evaporated milk, and 1 cup water. Raise heat to high and bring to a boil. Add potatoes, fish, salt, and pepper. Reduce heat to medium-low, cover and cook until fish and potatoes are tender and fish is opaque throughout, 10 to 12 minutes. Add bacon and cook 1 minute.

35   CHEDDAR AND BACON SOUP

Prep: 15 minutes   Cook: 13 to 17 minutes   Serves: 6

8 slices of bacon, diced	2 (14½-ounce) cans chicken
2 tablespoons vegetable oil	broth
2 medium carrots, chopped	¼ teaspoon pepper
1 medium onion, chopped	1 cup heavy cream
1 tablespoon Dijon mustard	2 cups shredded Cheddar
3 tablespoons flour	cheese (8 ounces)

1. In a wok, cook bacon over medium-high heat until very crisp, 4 to 6 minutes. Remove bacon to paper towels. Drain off fat from wok.

2. In same wok, heat oil over high heat. Add carrots and onion and cook, stirring, until soft, 3 to 5 minutes. Stir in mustard and flour. Cook 3 minutes, stirring. Add chicken broth, pepper, and 2 cups water. Bring to a boil and stir until thickened.

3. Stir in cream and cheese. Reduce heat to medium-low. Return bacon to wok. Stir over low heat until cheese is melted, about 3 minutes.

36   LIMA BEAN SOUP WITH SPINACH AND TOMATOES

Prep: 10 minutes   Cook: 41 to 45 minutes   Serves: 6

3 tablespoons olive oil	1 bay leaf
2 medium onions, chopped	1 teaspoon dried marjoram
1 celery rib, chopped	1½ teaspoons salt
2 garlic cloves, crushed	¼ teaspoon pepper
2 medium carrots, chopped	2 (10-ounce) packages frozen
1 (28-ounce) can crushed	chopped spinach, thawed
tomatoes	1 (10-ounce) package frozen
1 (14½-ounce) can chicken	lima beans
broth	

1. In a wok, heat olive oil over medium-high heat, swirling to coat sides of pan. Add onions, celery, and garlic and cook, stirring, until softened, 3 to 5 minutes.

2. Add carrots, tomatoes, chicken broth, bay leaf, marjoram, salt, pepper, and 1 cup water. Cook, covered, 30 minutes. Add spinach and lima beans and cook, covered, until beans are tender, 8 to 10 minutes.

37   NEW ENGLAND FISH CHOWDER
Prep: 10 minutes   Cook: 19 to 20 minutes   Serves: 4

1½ pounds red potatoes, peeled
    and cut into ½-inch cubes
1 large onion, chopped
1 celery rib, sliced
1 carrot, sliced
1 pound haddock fillets, cut
    into ½-inch cubes
1½ cups milk

1 (13-ounce) can evaporated
    skimmed milk
½ teaspoon dried thyme leaves
½ teaspoon salt
¼ teaspoon pepper
1 tablespoon cornstarch
¼ cup dry white wine

1. In a wok, combine potatoes, onion, celery, carrot, and 2 cups water. Bring to a boil. Reduce heat to medium-low, cover, and cook 10 minutes.

2. Add fish and cook, covered, until opaque, about 5 minutes. Add milk, evaporated milk, thyme, salt, and pepper. Cook 3 minutes longer.

3. Dissolve cornstarch in wine and stir into chowder. Cook over medium heat, stirring, until soup boils and thickens, 1 to 2 minutes.

38   EVERY BEAN IMAGINABLE BEAN SOUP
Prep: 5 minutes   Stands: 1 hour   Cook: 1½ to 2 hours   Serves: 6

1 (20-ounce) package 15 Bean
    Soup Mix (seasoning
    pack removed), rinsed
    well
2 carrots, quartered
1 large onion, quartered
1 celery rib, quartered

2 (14½-ounce) cans chicken
    broth
2 teaspoons salt
½ teaspoon pepper
1 bay leaf
    Few drops of liquid smoke
    (optional)

1. Place beans in a wok and add enough cold water to cover. Bring to a boil over high heat and cook 5 minutes. Remove from heat. Cover and let stand 1 hour; drain beans into a colander. Return to wok.

2. In a blender or food processor, puree carrots, onion, and celery until finely chopped. Add to beans in wok. Add chicken broth, salt, pepper, bay leaf, liquid smoke, and cold water to cover.

3. Return wok to high heat. Bring to a boil, skimming occasionally. Reduce heat to low. Cover and cook until beans are tender, 1½ to 2 hours.

39   FRENCH FARMHOUSE SOUP

Prep: 15 minutes   Cook: 37 to 41 minutes   Serves: 4 to 6

This aromatic soup is often served with French-bread croutons and grated Gruyère cheese in individual tureens.

6   slices of bacon, diced
3   tablespoons butter
2   medium carrots, coarsely
    chopped
2   celery ribs, coarsely
    chopped
2   medium turnips, peeled and
    coarsely chopped
2   medium leeks (white part
    only), chopped
4   cups (1 quart) chicken broth

1   teaspoon salt
¼   teaspoon pepper
1   medium fennel bulb,
    coarsely chopped
2   cups shredded green
    cabbage
¼   pound fresh green beans,
    cut into 1-inch pieces
2   medium potatoes, peeled
    and cut into ½-inch cubes

1. In a wok, cook bacon over medium-high heat until crisp, while stirring, 3 to 4 minutes. Remove bacon to paper towels. Drain off all but 1 tablespoon fat.

2. Add butter to wok and melt over medium-high heat. Add carrots, celery, turnips, and leeks and cook until softened, 4 to 5 minutes

3. Add chicken broth, salt, pepper, and 2 cups water. Bring to a boil; reduce heat to medium-low. Add fennel and cabbage, cover, and cook 20 minutes. Add green beans and potatoes. Return bacon to wok. Cook, covered, until potatoes are tender, 10 to 12 minutes.

40   DILLED POTATO LEEK SOUP

Prep: 10 minutes   Cook: 17 to 21 minutes   Serves: 6

3   tablespoons vegetable oil
3   medium russet potatoes,
    peeled and cut into
    ½-inch cubes
3   medium leeks (white and
    tender green), rinsed well
    and sliced

2   (14-ounce) cans chicken
    broth
1   tablespoon chopped fresh
    dill or 1 teaspoon dried
1   teaspoon salt
¼   teaspoon pepper

1. In a wok, heat oil over medium-high heat, swirling to coat sides of pan. Add potatoes and leeks and cook, stirring, until potatoes begin to turn translucent, 4 to 6 minutes.

2. Add chicken broth and 2 cups water. Bring to a boil. Reduce heat to medium-low, cover, and cook until potatoes are tender, 8 to 10 minutes.

3. With a slotted spoon, remove vegetables to a food processor or blender. Add 1 cup cooking liquid and puree until smooth. Return to wok. Add dill, salt, and pepper. Simmer 5 minutes. Serve hot or chilled.

41 SHRIMP GUMBO
Prep: 10 minutes   Cook: 9 to 12 minutes   Serves: 6

2 tablespoons olive oil
1 medium onion, chopped
1 celery rib, chopped
1 tomato, seeded and chopped
1 (10-ounce) package frozen
    okra, thawed
4 cups (1 quart) chicken broth
2 tablespoons chopped
    parsley

⅛ teaspoon cayenne
½ teaspoon salt
¼ teaspoon pepper
1 pound medium shrimp,
    shelled and deveined
1 (8-ounce) can corn kernels,
    drained

1. In a wok, heat olive oil over medium-high heat until hot. Add onion and celery and cook, stirring, until softened, 3 to 5 minutes. Add tomato and okra. Cook, stirring, 2 minutes.

2. Add chicken broth, parsley, cayenne, salt, and pepper. Bring to a boil, reduce heat to medium. Add shrimp. Cook until shrimp turn pink, 2 to 3 minutes. Add corn and cook 2 minutes longer. Serve hot.

42 HUNGARIAN BEEF SOUP
Prep: 10 minutes   Cook: 2 hours   Serves: 6

Try to use Hungarian sweet paprika for this soup. It really makes a difference. It can be found in many of the larger supermarkets.

3 tablespoons vegetable oil
1½ pounds boneless beef
    chuck, trimmed of fat and
    cut into 1-inch chunks
1 large onion, chopped
2 garlic cloves, minced
2 teaspoons imported sweet
    paprika
1 teaspoon dried marjoram

1 teaspoon salt
¼ teaspoon pepper
2 (14½-ounce) cans beef broth
1 cup dry red wine
1 (14-ounce) can Italian peeled
    tomatoes, broken up,
    juices reserved
1 (20-ounce) bag frozen
    potatoes and carrots

1. In a wok, heat 2 tablespoons oil over high heat until hot, swirling to coat sides of pan. Add beef chunks and cook, turning, until brown all over, 4 to 6 minutes. With a slotted spoon or skimmer, remove to a plate.

2. In same wok, heat remaining 1 tablespoon oil over medium-high heat. Add onion and garlic and cook, stirring, until soft, 3 to 5 minutes. Return meat to wok. Add paprika, marjoram, salt, and pepper. Cook, stirring 1 minute.

3. Add beef broth, wine, and tomatoes with their juices. Bring to a boil. Reduce heat to medium-low, cover, and cook 1½ hours. Add potatoes and carrots. Cook until meat and vegetables are tender, 15 to 20 minutes longer.

43   FLOUNDER AND CRAB CHOWDER
Prep: 15 minutes   Cook: 18 to 25 minutes   Serves: 6

3 tablespoons vegetable oil
1 large onion, diced
2 celery ribs, diced
1 medium carrot, diced
1 medium green bell pepper, diced
2 medium potatoes, peeled and cut into ½-inch cubes
3 cups bottled clam juice
1 (8-ounce) can crushed tomatoes, with their juice

1 bay leaf
Salt and freshly ground pepper
½ pound flounder fillets, cut into ¾-inch squares
½ pound lump crabmeat, picked over to remove shell and cartilage

1. In a wok, heat oil over medium-high heat, swirling to coat sides of pan. Add onion, celery, carrot, and green pepper and cook, stirring, until onion and celery are softened, 4 to 6 minutes. Add potatoes and cook, stirring, until potatoes begin to turn translucent, 3 to 5 minutes.

2. Add clam juice, tomatoes with their juice, bay leaf, salt, pepper, and 2 cups water. Bring to a boil. Reduce heat to medium-low.

3. Add flounder, cover, and cook until potatoes and fish are tender, 10 to 12 minutes. Remove bay leaf. Add crabmeat and simmer until heated through, 1 to 2 minutes.

44   HOT AND SOUR SOUP WITH VEGETABLES
Prep: 10 minutes   Cook: 13 to 15 minutes   Serves: 4

2 tablespoons vegetable oil
4 scallions, sliced
2 carrots, thinly sliced
2 garlic cloves, minced
¼ pound fresh mushrooms, sliced
2 (14½-ounce) cans chicken broth
¼ cup chopped cilantro or parsley

1 (6-ounce) package frozen Chinese pea pods, thawed
1 (8-ounce) can sliced water chestnuts, drained
¼ cup rice wine vinegar
2 tablespoons soy sauce
1 teaspoon Asian sesame oil

1. In a wok, heat oil over high heat until hot. Add scallions, carrots, and garlic and stir-fry until crisp-tender, 2 to 3 minutes. Add mushrooms. Cook, stirring, until softened, 2 to 3 minutes.

2. Add chicken broth and 1 cup water. Bring to a boil. Reduce heat to medium. Simmer 5 minutes. Add cilantro, pea pods, and water chestnuts. Cook 2 minutes.

3. Stir in vinegar, soy sauce, and sesame oil. Cook 2 minutes and serve.

45   MEATBALL VEGETABLE-JUICE SOUP

Prep: 5 minutes   Cook: 15 to 19 minutes   Serves: 4

1   pound ground sirloin
       (90% lean)
1   small onion, grated
1   garlic clove, minced
⅓   cup regular or quick-
       cooking oats
1   egg
1   tablespoon vegetable oil

3   cups vegetable-juice
       cocktail, such as V-8
1   (14½-ounce) can beef broth
1   (10-ounce) box frozen mixed
       vegetables
½   teaspoon salt
¼   teaspoon pepper

1. In a medium bowl, combine ground sirloin, onion, garlic, oats, and egg. Mix until well blended, preferably with your hands. Shape into balls 1 inch in diameter.

2. In a wok, heat oil over high heat until hot, swirling to coat sides of pan. Add meatballs and cook, turning, until browned all over, 5 to 7 minutes. Drain off fat.

3. Add vegetable-juice cocktail and beef broth. Bring to a boil. Add mixed vegetables, salt, and pepper. Reduce heat to medium-low. Partially cover and simmer until meatballs are cooked through, 10 to 12 minutes.

46   TOMATO SOUP WITH TARRAGON

Prep: 10 minutes   Cook: 26 to 28 minutes   Serves: 6

2   tablespoons vegetable oil
1   large onion, chopped
1   medium carrot, chopped
1   celery rib, chopped
3   cups chicken broth
1   (28-ounce) can Italian peeled
       tomatoes, with their
       juices

1   teaspoon salt
¼   teaspoon pepper
1   cup half-and-half or
       light cream
1½ tablespoons chopped fresh
       tarragon or 1 teaspoon
       dried

1. In a wok, heat oil over medium-high heat until hot, swirling to coat sides of pan. Add onion, carrot, and celery and cook, stirring, until softened, 4 to 6 minutes.

2. Add chicken broth, tomatoes with their juices, salt, and pepper. Bring to a boil. Reduce heat to low, cover, and cook 20 minutes. Remove from heat. Let cool 10 minutes.

3. Puree soup, in batches if necessary, in a food processor or blender. Return soup to wok.

4. Stir in half-and-half. Add tarragon. Cook over medium heat until hot, about 2 minutes.

47   STICK-TO-THE-RIBS SPLIT PEA SOUP

Prep: 10 minutes   Soak: 20 minutes   Cook: 1¾ to 2 hours
Serves: 6 to 8

Dried porcini mushrooms are sometimes labeled cèpes. They can be expensive and hard to find. While they are exceptionally flavorful, ½ to 1 ounce dried imported mushroom pieces would make a fine substitute.

3   dried porcini mushrooms
1   (16-ounce) package dried
      green split peas, rinsed
      well and drained
1   medium onion, finely
      chopped

1   medium carrot, finely
      chopped
1   celery rib, finely chopped
2   bay leaves
1   teaspoon salt
¼   teaspoon pepper

1. In a small bowl, combine dried mushrooms and ½ cup hot water. Let soak 20 minutes. Remove mushrooms. Discard stems and chop reconstituted mushrooms. Strain liquid through a sieve lined with a double layer of cheesecloth and reserve.

2. In a wok, combine split peas, onion, carrot, celery, bay leaves, salt, pepper, and chopped mushrooms. Add 8 cups (2 quarts) cold water plus reserved mushroom liquid. Bring to a boil over high heat. Skim off any impurities.

3. Reduce heat to low, cover, and cook until peas are very soft, the consistency of pureed vegetables, 1¾ to 2 hours.

48   EASTERN EUROPEAN MACARONI AND BEAN SOUP

Prep: 5 minutes   Cook: 16 to 21 minutes   Serves: 6

1½   tablespoons vegetable oil
1   medium onion, chopped
1½   teaspoons salt
¼   teaspoon pepper

1   (7-ounce) package elbow
      macaroni
2   (16-ounce) cans red kidney
      beans, undrained

1. In a wok, heat oil over medium-high heat until hot. Add onion and cook, stirring, until soft, 4 to 5 minutes. Remove to a bowl.

2. In same wok, bring 8 cups (2 quarts) water, salt, and pepper to a boil. Add macaroni and return to a boil. Cook 2 minutes. Add kidney beans and juice. Cook until macaroni is firm but still tender and some of liquid is evaporated, 10 to 12 minutes.

3. Add onion and cook until heated through, 1 to 2 minutes.

49   SPINACH TORTELLINI SOUP
Prep: 5 minutes   Cook: 9 to 13 minutes   Serves: 4

2 tablespoons olive oil
1 onion, chopped
1 carrot, thinly sliced
2 (10½-ounce) cans beef broth
1 (16-ounce) package frozen
    beef tortellini

1 (10-ounce) package frozen
    chopped spinach, thawed
¼ teaspoon grated nutmeg
½ teaspoon salt
¼ teaspoon pepper
¼ cup grated Parmesan cheese

1. In a wok, heat olive oil over high heat until hot, swirling to coat sides of pan. Add onion and carrot and cook, stirring, until softened, 4 to 6 minutes.

2. Add beef broth and 2 cups water. Raise heat to high and bring to a boil. Reduce heat to medium. Add tortellini and cook 3 minutes. Add spinach, nutmeg, salt, and pepper. Cook until tortellini are tender, 2 to 4 minutes.

3. To serve, ladle soup into bowls. Sprinkle with grated cheese.

50   SWEET POTATO, CORN, AND WHITE BEAN SOUP
Prep: 10 minutes   Cook: 31 to 40 minutes   Serves: 6

This is my adaptation of a recipe from a local restaurant that specializes in hearty soups and earthy, thick-crusted breads. I found it so delicious that I was determined to duplicate it—and I did!

3 tablespoons vegetable oil
1 medium onion, chopped
1 celery rib, chopped
3 medium sweet potatoes,
    peeled and chopped
3 cups chicken broth
1 tablespoon chopped fresh
    basil

1 bay leaf
2 medium carrots, chopped
1 (8-ounce) can corn kernels,
    undrained
1 (16-ounce) can white beans,
    undrained
Salt and freshly ground
    pepper

1. In a wok, heat oil over medium-high heat until hot. Add onion and celery and cook, stirring, until softened, 3 to 5 minutes.

2. Add sweet potatoes, chicken broth, basil, and bay leaf. Bring to a boil. Reduce heat to medium and cook, covered, until sweet potatoes are soft, 15 to 20 minutes. Remove bay leaf.

3. With a slotted spoon, remove onion, celery, and sweet potatoes to a food processor or blender. Add 1 cup cooking liquid and puree until smooth. Return to wok.

4. Add carrots, cover, and cook until soft, 8 to 10 minutes. Add corn, beans, salt, and pepper. Reduce heat to low and cook, covered, 5 minutes.

51   CREAM OF ONION SOUP
Prep: 5 minutes   Cook: 33 to 38 minutes   Serves: 6

4 tablespoons butter
3 large onions, sliced
2 (14½-ounce) cans beef broth
1 cup ditalini or other small
     pasta
1 cup heavy cream
1 egg yolk

½ teaspoon salt
¼ teaspoon pepper
1 cup shredded Swiss cheese
     (about 4 ounces)
6 slices of French bread,
     toasted

1. In a wok, melt butter over medium heat. Add onions and cook, stirring often, until softened, 4 to 6 minutes. Reduce heat to medium-low and cook, stirring occasionally, until golden, about 20 minutes. Add beef broth and bring to a boil. Stir in ditalini and cook until tender but still firm, 8 to 10 minutes.

2. In a medium bowl, whisk cream, egg yolk, salt, and pepper until blended. Whisk ¼ cup hot broth into cream mixture. Pour back into wok, whisking continuously.

3. Add Swiss cheese and cook, stirring, until cheese melts, 1 to 2 minutes. Place a slice of French bread in each of 6 soup bowls. Ladle soup over bread.

52   PUMPKIN CHEESE SOUP
Prep: 10 minutes   Cook: 20 to 23 minutes   Serves: 6

3 tablespoons vegetable oil
2 medium onions, chopped
2 medium carrots, chopped
1 celery rib, chopped
1 garlic clove, minced
4 cups chicken broth
½ cup dry white wine
1 teaspoon salt

¼ teaspoon pepper
½ teaspoon grated nutmeg
2 cups canned pumpkin puree
1 cup half-and-half
1 cup shredded Swiss cheese
     (about 4 ounces)
¼ cup chopped parsley

1. In a wok, heat oil over medium-high heat, swirling to coat sides of pan. Add onions, carrots, celery, and garlic and cook, stirring often, until onions and celery are softened, 4 to 6 minutes.

2. Add chicken broth, wine, salt, pepper, and nutmeg. Bring to a boil. Reduce heat to medium-low, cover, and cook 10 minutes.

3. With a slotted spoon, remove vegetables to a food processor or blender. Add 1 cup cooking liquid and puree until smooth. Return vegetable puree to wok. Add pumpkin and half-and-half. Simmer 5 minutes.

4. Add cheese and cook, stirring, until cheese melts, 1 to 2 minutes. Sprinkle with parsley and serve.

53   SPINACH, POTATO, AND LIMA BEAN SOUP

Prep: 10 minutes   Cook: 17 to 23 minutes   Serves: 6

2 tablespoons olive oil
1 medium onion, chopped
1 medium carrot, chopped
1 celery rib, sliced
1 garlic clove, minced
1 (28-ounce) can crushed
   tomatoes
1 (14½-ounce) can beef broth
1 (10-ounce) package frozen
   lima beans

2 medium potatoes, peeled
   and cut into ½-inch cubes
¼ cup chopped parsley
1 teaspoon dried marjoram
1 teaspoon salt
¼ teaspoon pepper
½ pound fresh spinach leaves,
   washed well

1. In a wok, heat olive oil over medium-high heat until hot, swirling to coat sides of pan. Add onion, carrot, celery, and garlic and cook, stirring, until onion and celery are softened, 3 to 5 minutes.

2. Add tomatoes, beef broth, and 2 cups water. Bring to a boil; reduce heat to medium-low. Add lima beans, potatoes, parsley, marjoram, salt, and pepper. Cook until potatoes are tender, 12 to 15 minutes. Add spinach. Cook, stirring, until wilted, 2 to 3 minutes.

54   STEAK, POTATO, AND MUSHROOM SOUP

Prep: 10 minutes   Cook: 36 to 44 minutes   Serves: 6

¼ cup vegetable oil
1 pound boneless top sirloin,
   cut into ½-inch cubes
4 scallions, chopped
½ pound sliced fresh
   mushrooms
2 large russet potatoes, peeled
   and cut into ½-inch cubes

2 (14½-ounce) cans beef broth
1 (14½-ounce) can crushed
   tomatoes
½ teaspoon dried thyme leaves
½ teaspoon salt
¼ teaspoon pepper

1. In a wok, heat 2 tablespoons oil over high heat until hot. Add steak cubes and cook, turning, until browned, 3 to 5 minutes. Remove to a plate.

2. In same wok, heat remaining 2 tablespoons oil over medium-high heat. Add scallions and mushrooms and cook, tossing, until tender, 3 to 4 minutes. Return steak to wok. Add potatoes.

3. Add beef broth, crushed tomatoes, thyme, salt, pepper, and 2 cups water. Bring to a boil. Reduce heat to medium, cover, and cook until meat and potatoes are tender, 30 to 35 minutes.

55   CHUNKY VEGETABLE, BEEF, AND ORZO SOUP

Prep: 10 minutes   Cook: 2 to 2½ hours   Serves: 6

Browning the vegetables and meat before adding the beef broth and tomatoes enhances the flavor of this nutritious and delicious soup. Orzo is a small rice-shaped pasta.

2 tablespoons olive oil	1 teaspoon dried thyme
1½ pounds beef shank	1 teaspoon salt
1 medium onion, chopped	½ teaspoon pepper
1 medium celery rib, chopped	1 (10-ounce) package frozen
1 garlic clove, minced	mixed vegetables
2 cups beef broth	¾ cup orzo
1 cup crushed tomatoes	

1. In a wok, heat 1 tablespoon olive oil over high heat until hot, swirling to coat sides of pan. Add beef shank and cook, turning, until brown all over, 6 to 8 minutes. Remove to a plate.

2. Add remaining 1 tablespoon oil to wok. Add onion, celery, and garlic and cook over medium-high heat, stirring occasionally until softened, 3 to 5 minutes. Return beef shank to wok.

3. Add beef broth, crushed tomatoes, thyme, salt, pepper, and 2 cups cold water. Bring to a boil. Reduce heat to low. Cook, partially covered, until meat is tender, 1½ to 2 hours. Remove beef and cut into bite-size pieces, discarding any bone and fat. Return meat to wok.

4. Add frozen mixed vegetables. Cook 5 minutes. Add orzo. Cook until tender, 10 to 12 minutes.

56   QUICK VEGETABLE SOUP WITH ROAST BEEF AND ELBOWS

Prep: 5 minutes   Cook: 10 to 12 minutes   Serves: 4

1 (10½-ounce) can beef broth	1½ cups cooked roast beef, cut
1 cup elbow macaroni	into ½-inch cubes
1 (10-ounce) package frozen	½ teaspoon salt
mixed vegetables	¼ teaspoon pepper

1. In a wok, bring beef broth and 2 cups water to a boil over medium-high heat. Add pasta. Cook 6 minutes. Add mixed vegetables. Return to a boil. Reduce heat to medium and cook, stirring occasionally, until vegetables are almost tender, 4 to 5 minutes.

2. Add roast beef, salt, and pepper. Cook 1 minute and serve hot.

57 EASY VEGETABLE, BEEF, AND BARLEY SOUP

Prep: 5 minutes   Cook: 86 to 91 minutes   Serves: 6

A great soup for a cold winter night. Serve with thick slices of multi-grain or black bread.

1 pound top rib (beef chuck),
    bone in
2 (14½-ounce) cans beef broth
2 tablespoons tarragon
    vinegar
1 teaspoon dried tarragon

1 teaspoon salt
¼ teaspoon pepper
½ cup quick-cooking barley
1 (10-ounce) package frozen
    mixed vegetables

1. Place beef and 4 cups cold water in a wok. Bring to a boil, skimming off fat as it accumulates. Add beef broth, vinegar, tarragon, salt, and pepper. Cover and cook over medium-low heat 1 hour.

2. Add barley and cook, covered, until tender, 20 to 25 minutes.

3. Add mixed vegetables. Cook until tender, about 6 minutes.

58 WINTER VEGETABLE SOUP

Prep: 10 minutes   Cook: 28 to 30 minutes   Serves: 6

3 tablespoons olive oil
2 medium leeks (white part
    only), chopped
1 medium carrot, chopped
1 celery rib, chopped
2 garlic cloves, minced
2 medium russet potatoes,
    peeled and cut into
    ½-inch cubes
1 medium turnip, peeled and
    cut into ½-inch cubes

2 (14½-ounce) cans beef broth
1 (16-ounce) can crushed
    tomatoes
¼ cup chopped parsley
1 bay leaf
1 teaspoon dried thyme
1 teaspoon salt
¼ teaspoon pepper
1 (10-ounce) package frozen
    baby lima beans

1. In a wok, heat olive oil over medium-high heat until hot, swirling to coat sides of pan. Add leeks, carrot, celery, and garlic and cook, stirring occasionally, until softened, 6 to 8 minutes. Add potatoes and turnip. Cook, stirring, 2 minutes.

2. Add beef broth, tomatoes, parsley, bay leaf, thyme, salt, pepper, and 3 cups water. Raise heat to high and bring to a boil. Add beans. Reduce heat to low, cover, and cook 20 minutes. Remove bay leaf and serve.

59   BEEF AND BARLEY VEGETABLE SOUP
Prep: 10 minutes   Stands: 1 hour   Cook: 2 hours   Serves: 6

1½ cups dried pea beans
1½ pounds top rib, bone in
1 large onion, peeled
2 celery ribs, sliced
2 carrots, diced
1 (16-ounce) can whole
   tomatoes, broken up,
   liquid reserved
2 teaspoons salt
¼ teaspoon pepper
½ cup medium barley
1 (8-ounce) can corn kernels
1 medium green bell pepper,
   chopped
1 medium potato, peeled and
   diced
¼ cup chopped parsley
½ teaspoon dried thyme leaves

1. Rinse beans thoroughly; drain and pick over to remove any defective beans and grit. Place beans in a wok. Add enough cold water to cover. Bring to a boil. Cover and cook 2 minutes. Remove from heat and let stand 1 hour. Drain beans into a colander. Rinse and return to wok.

2. Add meat to beans. Again add enough cold water to cover. Bring to a boil. Reduce heat to medium-low and cook, skimming off any impurities as necessary, until liquid is clear, about 15 minutes.

3. Add onion, celery, carrots, tomatoes, salt, and pepper. Simmer 45 minutes.

4. Add barley, corn, bell pepper, potato, parsley, and thyme. Simmer until meat is tender, about 1 hour. Remove onion and meat. Cut meat into small pieces and return to wok. Serve hot.

60   ZUCCHINI TOMATO SOUP WITH CORN AND BASIL
Prep: 10 minutes   Cook: 18 to 20 minutes   Serves: 6

2 tablespoons olive oil
1 large onion, chopped
1 medium green bell pepper,
   chopped
4 cups vegetable juice
   cocktail, such as V-8
1 cup dry white wine
2 small zucchini, grated
1 (16-ounce) can corn kernels,
   drained
2 tablespoons chopped fresh
   basil or 1 teaspoon dried
1 teaspoon salt
¼ teaspoon pepper
2 cups light cream or
   half-and-half

1. In a wok, heat olive oil over medium-high heat, swirling to coat sides of pan. Add onion and bell pepper and cook, stirring, until softened, 3 to 5 minutes.

2. Add vegetable juice cocktail, wine, and 1 cup water. Bring to a boil. Add zucchini, corn, basil, salt, and pepper. Reduce heat to medium-low. Cover and cook 15 minutes. Whisk in cream and serve.

Chapter 3

Stir-Frying American Style

This chapter is down-home and uptown. It's bell peppers and hot peppers. It's Northeast and Southwest. It combines the tried and true Eastern stir-fry technique with Western flavors and ingredients.

These recipes reflect the times. With so many people working, there isn't the time or desire to prepare complicated long-cooking meals. Fast and tasty are the main criteria here. The wok is perfect for this style of cooking. The broad surface area and depth facilitate the stirring and tossing over high heat that are so important.

In stir-frying, ingredients are cut into small pieces or strips; larger sections are pounded thin. Then they are cooked quickly over high heat as they are stirred and tossed continuously. The small amount of oil and/or butter required is spread over the bottom and up the sides of the wok with a spatula to prevent sticking. The most important thing in stir-frying is organization and preparing the ingredients before cooking.

Some of the all-American recipes include Stir-Fried Chicken and Broccoli with Sun-Dried Tomatoes, Fresh Salmon with Pineapple in Pineapple-Orange Sauce, Beef with Bell Peppers and Corn, and Leigh's Candlelight Chicken. There are also regional Southwestern recipes, such as Garlicky Salsa Chicken and Turkey Fajitas—full of tomatoes, salsa, and chile peppers; they are zesty with cilantro and lime.

61   GARLICKY SALSA CHICKEN
Prep: 10 minutes   Cook: 11 to 16 minutes   Serves: 4

½ cup yellow cornmeal
2 tablespoons chopped
   parsley
½ teaspoon salt
¼ teaspoon pepper
4 skinless, boneless
   chicken breast halves
   (4 to 5 ounces each),
   pounded to ¼-inch
   thickness
¼ cup corn oil

2 scallions, chopped
1 medium tomato, seeded and
   chopped
3 garlic cloves, crushed
1 jalapeño pepper, seeded and
   chopped
¼ cup tomato juice
1 tablespoon balsamic vinegar
¼ cup chopped cilantro
½ teaspoon salt
¼ teaspoon pepper

1. In a shallow dish, combine cornmeal, parsley, salt, and pepper. Lightly coat chicken on both sides, shaking off excess.

2. In a wok, heat 2 tablespoons oil over medium-high heat until hot, swirling to coat sides of pan. Arrange chicken extending up sides of pan without overlapping. Cook until brown on both sides, 6 to 8 minutes, turning and rotating for even cooking. Remove to a serving plate.

3. In same wok, heat remaining 2 tablespoons oil over medium-high heat. Add scallions, tomato, garlic, and jalapeño pepper and cook, stirring, until scallions are crisp-tender, 3 to 4 minutes. Add tomato juice, vinegar, cilantro, salt, and pepper. Cook, stirring, until most of liquid is evaporated, 2 to 4 minutes. Spoon salsa over chicken and serve.

62   THREE-ONION CHICKEN
Prep: 10 minutes   Cook: 9 to 12 minutes   Serves: 4

3 tablespoons vegetable oil
1¼ pounds skinless, boneless
   chicken breasts, cut into
   1-inch cubes
1 medium leek (white part
   only), chopped
1 small onion, chopped

2 scallions, chopped
1 garlic clove, minced
¼ cup dry white wine
¼ cup dry sherry
1 cup chicken broth
2 tablespoons soy sauce
1 tablespoon cornstarch

1. In a wok, heat 2 tablespoons oil over high heat until hot. Add chicken and stir-fry until meat is white throughout but still juicy, about 3 minutes. Remove to a plate.

2. In same wok, heat remaining 1 tablespoon oil over medium-high heat. Add leek, onion, scallions, and garlic and stir-fry until softened, 3 to 5 minutes. Return chicken to wok. Add white wine, sherry, chicken broth, and soy sauce. Cook 2 minutes.

3. Dissolve cornstarch in ¼ cup cold water and stir into wok. Cook over high heat, stirring, until sauce boils and thickens, 1 to 2 minutes.

63   STIR-FRIED CHICKEN LIVERS WITH ONIONS

Prep: 10 minutes   Cook: 12 to 17 minutes   Serves: 4

1 pound chicken livers	2 tablespoons red wine
3½ tablespoons vegetable oil	vinegar
2 medium onions, sliced and	½ teaspoon salt
separated into rings	¼ teaspoon pepper
1 garlic clove, minced	2 tablespoons chopped
¼ cup beef broth	parsley

1. Trim bits of fat and any spots from livers. Rinse and pat dry. Cut livers in half.

2. In a wok, heat 1½ tablespoons oil over high heat, swirling to coat sides of pan. Add onions and stir-fry until softened and beginning to color, 4 to 6 minutes. Add garlic and cook 1 minute longer. Remove to a plate.

3. In wok, heat 2 tablespoons oil over high heat. Add chicken livers and stir-fry until browned outside and pink in center, 3 to 5 minutes. Remove to plate with onions.

4. Add beef broth and vinegar to wok. Boil over high heat, scraping up browned bits from bottom of pan, 3 minutes. Return chicken livers and onions to wok. Season with salt and pepper. Cook, tossing, until heated through, 1 to 2 minutes. Serve garnished with chopped parsley.

64   STIR-FRIED CHICKEN AND BROCCOLI WITH SUN-DRIED TOMATOES

Prep: 10 minutes   Cook: 8 to 9 minutes   Serves: 4

3 tablespoons olive oil	6 sun-dried tomato halves
1¼ pounds skinless, boneless	(packed in oil), drained
chicken breasts, cut into	and chopped
1-inch pieces	1 teaspoon hot pepper sauce
2 cups broccoli florets	¼ teaspoon pepper
2 garlic cloves, minced	

1. In a wok, heat 1½ tablespoons olive oil over high heat until hot, swirling to coat sides of pan. Add chicken and stir-fry until meat is white throughout but still juicy, about 3 minutes. Remove to a plate.

2. In same wok, heat remaining 1½ tablespoons oil over medium-high heat. Add broccoli and stir-fry until crisp-tender, 3 to 4 minutes. Add garlic and cook 1 minute longer. Return chicken to wok. Add sun-dried tomatoes, hot sauce, and pepper. Cook, stirring, 1 minute. Serve hot.

65 CHICKEN WITH YELLOW PEPPERS AND SUN-DRIED TOMATOES

Prep: 10 minutes   Cook: 10 to 14 minutes   Serves: 4

3 tablespoons olive oil
1¼ pounds boneless, skinless
    chicken breasts, cut
    crosswise into ¼-inch
    strips
1 medium yellow bell pepper,
    chopped
1 medium onion, chopped
2 garlic cloves, minced
1 tomato, chopped
4 sun-dried tomatoes packed
    in oil, drained and
    chopped

½ cup dry white wine
½ teaspoon dried thyme
½ teaspoon salt
¼ teaspoon pepper
2 tablespoons butter, cut into
    small pieces
2 tablespoons chopped
    parsley

1. In a wok, heat 1½ tablespoons olive oil over high heat until hot, swirling to coat sides of pan. Add chicken and stir-fry until white throughout but still juicy, 3 to 4 minutes. Remove to a plate.

2. In same wok, heat remaining 1½ tablespoons oil over high heat. Add bell pepper, onion, and garlic and stir-fry until soft, 3 to 5 minutes. Add fresh and sun-dried tomatoes. Cook 1 minute. Remove to plate with chicken.

3. Add wine, thyme, salt, and pepper to wok. Boil over high heat, scraping up browned bits from bottom of pan, until liquid is reduced by half, 2 to 3 minutes.

4. Whisk in butter, a few pieces at a time, until melted. Return chicken and vegetables to wok. Cook, stirring, until heated through, 1 minute. Serve garnished with chopped parsley.

66 SPICY CHICKEN THIGHS IN TEQUILA

Prep: 10 minutes   Marinate: 1 hour
Cook: 45 to 52 minutes   Serves: 4

6 chicken thighs, about
    6 ounces each
5 tablespoons olive oil
2 garlic cloves, crushed
1 serrano pepper, seeded and
    minced
1 teaspoon imported hot
    paprika

1 teaspoon cayenne
1 teaspoon ground cumin
1 teaspoon ground coriander
½ teaspoon salt
¼ teaspoon crushed hot red
    pepper
½ cup tomato juice
½ cup tequila

1. In a large bowl, combine chicken thighs, 3 tablespoons olive oil, garlic, serrano pepper, paprika, cayenne, cumin, coriander, salt, and hot pepper. Toss to coat. Cover with plastic wrap and marinate for 1 hour at room temperature.

2. In a wok, heat remaining 2 tablespoons oil over medium-high heat until hot, swirling to coat sides of pan. Arrange chicken thighs extending up sides of pan without overlapping. Cook, turning, until browned all over, 5 to 7 minutes.

3. Add tomato juice and tequila. Reduce heat to medium-low, cover, and cook until chicken is tender and juices run clear when pricked near bone, 40 to 45 minutes.

67   CHICKEN AND SALMON STIR-FRY
Prep: 15 minutes   Marinate: 30 minutes   Cook: 9 to 12 minutes
Serves: 6

This combination of Dijon-marinated chicken and fresh salmon in an orange-flavored soy sauce is one of my friend W. Michael Boyer's favorite dishes. He first tasted it in a posh restaurant in Philadelphia, and I was delighted to re-create it at home. Note that the salmon and chicken are marinated separately. Serve with plenty of hot steamed rice.

½ **cup dry white wine**
3 **tablespoons Dijon mustard**
2 **tablespoons honey**
3 **tablespoons cornstarch**
1 **pound skinless, boneless chicken breasts, cut into ¾-inch pieces**
1 **pound salmon fillets, skin removed, cut into ¾-inch pieces**

¼ **cup vegetable oil**
1 **medium red bell pepper, chopped**
1 **medium carrot, sliced**
1½ **cups broccoli florets**
3 **scallions, sliced**
1 **garlic clove, minced**
½ **cup orange juice**
2 **tablespoons soy sauce**

1. Combine the wine, Dijon mustard, honey, and cornstarch in a mixing bowl and whisk to blend well. Divide the marinade between two medium bowls. Add chicken pieces to one bowl and toss to coat. Add salmon pieces to other bowl and toss gently to coat. Let marinate at room temperature 30 minutes.

2. In a wok, heat 2 tablespoons oil over high heat until hot, swirling to coat sides of pan. Add bell pepper, carrot, broccoli, scallions, and garlic and stir-fry until crisp-tender, 4 to 5 minutes. Remove to a bowl.

3. In same wok, heat remaining 2 tablespoons oil over medium-high heat. Add marinated chicken and salmon and stir-fry until chicken is white throughout and salmon is opaque throughout, 3 to 5 minutes. Return vegetables to wok.

4. Add orange juice and soy sauce. Cook, stirring gently, 2 minutes. Serve at once.

68   LEIGH'S CANDLELIGHT CHICKEN
Prep: 10 minutes   Cook: 7 to 11 minutes   Serves: 4

After tasting this delicious chicken and pasta dish in a restaurant, my daughter Leigh re-created the following version for us to enjoy at home.

1 **cup peach wine or peach nectar**
½ **cup apricot preserves**
1 **tablespoon Dijon mustard**
1 **(9-ounce) package fresh angel hair pasta**
3 **tablespoon olive oil**
1¼ **pounds skinless, boneless chicken breasts, cut into 1-inch cubes**

¼ **pound snow peas, stemmed and stringed**
1 **medium red bell pepper, cut into ¼-inch-wide strips**
4 **scallions, chopped**
1 **garlic clove, minced**
½ **teaspoon salt**
¼ **teaspoon pepper**

1. In a bowl, combine wine, preserves, and Dijon mustard. Whisk until blended. Set aside.

2. In a large pot of boiling salted water, cook angel hair pasta until just tender, 1 to 2 minutes. Drain into a colander and rinse under cold running water; drain well.

3. In a wok, heat 1½ tablespoons olive oil over high heat until hot, swirling to coat sides of pan. Add chicken and stir-fry until meat is white throughout but still juicy, 3 to 4 minutes. Remove to a plate.

4. In same wok, heat remaining 1½ tablespoons oil over high heat. Add snow peas, bell pepper, scallions, garlic, salt, and pepper. Stir-fry until vegetables are crisp-tender, 2 to 3 minutes. Add chicken and pasta. Mix in reserved mustard-fruit sauce. Cook, tossing, until heated through, 1 to 2 minutes.

69   OLYMPIC CHICKEN
Prep: 10 minutes   Cook: 9 to 13 minutes   Serves: 4

3 **tablespoons olive oil**
1 **pound skinless, boneless chicken breasts, cut into 1-inch pieces**
1 **medium onion, chopped**
1 **garlic clove, minced**
½ **teaspoon oregano**
1 **medium red bell pepper, cut into thin strips**

1 **medium green bell pepper, cut into thin strips**
1 **small yellow bell pepper, cut into thin strips**
¼ **cup orange juice**
1 **(8-ounce) can mandarin oranges, with their juice**

1. In a wok, heat 1½ tablespoons olive oil over high heat until hot, swirling to coat sides of pan. Add chicken and stir-fry until cooked through but still juicy, 3 to 4 minutes. Remove to a plate.

2. In same wok, heat remaining 1½ tablespoons oil over high heat. Add onion, garlic, oregano, and bell peppers and stir-fry until soft, 3 to 5 minutes. Return chicken to wok.

3. Add orange juice and mandarin oranges and their juice. Cook until liquid is slightly reduced, 2 to 3 minutes.

---

70   SHERRIED CHICKEN WITH ASPARAGUS, CARROTS, AND NOODLES

Prep: 10 minutes   Cook: 16 to 19 minutes   Serves: 4

3 tablespoons vegetable oil	1 tablespoon butter
1 small onion, minced	1 cup fine egg noodles
½ pound fresh asparagus, cut diagonally into ½-inch slices	1 cup chicken broth
	1 cup dry sherry
1 carrot, cut diagonally into thin slices	¼ cup chopped parsley
	½ teaspoon salt
1 pound skinless, boneless chicken breasts, cut into ½-inch dice	¼ teaspoon pepper

1. In a wok, heat 1½ tablespoons oil over high heat until hot, swirling to coat sides of pan. Add onion, asparagus, and carrot and stir-fry until crisp-tender, about 3 minutes. Remove to a plate.

2. In same wok, heat remaining 1½ tablespoons oil over high heat. Add chicken and stir-fry until meat is white throughout but still juicy, 2 to 3 minutes. Remove to plate with vegetables.

3. Add butter to wok and heat over medium-high heat until melted. Add uncooked noodles and cook, tossing to coat, 1 minute. Return chicken and vegetables to wok.

4. Add chicken broth, sherry, parsley, salt, and pepper. Bring to a boil. Reduce heat to medium-low, cover, and cook until noodles are tender and most of liquid is absorbed, 10 to 12 minutes.

71   CHICKEN AND BROCCOLI IN WHITE WINE
Prep: 10 minutes   Cook: 12 to 15 minutes   Serves: 6

3 tablespoons vegetable oil
1½ pounds boneless, skinless
    chicken breasts, cut into
    1-inch pieces
2 cups broccoli florets
4 scallions, sliced
1 garlic clove, minced

½ cup dry white wine
¼ cup chicken broth
2 tablespoons white wine
    vinegar
½ teaspoon salt
¼ teaspoon pepper

1. In a wok, heat 1½ tablespoons oil over high heat until hot, swirling to coat sides of pan. Add chicken and stir-fry until meat is white throughout but still juicy, 3 to 4 minutes. Remove to a plate.

2. In same wok, heat remaining 1½ tablespoons oil over medium-high heat. Add broccoli and scallions and stir-fry until broccoli is crisp-tender, 3 to 4 minutes. Add garlic and cook, stirring, 2 minutes longer. Remove to plate with chicken.

3. Add wine, chicken broth, vinegar, salt, and pepper to wok. Cook over high heat, scraping up browned bits from bottom of wok, 3 minutes. Return chicken and vegetables to wok. Cook until heated through, 1 to 2 minutes.

72   CHICKEN AND NOODLE SUNDAY SUPPER
Prep: 10 minutes   Cook: 14 to 20 minutes   Serves: 4

3 tablespoons vegetable oil
2 carrots, sliced
1 medium onion, chopped
1 celery rib, sliced
½ pound fresh spinach leaves,
    rinsed well and drained
1 pound skinless, boneless
    chicken breasts, cut into
    ½-inch cubes

2 (14½-ounce) cans chicken
    broth
½ cup dry white wine
1 (9-ounce) package fresh
    spinach fettuccine
½ teaspoon salt
¼ teaspoon pepper
¼ teaspoon grated nutmeg

1. In a wok, heat 2 tablespoons oil over high heat until hot, swirling to coat sides of pan. Add carrots, onion, and celery and stir-fry until softened, 3 to 5 minutes. Add spinach and cook, stirring, until wilted, 1 to 2 minutes. Remove vegetables to a plate.

2. In same wok, heat remaining 1 tablespoon oil over high heat. Add chicken and stir-fry until meat is white throughout but still juicy, about 3 minutes. Remove to plate with vegetables.

3. Add chicken broth, wine, and 1 cup water to wok. Bring to a boil. Add fettuccine. Cook over medium heat, stirring occasionally, until tender and most of liquid is absorbed, 6 to 8 minutes. Return chicken and vegetables to wok. Add salt, pepper, and nutmeg. Cook, stirring, until heated through, 1 to 2 minutes.

73 TURKEY FAJITAS

Prep: 10 minutes Marinate: 1 hour Cook: 7 to 10 minutes
Serves: 6

These deluxe fajitas are great for family dinners and casual entertaining. Serve with a variety of garnishes and toppings: shredded lettuce, onions, and tomatoes. Top with guacamole and/or salsa.

½ cup dry white wine
½ cup pineapple juice
2 tablespoons lime juice
¼ cup chopped cilantro
2 tablespoons minced, seeded jalapeño pepper
1 garlic clove, minced

1½ pounds skinless, boneless turkey cutlets, cut into 2 x ¼-inch strips
¼ cup vegetable oil
1 medium white onion, sliced
6 flour tortillas, 7 inches in diameter, warmed

1. In a medium bowl, combine wine, pineapple juice, lime juice, cilantro, jalapeño pepper, and garlic. Add turkey strips and toss to coat. Marinate, covered, in refrigerator, 1 hour.

2. In a wok, heat 2 tablespoons oil over medium-high heat until hot, swirling to coat sides of pan. Remove turkey from marinade and add to wok. Stir-fry until meat is white throughout but still juicy, 3 to 5 minutes. Remove to a plate.

3. In same wok, heat remaining 2 tablespoons oil over high heat until hot. Add onion and stir-fry until softened, 3 to 4 minutes. Return turkey to wok. Cook, stirring, until heated through, about 1 minute. Serve wrapped in tortillas.

74 GROUND TURKEY WITH ORZO, ZUCCHINI, AND FRESH BASIL

Prep: 10 minutes Cook: 16 to 20 minutes Serves: 6

1 tablespoon olive oil
1 medium onion, chopped
1 garlic clove, minced
1½ pounds ground turkey
1 (16-ounce) can Italian crushed tomatoes

2 medium zucchini, sliced
¼ cup chopped fresh basil
½ teaspoon salt
¼ teaspoon pepper
1 cup orzo (rice-shaped pasta)
⅓ cup grated Parmesan cheese

1. In a wok, heat olive oil over medium-high heat until hot, swirling to coat sides of pan. Add onion and garlic and cook, stirring, until softened, about 3 minutes. Add ground turkey and cook, stirring, until meat loses its pink color, 5 to 7 minutes.

2. Add crushed tomatoes, zucchini, basil, salt, pepper, and 1 cup water. Bring to a boil. Stir in orzo. Reduce heat to medium-low, cover, and cook until orzo is tender and most of sauce is absorbed, 8 to 10 minutes. Stir in cheese.

75   STIR-FRIED TURKEY AND BROCCOLI ASIAN-STYLE

Prep: 5 minutes   Cook: 13 to 16 minutes   Serves: 4

2 tablespoons corn oil
1 pound skinless, boneless
     turkey breast, cut into
     2 x ½-inch strips
1 cup broccoli florets
3 scallions, sliced
1 teaspoon minced fresh
     ginger

1 garlic clove, minced
¼ cup dry white wine
2 tablespoons soy sauce
2 teaspoons cornstarch
¼ cup chicken broth
1 (8-ounce) can sliced water
     chestnuts, drained

1. In a wok, heat 1 tablespoon oil over medium-high heat until hot, swirling to coat sides of pan. Add turkey and stir-fry until meat is white throughout but still juicy, 4 to 5 minutes. Remove to a plate.

2. In same wok, heat remaining 1 tablespoon oil over medium-high heat. Add broccoli. Stir-fry 2 minutes. Add scallions, ginger, and garlic. Stir-fry until broccoli is crisp-tender, 3 to 4 minutes. Add wine and soy sauce. Cook 2 minutes.

3. Dissolve cornstarch in chicken broth and stir into wok. Cook over high heat, stirring, until sauce boils and thickens, 1 to 2 minutes. Return turkey to wok. Add water chestnuts. Cook until heated through, about 1 minute.

76   PEPPER CUBE STEAK

Prep: 10 minutes   Cook: 14 to 18 minutes   Serves: 4

3 tablespoons vegetable oil
1 pound cube steak, cut into
     ½-inch cubes
1 small green bell pepper, cut
     into wedges
1 small red bell pepper, cut
     into wedges

1 large onion, cut into wedges
1 garlic clove, minced
½ teaspoon seasoned salt
¼ teaspoon pepper
1 (10¾ ounce) can beef gravy
     with onions

1. In a wok, heat 1½ tablespoons oil over high heat until hot, swirling to coat sides of pan. Add cube steak and stir-fry until meat loses its red color, 3 to 4 minutes. Remove to a plate.

2. In same wok, heat remaining 1½ tablespoons oil over high heat. Add bell peppers, onion, garlic, seasoned salt, and pepper. Stir-fry until crisp-tender, 3 to 4 minutes. Return meat and any juices that have collected on plate to wok.

3. Add gravy, cover, and cook until meat is tender, 8 to 10 minutes.

77 BEEF WITH BELL PEPPERS AND CORN
Prep: 10 minutes   Cook: 14 to 18 minutes   Serves: 4

Partially freezing the meat ensures easier slicing. This dish tastes great over lots of steamed rice.

1 pound boneless sirloin steak	1 cup beef broth
3 tablespoons corn oil	2 tablespoons soy sauce
1 small onion, chopped	2 tablespoons hoisin sauce
1 medium red bell pepper, cut into ¼-inch strips	¼ teaspoon pepper
	1 (10-ounce) package frozen corn kernels, thawed
1 medium green bell pepper, cut into ¼-inch strips	2 teaspoons cornstarch

1. Cut steak across grain on a slight diagonal into thin strips. In a wok, heat 1½ tablespoons oil over high heat until hot, swirling to coat sides of pan. Add beef and stir-fry until meat loses its red color, 2 to 3 minutes. Remove to a plate.

2. In same wok, heat remaining 1½ tablespoons oil over high heat. Add onion and red and green bell peppers. Stir-fry until peppers are crisp-tender, 3 to 5 minutes. Return meat to wok.

3. Add beef broth, soy sauce, hoisin sauce, and pepper. Bring to a boil. Reduce heat to medium. Cook 5 minutes. Add corn and cook 3 minutes.

4. Dissolve cornstarch in ¼ cup cold water and stir into wok. Cook over high heat, stirring, until sauce boils and thickens, 1 to 2 minutes.

78 TEX MEX POT CHILI WITH RICE
Prep: 10 minutes   Cook: 29 to 33 minutes   Serves: 6

2 tablespoons olive oil	1 cup white rice
1 medium onion, chopped	1 (16-ounce) can crushed tomatoes
1 medium green bell pepper, chopped	2 teaspoons chili powder
1 garlic clove, minced	½ teaspoon ground cumin
1½ pounds ground chuck (80% lean)	½ teaspoon salt
	¼ teaspoon pepper

1. In a wok, heat olive oil over medium-high heat until hot, swirling to coat sides of pan. Add onion, bell pepper, and garlic and cook, stirring, until softened, 3 to 4 minutes.

2. Add ground chuck and cook, stirring, until meat is brown and crumbly, 5 to 6 minutes. Add rice and cook, stirring to coat, 2 minutes.

3. Add tomatoes, chili powder, cumin, salt, pepper, and 1 cup water. Bring to a boil. Reduce heat to low, cover, and cook until rice is absorbed, 18 to 20 minutes.

79   CITRUSY BEEF WITH ASPARAGUS
Prep: 10 minutes   Marinate: 1 hour   Cook: 8 minutes   Serves: 4

1 pound flank steak
2 tablespoons soy sauce
2 tablespoons lemon juice
1 egg white
1 tablespoon honey
1 tablespoon cornstarch
½ teaspoon lemon pepper
   seasoning
½ teaspoon ground ginger
3 tablespoons vegetable oil
½ pound fresh asparagus, cut
   diagonally into ½-inch
   slices
4 scallions, sliced
⅓ cup dry white wine
⅓ cup orange juice

1. Cut steak across grain on a slight diagonal into thin strips. In a medium bowl, combine soy sauce, lemon juice, egg white, honey, cornstarch, lemon pepper seasoning, and ginger. Add beef slices and toss to coat. Let marinate at room temperature for 1 hour.

2. In a wok, heat 1½ tablespoons oil over medium-high heat until hot, swirling to coat sides of pan. Add asparagus and scallions and stir-fry until crisp-tender, about 3 minutes. Remove to a plate.

3. In same wok, heat remaining 1½ tablespoons oil over high heat. Add beef and stir-fry until meat loses its red color, about 3 minutes. Return vegetables to wok.

4. Stir in wine and orange juice. Cook, tossing, 2 minutes.

80   PORK IN CHUNKY CHILE TOMATO SAUCE
Prep: 10 minutes   Cook: 17 to 21 minutes   Serves: 4

3 tablespoons vegetable oil
1 pound lean boneless pork
   loin, cut into 2 x ½-inch
   strips
1 medium onion, chopped
1 (4-ounce) can diced green
   chiles
1 (8-ounce) can tomato sauce
1 teaspoon Worcestershire
   sauce
1 teaspoon chili powder

1. In a wok, heat 1 tablespoon oil over high heat until hot, swirling to coat sides of pan. Add pork and stir-fry until browned outside and white in center, 3 to 5 minutes. Remove to a plate.

2. In same wok, heat remaining 2 tablespoons oil over high heat. Add onion and cook, stirring, until soft, 3 to 4 minutes. Add chiles, tomato sauce, Worcestershire sauce, chili powder, and ½ cup water. Bring to a boil, reduce heat to medium, and cook 10 minutes.

3. Return pork to wok and cook until heated through, 1 to 2 minutes.

81   BEEF WITH MUSHROOMS AND NOODLES
Prep: 10 minutes   Cook: 17 to 22 minutes   Serves: 4 to 6

12 ounces egg noodles
3 tablespoons vegetable oil
1½ pounds boneless sirloin
   steak, cut into ½-inch
   strips
½ pound fresh mushrooms,
   sliced

3 scallions, sliced
1 garlic clove, minced
½ cup beef broth
¼ cup hoisin sauce
3 tablespoons soy sauce
1 tablespoon Asian sesame oil

1. In a large pot of boiling salted water, cook noodles until tender but still firm, 10 to 12 minutes. Drain and rinse under cold running water; drain well.

2. In a wok, heat 1½ tablespoons oil over high heat until hot, swirling to coat sides of pan. Add beef and stir-fry until meat loses its red color, about 3 minutes. Remove to a plate.

3. In same wok, heat remaining 1½ tablespoons oil over high heat. Add mushrooms, scallions, and garlic and stir-fry until mushrooms are tender, 3 to 5 minutes. Return meat to wok. Add noodles.

4. In a small bowl, combine beef broth, hoisin sauce, soy sauce, and sesame oil. Whisk to blend well. Pour into wok, and cook, stirring until heated through, 1 to 2 minutes.

82   NO-MEAT CHILI
Prep: 10 minutes   Cook: 15 to 22 minutes   Serves: 6

3 tablespoons olive oil
2 medium green bell peppers,
   chopped
2 medium onions, chopped
2 medium carrots, chopped
¼ pound fresh mushrooms,
   chopped
2 garlic cloves, crushed
2 tablespoons minced fresh
   green chiles
2 tablespoons chili powder

2 teaspoons cumin
½ teaspoon salt
¼ teaspoon pepper
1 (28-ounce) can Italian peeled
   tomatoes, broken up,
   juice reserved
1 (16-ounce) can chick-peas
   (garbanzo beans), liquid
   reserved
1 (16-ounce) can red kidney
   beans, liquid reserved

1. In a wok, heat olive oil over medium-high heat until hot, swirling to coat sides of pan. Add bell peppers, onions, carrots, mushrooms, and garlic. Cook, stirring, until onions are softened, 4 to 5 minutes. Add chiles, chili powder, cumin, salt, and pepper. Cook, stirring, 1 to 2 minutes.

2. Add tomatoes, chick-peas, and kidney beans, along with reserved juices. Heat to boiling. Reduce heat to medium and cook until sauce has reduced by one-third, 10 to 15 minutes.

83   STIR-FRIED BEEF AND PEACHES

Prep: 10 minutes   Marinate: 2 hours   Cook: 6 to 9 minutes
Serves: 4

While beef and fruit may sound unusual at first glance, the savory-sweet combination is popular in many different cuisines, especially African and Middle Eastern. The Asian seasonings add an "East meets West" flavor that is very appealing.

1 pound flank steak	1 large leek (white part only),
½ cup peach nectar	rinsed well and chopped
2 tablespoons hoisin sauce	2 garlic cloves, minced
1 tablespoon brown sugar	1 cup sliced fresh or frozen
1 teaspoon Asian sesame oil	peaches
½ teaspoon ground ginger	2 teaspoons cornstarch
3 tablespoons vegetable oil	

1. Cut steak across grain on a diagonal into thin strips. In a medium bowl, combine peach nectar, hoisin sauce, brown sugar, sesame oil, and ginger. Stir to blend well. Add meat slices and toss to coat. Refrigerate, turning occasionally, 2 hours.

2. In a wok, heat 1½ tablespoons oil over medium-high heat until hot, swirling to coat sides of pan. Add leek and garlic. Stir-fry until softened, 3 to 5 minutes. Remove to a plate.

3. Remove meat from marinade and pat dry. Reserve marinade. In same wok, heat remaining 1½ tablespoons oil over high heat. Add beef and stir-fry until meat loses its red color, about 2 minutes. Return leek to wok. Add peaches and reserved marinade. Cook 2 minutes.

4. Dissolve cornstarch in ¼ cup cold water. Add to stir-fried mixture and cook, stirring, until sauce boils and thickens, 1 to 2 minutes.

84   FRESH SALMON WITH PINEAPPLE IN PINEAPPLE-ORANGE SAUCE

Prep: 10 minutes   Cook: 9 to 13 minutes   Serves: 6

¼ cup vegetable oil	1 (8-ounce) can unsweetened
1 celery rib, sliced	pineapple chunks,
1 medium onion, chopped	drained, juice reserved
1 garlic clove, minced	2 teaspoons minced fresh
1½ pounds salmon fillets, skin	ginger
removed, cut into 1-inch	1 teaspoon grated orange zest
chunks	2 teaspoons cornstarch
½ cup orange juice	

1. In a wok, heat 2 tablespoons oil over high heat until hot, swirling to coat sides of pan. Add celery, onion, and garlic and stir-fry until crisp-tender, 2 to 3 minutes. Remove to a plate.

2. In same wok, heat remaining 2 tablespoons oil over medium-high heat. Add salmon and stir-fry until opaque and cooked through, 4 to 6 minutes. Remove to plate with vegetables.

3. Add orange juice, reserved pineapple juice, ginger, and orange zest to wok. Cook over medium-high heat 2 minutes. Return salmon and vegetables to wok. Add pineapple chunks.

4. Dissolve cornstarch in ¼ cup cold water and stir into wok. Cook over high heat, stirring, until sauce boils and thickens, 1 to 2 minutes.

---

85   BLACKENED TUNA STEAKS
Prep: 10 minutes   Cook: 8 to 12 minutes   Serves: 4

This seasoning mix works very well with other full-flavored fish, such as swordfish, shark, or tuna. Use the same size steaks when preparing the recipe. If you have an exhaust fan in the kitchen, turn it on—there will be smoke.

¼ cup orange juice
¼ cup white wine vinegar
1 tablespoon honey
¼ cup olive oil
1 teaspoon paprika
1 teaspoon pepper
1 teaspoon garlic powder
1 teaspoon salt
1½ teaspoons minced fresh thyme, or ½ teaspoon dried

1½ teaspoons minced fresh oregano, or ½ teaspoon dried
½ teaspoon onion powder
½ teaspoon cayenne
4 tuna steaks, 8 ounces each

1. In a small bowl, combine orange juice, vinegar, and honey. Whisk to blend well.

2. In a shallow dish, combine olive oil, paprika, pepper, garlic powder, salt, thyme, oregano, onion powder, and cayenne. Blend well. Brush seasoned oil onto both sides of tuna steaks.

3. Heat wok over high heat until very hot. Arrange coated tuna steaks extending up sides of pan without overlapping and cook until dark brown on bottom, 3 to 4 minutes, rotating for even cooking. Turn and cook until well browned on other side, 2 to 3 minutes.

4. Add orange juice mixture and cook until fish is just opaque in center, 3 to 5 minutes. Serve hot, with pan juices spooned over tuna.

86   SESAME-COATED COD AND CABBAGE
Prep: 10 minutes   Cook: 9 to 12 minutes   Serves: 3

½ cup sesame seeds
½ cup dried bread crumbs
1 egg
1 tablespoon Asian sesame oil
1 pound cod fillets, cut into
    1-inch chunks
6 tablespoons vegetable oil
2 cups shredded cabbage

3 scallions, sliced
1 garlic clove, crushed
2 tablespoons rice vinegar
1 tablespoon honey
1 teaspoon minced fresh
    ginger
2 tablespoons soy sauce

1. Mix sesame seeds and bread crumbs in a shallow dish. In a small bowl, beat egg with sesame oil. Dip cod pieces first in egg, then in sesame mixture. Arrange on a plate and refrigerate while cooking cabbage.

2. In a wok, heat 1½ tablespoons oil over high heat until hot, swirling to coat sides of pan. Stir-fry cabbage, scallions, and garlic until cabbage is crisp-tender, 3 to 5 minutes. Remove to a plate.

3. In same wok, heat 1½ tablespoons oil over medium-high heat. Add cod in one layer and cook until golden brown on bottom, 3 to 4 minutes. Turn and cook until brown on other side, about 2 minutes. Return vegetables to wok.

4. In a small bowl, whisk together vinegar, honey, ginger, soy sauce, and remaining 3 tablespoons oil. Pour into wok. Cook, stirring gently, 1 minute.

87   TUNA AND BRUSSELS SPROUTS FRIED RICE
Prep: 10 minutes   Cook: 12 to 14 minutes   Serves: 4

3 tablespoons vegetable oil
1 egg, beaten
1 (10-ounce) package frozen
    brussels sprouts, thawed,
    drained, and halved
1 medium onion, chopped
1 garlic clove, minced

1 cup chicken broth
1 (7-ounce) can tuna, drained
    and flaked
¼ teaspoon pepper
2 teaspoons Asian sesame oil
2 cups cooked rice
2 tablespoons soy sauce

1. In a wok, heat 1 tablespoon oil over high heat until hot. Add egg and cook, stirring, until firm. Remove to a plate. Cut into small pieces.

2. In same wok, heat remaining 2 tablespoons oil over high heat. Add brussels sprouts, onion, and garlic and stir-fry until sprouts are crisp-tender, 5 to 6 minutes. Reduce heat to medium-low. Add ¾ cup chicken broth and cook, covered, until sprouts are tender, 3 to 4 minutes.

3. Raise heat to high and add tuna, pepper, sesame oil, rice, and cooked egg. Stir-fry 2 minutes. Add remaining ¼ cup chicken broth and soy sauce. Cook, stirring, 2 minutes.

88   SNAPPER WITH SALSA
Prep: 10 minutes   Cook: 11 to 14 minutes   Serves: 4

Here's an instant Southwestern seafood dish the whole family will enjoy. Serve with rice or roll up in warmed flour tortillas to make snapper burritos.

2   tablespoons vegetable oil
1   medium onion, chopped
1   celery rib, chopped
1   (12-ounce) jar salsa
2   tablespoons lemon juice

¼   teaspoon pepper
¼   teaspoon Worcestershire
     sauce
1½   pounds snapper fillets, cut
     into 1-inch chunks

1. In a wok, heat oil over high heat until hot. Add onion and celery and stir-fry until softened, 3 to 4 minutes.

2. Add salsa, lemon juice, pepper, and Worcestershire sauce. Bring to a boil.

3. Add snapper. Reduce heat to medium-low. Cook, stirring occasionally, until fish is tender and opaque throughout, 8 to 10 minutes.

---

89   STIR-FRIED SALMON WITH ZUCCHINI, MUSHROOMS, AND SHALLOTS
Prep: 10 minutes   Cook: 10 to 15 minutes   Serves: 4

This dish is fine for company as well as for family fare. Be sure the zucchini is dry before adding to the wok to avoid splattering.

3   tablespoons vegetable oil
1   pound salmon fillets, skin
     removed, cut into 1-inch
     chunks
1   medium zucchini, coarsely
     shredded, patted dry
3   shallots, chopped
¼   pound fresh mushrooms,
     sliced

¾   cup bottled clam juice
2   tablespoons lemon juice
2   tablespoons chopped dill
2   tablespoons grated lemon
     zest
½   teaspoon salt
¼   teaspoon pepper
2   tablespoons butter, cut into
     small pieces

1. In a wok, heat 1½ tablespoons oil over medium-high heat until hot, swirling to coat sides of pan. Add salmon and stir-fry until opaque and cooked through, 3 to 4 minutes. Remove to a plate.

2. In same wok, heat remaining 1½ tablespoons oil over medium-high heat. Add zucchini, shallots, and mushrooms and stir-fry until crisp-tender, 3 to 4 minutes. Remove to plate with salmon.

3. Add clam juice, lemon juice, dill, lemon zest, salt, and pepper to wok. Cook, scraping up browned bits from bottom of wok, until reduced by half, 3 to 5 minutes. Add butter, a few pieces at a time, whisking until incorporated before adding more butter. Return salmon and vegetables to wok. Cook, stirring, until heated through, 1 to 2 minutes.

90 SHRIMP DRENCHED IN BUTTERED BREAD CRUMBS
Prep: 10 minutes   Cook: 8 to 9 minutes   Serves: 4

These taste like baked stuffed shrimp, with the filling on the outside. You'll find they are extremely popular—with family and guests. Serve with rice and a fresh tomato and basil salad.

4 tablespoons butter	¼ teaspoon salt
3 tablespoons olive oil	⅛ teaspoon freshly ground
2 shallots, minced	pepper
2 garlic cloves, crushed	Dash of cayenne
¾ cup fresh bread crumbs	1½ pounds medium shrimp,
¼ cup minced parsley	shelled and deveined
¼ teaspoon dried thyme leaves	1½ teaspoons lemon juice

1. In a wok, melt butter in 1½ tablespoons olive oil over medium heat. Add shallots and cook until softened, about 2 minutes. Add garlic and cook 30 seconds longer. Add bread crumbs and cook, stirring often, until golden brown and toasted, 3 to 5 minutes. Toss with parsley, thyme, salt, pepper, and cayenne. Remove seasoned crumbs to a bowl. Wipe out wok.

2. Heat remaining 1½ tablespoons oil in wok over high heat. Add shrimp and stir-fry until shrimp are pink and curled, 2 to 3 minutes. Add bread crumbs and toss. Sprinkle with lemon juice and serve at once.

91 SHRIMP IN WHITE WINE
Prep: 15 minutes   Cook: 8 to 11 minutes   Serves: 4

Here's a quick, light shrimp dish that pairs well with rice and lightly sautéed zucchini.

1 tablespoon butter	½ cup dry white wine
3 tablespoons olive oil	¼ cup chicken broth
1½ pounds medium shrimp,	½ teaspoon salt
shelled and deveined	¼ teaspoon pepper
1 medium onion, chopped	1 tablespoon lemon juice
1 garlic clove, minced	¼ cup chopped parsley

1. In a wok, melt butter in 1 tablespoon olive oil over high heat until hot, swirling to coat sides of pan. Add shrimp and stir-fry until shrimp are pink and curled, 2 to 3 minutes. Remove to a plate.

2. In same wok, heat remaining 2 tablespoons oil over medium-high heat. Add onion and garlic. Stir-fry until soft, 3 to 5 minutes.

3. Add wine, chicken broth, salt, pepper, and lemon juice. Boil over high heat until reduced by one-third, about 3 minutes. Return shrimp to wok. Cook, tossing, for 30 seconds to heat through. Add parsley and serve.

92   STIR-FRIED SHRIMP AND GRAPEFRUIT
Prep: 10 minutes   Cook: 6 to 8 minutes   Serves: 4

3 tablespoons vegetable oil
1½ pounds medium shrimp,
    shelled and deveined
3 scallions, chopped
1 garlic clove, crushed
½ cup dry white wine
½ cup unsweetened grapefruit
    sections, drained, juice
    reserved

½ teaspoon salt
¼ teaspoon pepper
2 tablespoons soy sauce
3 tablespoon unsalted butter,
    cut into small pieces

1. In a wok, heat 2 tablespoons oil over high heat until hot, swirling to coat sides of pan. Add shrimp and stir-fry until shrimp are pink and curled, 2 to 3 minutes. Remove to a serving plate.

2. In same wok, heat remaining 1 tablespoon oil over medium-high heat. Add scallions and garlic and stir-fry until softened, 1 to 2 minutes.

3. Add wine, grapefruit juice, salt, and pepper. Heat to boiling. Cook 2 minutes. Reduce heat to medium-low. Add soy sauce and butter. Cook, stirring, until butter is melted and sauce is smooth about 1 minute. Add grapefruit sections and pour sauce over shrimp. Serve at once.

93   CURRIED SHRIMP STROGANOFF
Prep: 10 minutes   Cook: 13 to 16 minutes   Serves: 4 to 6

Frozen shrimp are convenient to use, and no shelling is required. Make sure they're dry before cooking to prevent splattering. Serve with rice or pasta to soak up the delicious sauce.

1 tablespoon butter
3 tablespoons vegetable oil
1 medium onion, chopped
1 celery rib, chopped
1 pound medium shrimp,
    shelled and deveined
1 tablespoon curry powder

½ teaspoon ground ginger
¼ teaspoon white pepper
1 (10¾-ounce) can cream of
    mushroom soup
1 cup sour cream
2 tablespoons lemon juice

1. In a wok, melt butter in 2 tablespoons oil over medium-high heat until hot. Add onion and celery and stir-fry until softened, 3 to 5 minutes. Remove to a plate.

2. In same wok, heat remaining 1 tablespoon oil over medium-high heat. Add shrimp, curry powder, ginger, and pepper. Cook, stirring, until shrimp are pink and curled, 3 minutes.

3. Add soup, sour cream and lemon juice. Reduce heat to low. Cook, stirring, until heated through, about 5 minutes. Return vegetables to wok. Cook until vegetables are hot, 1 to 2 minutes.

94 BLACKENED SHRIMP WITH SOUTHERN VEGETABLES

Prep: 15 minutes   Cook: 12 to 16 minutes   Serves: 6

In the South, especially Louisiana, crawfish would be used in place of shrimp. If you are lucky enough to find them, substitute 1½ pounds crawfish (same size as shrimp) for the shellfish in this recipe. Serve with red beans and rice and hush puppies for an extraordinary meal.

¼ cup plus 2 tablespoons vegetable oil
1 teaspoon paprika
½ teaspoon dried oregano
½ teaspoon ground cumin
½ teaspoon chili powder
½ teaspoon garlic powder
¼ teaspoon black pepper
¼ teaspoon cayenne
2 pounds medium shrimp, shelled and deveined

1 medium green bell pepper, diced
1 (10-ounce) box frozen sliced okra, thawed
1 medium onion, chopped
1 (8-ounce) can corn kernels, drained
1 (8-ounce) can stewed tomatoes
¼ teaspoon hot pepper sauce, or more to taste

1. In a shallow dish, combine ¼ cup oil, paprika, oregano, cumin, chili powder, garlic powder, black pepper, and cayenne. Add shrimp and toss to coat thoroughly.

2. Heat wok over high heat until hot. Add coated shrimp and stir-fry until shrimp are pink and curled, 2 to 3 minutes. Remove to a serving plate.

3. In same wok, heat remaining 2 tablespoons oil over medium-high heat. Add bell pepper, okra, and onion and cook, stirring, until soft, 4 to 6 minutes.

4. Add corn, stewed tomatoes, and hot sauce. Cook until slightly thickened, 3 to 4 minutes. Return shrimp to wok and cook, stirring, until heated through, about 1 minute. Serve at once.

95 PINEAPPLE WALNUT SHRIMP

Prep: 15 minutes   Cook: 7 to 10 minutes   Serves: 4

1 cup walnuts
2½ tablespoons vegetable oil
1 pound medium shrimp, shelled and deveined
3 scallions, chopped
1 celery rib, sliced
1 medium red bell pepper, cut into thin strips

2 garlic cloves, minced
2 teaspoons minced fresh ginger
1 (8-ounce) can unsweetened pineapple chunks, juice reserved
2 teaspoons cornstarch

1. Heat wok over medium-high heat until hot. Add walnuts, reduce heat to medium, and cook, tossing constantly, until nuts are lightly toasted. Remove to a bowl and set aside.

2. In wok, heat 1½ tablespoons oil over high heat, swirling to coat sides of pan. Add shrimp and stir-fry until shrimp are pink and curled, 2 to 3 minutes. Remove to a plate.

3. In same wok, heat remaining 1 tablespoon oil over medium-high heat. Add scallions, celery, and bell pepper. Stir-fry until crisp-tender, 3 to 4 minutes. Add garlic and ginger. Cook 1 minute. Add pineapple chunks and return shrimp to wok.

4. Dissolve cornstarch in reserved pineapple juice and stir into wok. Cook over high heat, stirring, until sauce boils and thickens, 1 to 2 minutes. Stir in walnuts and serve.

96   SHRIMP AND PEPPER QUESADILLAS
Prep: 10 minutes   Cook: 10 to 13 minutes   Serves: 4 to 6

My daughter's friend Adam is one of that new breed of young men who like to cook. This is his special recipe.

5 tablespoons vegetable oil
2 garlic cloves, minced
¾ pound small or medium shrimp, shelled and deveined
1 small red bell pepper, cut into ½-inch dice
1 small yellow bell pepper, cut into ½-inch dice

1 small zucchini, cut into ½-inch dice
3 tablespoons chopped cilantro or parsley
3 tablespoons dry white wine
6 flour tortillas (7-inch), warmed
1 cup shredded Monterey Jack cheese (4 ounces)

1. In a wok, heat 1½ tablespoons oil over medium-high heat until hot, swirling to coat sides of pan. Add 1 garlic clove and shrimp and cook, stirring, until shrimp are pink and curled, about 2 minutes. Remove to a plate.

2. In same wok, heat 1½ tablespoons oil over medium-high heat. Add bell peppers, zucchini, and remaining garlic. Cook, stirring, until softened, 4 to 6 minutes. Add cilantro and wine. Cook 2 minutes.

3. On one half of each tortilla, make layers of cheese, shrimp, vegetables, and more cheese. Fold tortillas in half, pressing edges together to seal.

4. In same wok, heat remaining 2 tablespoons oil over medium-high heat. Arrange quesadillas extending up sides of pan without overlapping. Cook until light brown in color, rotating for even cooking as needed, 1 to 2 minutes. Turn and brown on other side, 1 minute.

97   HAWAIIAN SHRIMP WITH PINEAPPLE
Prep: 10 minutes   Cook: 9 to 11 minutes   Serves: 4 to 6

2 tablespoons vegetable oil
1 garlic clove, minced
2 teaspoons minced fresh
   ginger
2 pounds medium shrimp,
   shelled and deveined

¾ cup orange juice
1 (8-ounce) can unsweetened
   pineapple chunks,
   drained, juice reserved
1 tablespoon lemon juice
2 teaspoons cornstarch

1. In a wok, heat oil over high heat until hot, swirling to coat sides of pan. Add garlic and ginger. Stir-fry 30 seconds. Add shrimp and stir-fry 2 minutes.

2. Add orange juice, reserved pineapple juice, and lemon juice to wok. Cook 2 minutes. Add pineapple chunks.

3. Dissolve cornstarch in ¼ cup cold water and stir into wok. Cook over high heat, stirring, until sauce boils and thickens, 1 to 2 minutes.

Chapter 4

Chinese Stir-Fry Classics

Re-create your favorite restaurant dishes quickly and easily in your wok. This chapter takes many traditional Chinese classics and adapts them for the American kitchen. Recipes like Stir-Fried Chicken with Broccoli and Peanuts, Chinese Pepper Steak, Spicy Orange-Flavored Lamb, Chicken Fried Brown Rice, Stir-Fried Chicken with Black Bean–Garlic Sauce, and Stir-Fried Shrimp with Water Chestnuts and Peas will have your family printing up their own menus.

For proper stir-frying, a small amount of oil is heated in the wok until very hot but not smoking. The oil is swirled around to coat the sides of the wok as well, so that the food can be moved around and around. The food is cooked quickly over high heat, with continuous stirring and tossing, which yields maximum flavor in a minimum amount of time.

To get the best results from stir-frying, it is best to cut the food into relatively small pieces:

Dice—usually ½- to 1-inch cubes
Strips—¼ to ½ inch wide by up to 3 inches long
Slivers—thinner than strips and usually shorter

For the most efficient stir-frying, good preparation is crucial. It's important to assemble all the necessary ingredients and cut them up before cooking. Group ingredients according to when they will be added to the wok. One or two medium-sized bowls and several small bowls are usually helpful here.

Most of the recipes in this chapter use a pound of meat or chicken. Many of them take a pound farther than you might believe possible, to feed four and sometimes six people. Of course, if you make several dishes, you can count on stretching them even farther. And all that's needed to complete the meal is hot steamed rice and chopsticks.

98   STIR-FRIED CHICKEN WITH BROCCOLI AND PEANUTS

Prep: 10 minutes   Cook: 26 to 32 minutes   Serves: 4 to 6

Pull out your chopsticks and relax as you tuck into this tasty one-pot meal. This is a dish the entire family is guaranteed to love, and is, in fact, my son David's most frequently requested dinner.

¼ **cup vegetable oil**
2 **cups broccoli florets**
2 **medium carrots, sliced**
1 **celery rib, sliced**
3 **scallions, sliced**
1 **garlic clove, crushed**
1 **teaspoon grated fresh ginger**
1½ **pounds skinless, boneless chicken breasts, cut into ½-inch chunks**

1 **(14½-ounce) can chicken broth**
¼ **cup dry sherry**
2 **tablespoons soy sauce**
1 **cup long-grain white rice**
½ **cup dry-roasted peanuts**

1. In a wok, heat 2 tablespoons oil over high heat until hot, swirling to coat sides of pan. Add broccoli, carrots, celery, scallions, garlic, and ginger and stir-fry until crisp-tender, 4 to 6 minutes. Remove to a bowl.

2.. In same wok, heat remaining 2 tablespoons oil over high heat. Add chicken and stir-fry until meat is white throughout but still juicy, 3 to 4 minutes. Remove to bowl with vegetables.

3. Add chicken broth, sherry, and soy sauce to wok. Heat to boiling, Add rice. Reduce heat to low, cover, and cook until rice is tender, 18 to 20 minutes. Return chicken and vegetables to wok and add peanuts. Cook, stirring, until heated through, 1 to 2 minutes.

99   CHICKEN WITH CHINESE CHILI GARLIC SAUCE

Prep: 10 minutes   Cook: 6 to 8 minutes   Serves: 4

1 **egg white**
1 **tablespoon plus 2 teaspoons cornstarch**
2 **tablespoons soy sauce**
1 **garlic clove, minced**
1 **pound boneless, skinless chicken breasts, cut into ½-inch cubes**

¼ **cup chicken broth**
1 **tablespoon rice wine vinegar**
¼ **cup Chinese chili paste with garlic**
1 **tablespoon Asian sesame oil**
3 **tablespoons vegetable oil**
1 **medium onion, chopped**

1. In a medium bowl, combine egg white, 1 tablespoon cornstarch, soy sauce, and garlic. Blend well. Add chicken and toss to coat.

2. In a small bowl, dissolve remaining 2 teaspoons cornstarch in ¼ cup cold water. Add chicken broth, vinegar, chili paste, and sesame oil; stir to blend. Set sauce aside.

3. In a wok, heat 1 tablespoon vegetable oil over high heat until hot. Add onion and stir-fry until softened, 2 to 3 minutes. Remove to a plate.

4. In same wok, heat remaining 2 tablespoons oil over high heat, swirling to coat sides of pan. Add chicken mixture and stir-fry until meat is white throughout and cooked through, about 3 minutes. Return onion to wok.

5. Stir sauce and add to wok. Cook over high heat, stirring, until sauce boils and thickens, 1 to 2 minutes.

---

100   CHICKEN WITH CASHEWS, MUSHROOMS, AND BEAN SPROUTS

Prep: 10 minutes   Cook: 9 to 11 minutes   Serves: 4

6 dried shiitake mushrooms	1 cup cashews
3 tablespoons soy sauce	4 scallions, sliced
2 tablespoons dry sherry	¼ pound fresh mushrooms, sliced
1 teaspoon sugar	
1 pound skinless, boneless chicken breasts, cut crosswise into ½-inch strips	1 garlic clove, minced
	½ cup fresh bean sprouts
	½ cup chicken broth
3 tablespoons vegetable oil	2 teaspoons cornstarch

1. Place shiitakes in a small heatproof bowl. Add boiling water to cover and let soak 20 minutes. Remove mushrooms and squeeze dry. Cut off and discard stems; slice caps.

2. In a medium bowl, combine soy sauce, sherry, and sugar. Add chicken and toss to coat. Set aside.

3. In a wok, heat 1½ tablespoons oil over medium heat until hot, swirling to coat sides of pan. Add cashews and stir-fry until lightly toasted, about 2 minutes. Remove with a slotted spoon and drain on paper towels.

4. Raise heat to high. Add scallions, mushrooms, and garlic. Stir-fry until mushrooms are tender, 2 to 3 minutes. Remove to a plate.

5. Add remaining 1½ tablespoons oil to wok and heat over high heat. Add chicken and stir-fry until meat is white throughout but still juicy, about 3 minutes. Return vegetables and cashews to wok. Add sliced shiitakes, bean sprouts, and chicken broth. Cook 1 minute.

6. Dissolve cornstarch in ¼ cup cold water and stir into wok. Cook over high heat, stirring, until sauce boils and thickens, 1 to 2 minutes.

101 STIR-FRIED CHICKEN WITH BLACK BEAN–GARLIC SAUCE

Prep: 10 minutes   Cook: 4 to 7 minutes   Serves: 4

3 tablespoons vegetable oil
1 pound skinless, boneless chicken breasts, cut crosswise into ½-inch strips
2 tablespoons Chinese fermented black beans, rinsed and drained
3 scallions, chopped

2 garlic cloves, minced
1 teaspoon minced fresh ginger
½ cup chicken broth
¼ cup dry sherry
2 tablespoons soy sauce, preferably mushroom soy
1 teaspoon Asian sesame oil
2 teaspoons cornstarch

1. In a wok, heat 2 tablespoons vegetable oil over high heat until hot, swirling to coat sides of pan. Add chicken and stir-fry until meat is white throughout but still juicy, 2 to 3 minutes. Remove to a plate.

2. In same wok, heat remaining 1 tablespoon vegetable oil over medium-high heat until hot. Add black beans, scallions, garlic, and ginger. Stir-fry until garlic is softened but not browned, 1 to 2 minutes. Add chicken broth, sherry, soy sauce, and sesame oil. Bring to a boil. Return chicken to wok.

3. Dissolve cornstarch in ¼ cup cold water and stir into wok. Cook over high heat, stirring, until sauce boils and thickens, 1 to 2 minutes.

102 SPICY GARLIC CHICKEN WITH MUSHROOMS

Prep: 10 minutes   Marinate: 1 hour   Cook: 8 to 11 minutes Serves: 4

1¼ pounds skinless, boneless chicken breasts, cut crosswise into ½-inch slices
1 egg white
1 tablespoon plus 2 teaspoons cornstarch
2 tablespoons soy sauce
¼ cup chicken broth

1 tablespoon rice wine vinegar
1 tablespoon Asian sesame oil
3½ tablespoons vegetable oil
½ pound fresh mushrooms, sliced
3 scallions, chopped
¼ cup Chinese chili paste with garlic

1. Place chicken in a medium bowl. Add egg white, 1 tablespoon cornstarch, 1 tablespoon soy sauce, and 2 tablespoons cold water. Toss to coat. Cover and marinate in refrigerator 1 hour.

2. In a small bowl, whisk together chicken broth, vinegar, sesame oil, and remaining 2 teaspoons cornstarch and 1 tablespoon soy sauce. Set aside.

3. In a wok, heat 2 tablespoons vegetable oil over high heat, swirling to coat sides of pan. Add chicken and stir-fry until meat is white throughout but still juicy, 3 to 4 minutes. Remove to a plate.

4. In same wok, heat remaining 1½ tablespoons vegetable oil over high heat. Add mushrooms and scallions and stir-fry until tender, 2 to 3 minutes. Add chili paste. Cook 2 minutes. Return chicken to wok.

5. Add vinegar–sesame oil mixture and cook until sauce boils and thickens, 1 to 2 minutes.

---

103 STIR-FRIED CHICKEN WITH TOMATOES IN OYSTER SAUCE

Prep: 10 minutes   Stands: 20 minutes   Cook: 8 to 10 minutes
Serves: 4

6 dried shiitake mushrooms	2 medium tomatoes, cut into 6 wedges each
1 pound skinless, boneless chicken breasts, cut into 1-inch cubes	2 teaspoons minced fresh ginger
2 tablespoons dry sherry	⅓ cup chicken broth or water
2 tablespoons soy sauce	2 tablespoons oyster sauce
1 tablespoon cornstarch	¼ teaspoon pepper
3 tablespoons vegetable oil	
1 medium white onion, thickly sliced	

1. Place shiitakes in a small heatproof bowl. Add boiling water to cover and let soak 20 minutes. Remove mushrooms and squeeze dry. Cut off and discard stems; slice caps.

2. In a medium bowl, combine chicken, sherry, 1 tablespoon soy sauce, and cornstarch. Toss to coat chicken evenly. Let stand at room temperature 10 to 20 minutes.

3. In a wok, heat 1½ tablespoons oil over high heat until hot, swirling to coat sides of pan. Add chicken and stir-fry until meat is white throughout but still juicy, about 3 minutes. Remove to a plate.

4. Add remaining 1½ tablespoons oil to wok and heat over medium-high heat. Add onion and stir-fry until crisp-tender, about 3 minutes. Add tomato wedges and ginger and cook, stirring gently, until heated through and just beginning to soften, 1 to 2 minutes. Return chicken to wok. Add sliced shiitakes.

5. Add remaining 1 tablespoon soy sauce, chicken broth, oyster sauce, and pepper to wok. Cook, stirring, until sauce boils and thickens slightly, 1 to 2 minutes.

104   DOUBLE GINGER CHICKEN STRIPS

Prep: 5 minutes   Marinate: 30 minutes   Cook: 5 to 8 minutes
Serves: 4

⅓ cup ginger preserves
1 tablespoon cornstarch
2 tablespoons soy sauce
2 teaspoons Asian sesame oil
1 pound skinless, boneless
   chicken breasts, cut
   crosswise into ½-inch
   strips

3 tablespoons vegetable oil
1 garlic clove, minced
1 ½-inch piece peeled fresh
   ginger, minced
3 scallions, sliced
2 tablespoons rice wine
   vinegar

1. In a medium bowl, combine ginger preserves, cornstarch, soy sauce, and 2 tablespoons cold water. Whisk in sesame oil. Add chicken and toss to coat. Let marinate 30 minutes at room temperature.

2. In a wok, heat 2 tablespoon vegetable oil over high heat until hot, swirling to coat sides of pan. Add chicken with marinade and stir-fry until meat is white throughout but still juicy, 3 to 4 minutes. Remove to a plate.

3. In same wok, heat remaining 1 tablespoon oil over high heat. Add garlic, fresh ginger, and scallions and stir-fry until fragrant 1 to 2 minutes. Return chicken to wok. Stir in vinegar and cook until chicken is heated through, 1 to 2 minutes.

105   CHICKEN WITH TOASTED PEANUTS AND CHINESE VEGETABLES

Prep: 10 minutes   Cook: 8 to 9 minutes   Serves: 4

3½ tablespoons peanut oil
1 pound skinless, boneless
   chicken breasts, cut into
   ½-inch cubes
1 (6-ounce) package frozen
   Chinese pea pods,
   thawed
¼ pound fresh mushrooms,
   sliced

1 (8-ounce) can bamboo
   shoots, rinsed and
   drained
½ cup chicken broth
2 tablespoons soy sauce
1 teaspoon sugar
2 teaspoons cornstarch
1 cup dry-roasted peanuts

1. In a wok, heat 2 tablespoons oil over high heat until hot, swirling to coat sides of pan. Add chicken and stir-fry until meat is white throughout but still juicy, about 3 minutes. Remove to a plate.

2. Add remaining 1½ tablespoons oil to wok and heat over high heat. Add pea pods, mushrooms, and bamboo shoots and stir-fry until crisp-tender, about 2 minutes. Add broth, soy sauce, and sugar. Cook, stirring, 2 minutes longer. Return chicken to wok.

3. Dissolve cornstarch in 2 tablespoons cold water and stir into wok. Cook over high heat, stirring, until sauce boils and thickens, 1 to 2 minutes. Add peanuts and serve.

---

106   STIR-FRIED CHICKEN WITH COLORFUL VEGETABLES

Prep: 10 minutes   Cook: 9 to 13 minutes   Serves: 4

3   tablespoons vegetable oil
1   medium onion, sliced
1   carrot, thinly sliced
1   medium green bell pepper, cut into thin strips
2   garlic cloves, minced
1   teaspoon minced fresh ginger
1   pound skinless, boneless chicken breasts, cut crosswise into ½-inch strips

1   can (14 ounces) whole baby corn, drained
½   cup chicken broth
½   cup dry sherry
2   tablespoons soy sauce
2   tablespoons hoisin sauce
¼   teaspoon pepper
2   teaspoons cornstarch

1. In a wok, heat 2 tablespoons oil over high heat until hot, swirling to coat sides of pan. Add onion, carrot, and bell pepper. Stir-fry until onion and pepper are softened, 4 to 6 minutes. With a slotted spoon, remove to a plate.

2. In same wok, heat remaining 1 tablespoon oil over high heat. Add garlic and ginger and stir-fry 30 seconds. Add chicken and stir-fry until meat is barely white throughout, 2 to 3 minutes.

3. Add corn, chicken broth, sherry, soy sauce, hoisin sauce, and pepper. Cook over medium heat 2 minutes. Return vegetables to wok.

4. Dissolve cornstarch in ¼ cup cold water and stir into wok. Cook over high heat, stirring, until sauce boils and thickens, 1 to 2 minutes.

107   CHICKEN AND CUCUMBERS WITH CASHEWS

Prep: 10 minutes   Cook: 7 to 11 minutes   Serves: 4

Cucumbers taste delightful when lightly cooked. Try this twist on a familiar vegetable prepared in a different manner. Hoisin sauce is available in Chinese groceries and in the Asian foods section of most supermarkets.

2   tablespoons dry sherry
2   tablespoons soy sauce
1   tablespoon plus 2 teaspoons cornstarch
1   pound skinless, boneless chicken breasts, cut into ½-inch cubes
¼   cup chicken broth

2   tablespoons hoisin sauce
1   teaspoon sugar
¼   teaspoon pepper
3   tablespoons vegetable oil
3   scallions, sliced
1   cup cucumber, cut into ½-inch dice
½   cup cashews

1. In a medium bowl, blend sherry, soy sauce, and 1 tablespoon cornstarch. Add chicken and toss to coat.

2. In a small bowl, dissolve remaining 2 teaspoons cornstarch in 1 tablespoon cold water. Add chicken broth, hoisin sauce, sugar, and pepper and stir to blend. Set sauce aside.

3. In a wok, heat 2 tablespoons oil over high heat until hot, swirling to coat sides of pan. Add chicken mixture and cook, tossing, until meat is white and cooked through, 3 to 4 minutes. Remove to a plate.

4. In same wok, heat remaining 1 tablespoon oil over medium-high heat. Add scallions. Stir-fry until scallions are soft, 2 to 3 minutes. Add cucumber. Cook until heated through, 1 to 2 minutes.

5. Return chicken to wok. Add reserved sauce. Cook over high heat, stirring, until sauce boils and thickens, 1 to 2 minutes. Stir in cashews and serve.

108   STIR-FRIED BEEF AND BROCCOLI

Prep: 10 minutes   Cook: 9 to 11 minutes   Serves: 4

1   pound boneless sirloin steak
2   tablespoons dry sherry
2   tablespoons soy sauce
1   garlic clove, minced
½   teaspoon ground ginger
3   tablespoons vegetable oil
1   small bunch of broccoli, separated into florets

3   scallions, chopped
¼   pound fresh mushrooms, sliced
2   teaspoons cornstarch
½   cup beef broth

1. Cut steak across grain on a slight diagonal into thin strips. In a medium bowl, combine sherry, soy sauce, garlic, and ginger. Add beef slices and toss to coat.

2. In a wok, heat 1½ tablespoons oil over high heat until hot, swirling to coat sides of pan. Add beef and stir-fry until meat loses its red color, about 3 minutes. Remove to a plate.

3. Add remaining 1½ tablespoons oil to wok and heat over high heat. Add broccoli. Stir-fry until crisp-tender, 3 to 4 minutes. Add scallions and mushrooms. Stir-fry 2 minutes. Return beef to wok.

4. Dissolve cornstarch in beef broth and stir into wok. Cook over high heat, stirring, until sauce boils and thickens, 1 to 2 minutes.

109 SPICY CHICKEN
Prep: 10 minutes   Cook: 4 to 6 minutes   Serves: 4

This dish is *hot!* Serve with lots of rice—white or brown—to absorb the fire and accompany with a Chinese vegetable or Western-style sautéed sugar-snap peas and carrots.

1 **egg white**
1 **tablespoon cornstarch**
3 **tablespoons soy sauce**
1 **pound skinless, boneless**
   chicken breasts, cut into
   ½-inch cubes
¼ **cup Chinese chili paste with**
   garlic

¼ **cup chicken broth**
1 **tablespoon white wine**
   vinegar
2 **teaspoons Asian sesame oil**
1 **teaspoon sugar**
½ **teaspoon salt**
2 **tablespoons corn oil**

1. In a medium bowl, mix together egg white, cornstarch, 1 tablespoon soy sauce, and 1 tablespoon cold water until smooth. Add chicken pieces and toss to coat well.

2. In a small bowl, combine chili paste, chicken broth, vinegar, sesame oil, sugar, salt, and remaining 2 tablespoons soy sauce. Set sauce aside.

3. In a wok, heat oil over high heat until hot, swirling to coat sides of pan. Add chicken mixture and stir-fry until meat is white throughout but still juicy, 3 to 4 minutes. Add reserved sauce and stir until mixture boils and thickens, 1 to 2 minutes.

110 THAI CHICKEN
Prep: 15 minutes   Cook: 11 to 13 minutes   Serves: 4

Obviously, this is not a Chinese recipe, but it is one of my favorite Asian chicken stir-fries, so I couldn't resist including it in this collection.

3 tablespoons vegetable oil
1 pound skinless, boneless chicken breasts, cut crosswise into ½-inch strips
1 medium onion, chopped
2 garlic cloves, crushed
¼ cup red curry paste*
2 tablespoons fish sauce (nam pla)*
2 teaspoons grated lime zest

1½ teaspoons minced fresh ginger
4 green serrano peppers or other fresh hot chiles, seeded and thinly sliced
1 teaspoon instant tamarind concentrate,* dissolved in 2 tablespoons hot water
2 teaspoons sugar
¼ cup chopped fresh mint

1. In a wok, heat 1½ tablespoons oil over high heat until hot, swirling to coat sides of pan. Add chicken and stir-fry until meat is white throughout but still juicy, 3 to 4 minutes. Remove to a plate.

2. In same wok, heat remaining 1½ tablespoons oil over medium-high heat until hot. Add onion and garlic and stir-fry until softened, 3 to 4 minutes. Return chicken to wok.

3. Mix curry paste with fish sauce, lime zest, and ginger and add to chicken; stir-fry 3 minutes. Add serrano peppers, tamarind, and sugar. Stir-fry 2 minutes. Sprinkle with mint and serve.

* *Available in Asian markets or specialty food stores.*

111 STIR-FRIED SHRIMP WITH WATER CHESTNUTS AND PEAS
Prep: 15 minutes   Cook: 5 to 7 minutes   Serves: 4

½ cup dry sherry
2 tablespoons hoisin sauce
1 egg white
1 tablespoon cornstarch
1 pound medium shrimp, shelled and deveined
3 tablespoons vegetable oil

1 medium onion, chopped
1 medium carrot, chopped
1 (8-ounce) can sliced water chestnuts, drained
1 (10-ounce) package frozen small peas, thawed
2 teaspoons Asian sesame oil

1. In a small bowl, combine sherry, hoisin sauce, egg white, and cornstarch. Add shrimp and toss to coat.

2. In a wok, heat 2 tablespoons vegetable oil over high heat until hot, swirling to coat sides of pan. Add onion and carrot and stir-fry until onion is softened, 2 to 3 minutes. Remove to a plate.

3. In same wok, heat remaining 1 tablespoon vegetable oil over high heat. Add shrimp and stir-fry until shrimp are pink and curled, 2 to 3 minutes. Return vegetables to wok.

4. Add water chestnuts, peas, and sesame oil. Cook until heated through, about 1 minute.

112 SHRIMP WITH BLACK BEAN SAUCE
Prep: 10 minutes   Cook: 7 to 9 minutes   Serves: 4

3 tablespoons vegetable oil
1 pound medium shrimp,
   shelled and deveined
1 tablespoon Chinese
   fermented black beans,
   rinsed and drained
2 garlic cloves, minced
2 scallions, minced

½ green bell pepper, minced
½ cup chicken broth
¼ cup dry sherry
1 tablespoon soy sauce
1 tablespoon oyster sauce
¼ teaspoon pepper
1 teaspoon Asian sesame oil
2 teaspoons cornstarch

1. In a wok, heat 2 tablespoons vegetable oil over high heat until hot, swirling to coat sides of pan. Add shrimp and stir-fry until shrimp are pink and curled, 2 to 3 minutes. Remove to a plate.

2. In same wok, heat remaining 1 tablespoon vegetable oil over medium-high heat. Add black beans, garlic, scallions, and bell pepper. Stir-fry 2 minutes. Add chicken broth, sherry, soy sauce, oyster sauce, pepper, and sesame oil. Cook 2 minutes. Return shrimp to wok.

3. Dissolve cornstarch in 2 tablespoons cold water and stir into wok. Cook over high heat, stirring, until sauce boils and thickens, 1 to 2 minutes.

113   ORANGE-FLAVORED FLANK STEAK AND SCALLIONS

Prep: 10 minutes   Cook: 6 to 9 minutes   Serves: 4

1   **pound flank steak**
3   **tablespoons vegetable oil**
5   **scallions—4 cut into 1-inch lengths, 1 chopped**
1   **garlic clove, minced**
¼   **cup orange juice**
2   **tablespoons rice wine vinegar**

2   **tablespoons soy sauce**
1   **tablespoon honey**
1   **teaspoon Asian sesame oil**
1   **teaspoon grated orange zest**
2   **teaspoons cornstarch**

1. Cut steak across grain on a slight diagonal into thin strips. In a wok, heat 2 tablespoons vegetable oil over high heat until hot, swirling to coat sides of pan. Add beef strips and stir-fry until meat is browned outside but still pink inside, about 2 minutes. Remove to a plate.

2. In same wok, heat remaining 1 tablespoon oil over high heat. Add 4 cut scallions and stir-fry until just softened, 1 to 2 minutes. Add garlic and stir-fry 1 minute. Return meat to wok.

3. Add orange juice, vinegar, soy sauce, honey, sesame oil, and orange zest. Cook 2 minutes.

4. Dissolve cornstarch in ¼ cup cold water and stir into wok. Cook over high heat, stirring, until sauce boils and thickens, 1 to 2 minutes. Sprinkle on chopped scallion and serve.

114   STIR-FRIED FLANK STEAK WITH RAINBOW PEPPERS

Prep: 10 minutes   Cook: 13 to 17 minutes   Serves: 4 to 6

¼   **cup vegetable oil**
1   **medium red bell pepper, cut into ½-inch dice**
1   **medium green bell pepper, cut into ½-inch dice**
1   **medium yellow bell pepper, cut into ½-inch dice**
1   **medium leek (white part only), chopped**
2   **garlic cloves, minced**

1½   **pounds flank steak, cut crosswise on diagonal into ¼-inch-thick strips**
1   **cup beef broth**
2   **tablespoons soy sauce**
2   **tablespoons rice wine vinegar**
2   **teaspoons Asian sesame oil**
¼   **teaspoon pepper**
2   **teaspoons cornstarch**

1. In a wok, heat 2 tablespoons vegetable oil over high heat until hot, swirling to coat sides of pan. Add red, green, and yellow bell peppers, leek, and garlic. Stir-fry until peppers are crisp-tender, about 3 minutes. Remove to a plate.

2. In same wok, heat remaining 2 tablespoons vegetable oil over high heat. Add steak and stir-fry until meat just loses its red color, 2 to 3 minutes.

3. Return vegetables to wok. Add beef broth, soy sauce, vinegar, sesame oil, and pepper. Cook 5 minutes.

4. Dissolve cornstarch in ¼ cup cold water and stir into wok. Cook over high heat, stirring, until sauce boils and thickens, 1 to 2 minutes.

---

115 BEEF AND PEPPERS IN HOT MUSTARD SAUCE

Prep: 10 minutes   Cook: 8 to 10 minutes   Serves: 4

1 pound flank steak
1 egg white
1 tablespoon cornstarch
2 tablespoons lemon juice
3 tablespoons soy sauce
3 tablespoons dry mustard
⅓ cup white wine vinegar
2 tablespoons vegetable oil

1 medium red bell pepper, cut into ¼-inch strips
1 medium green bell pepper, cut into ¼-inch strips
3 scallions, chopped
2 tablespoons dry sherry
2 teaspoons Asian sesame oil

1. Cut steak across grain on a diagonal into thin strips. In a medium bowl, mix together egg white, cornstarch, lemon juice, and 2 tablespoons soy sauce. Add beef slices and toss to coat.

2. In a small bowl, combine mustard powder, ⅓ cup cold water, vinegar, and remaining 1 tablespoon soy sauce. Stir to blend well. Set sauce aside.

3. In a wok, heat 1 tablespoon oil over high heat until hot, swirling to coat sides of pan. Add beef and stir-fry until meat loses its red color, about 3 minutes. Remove to a plate.

4. In same wok, heat remaining 1 tablespoon oil over high heat. Add bell peppers and scallions and stir-fry until crisp-tender, 3 to 4 minutes. Add sherry and sesame oil. Cook 1 minutes. Return beef to wok.

5. Add reserved mustard sauce and cook until heated through, 1 to 2 minutes.

116   STIR-FRIED BEEF WITH ASPARAGUS
Prep: 10 minutes   Cook: 7 to 10 minutes   Serves: 4

1 **pound flank steak**
2 **tablespoons dry sherry**
2 **tablespoons soy sauce**
1 **garlic clove, minced**
¼ **cup vegetable oil**
1 **pound fresh asparagus, cut on diagonal into ½-inch lengths**

3 **scallions, chopped**
½ **teaspoon salt**
¼ **teaspoon pepper**
2 **teaspoons cornstarch**
½ **cup beef broth**

1. Cut steak across grain on a slight diagonal into thin strips. In a medium bowl, combine sherry, soy sauce, and garlic. Add beef slices and toss to coat.

2. In a wok, heat 2 tablespoons oil over high heat until hot, swirling to coat sides of pan. Add beef and stir-fry until meat loses its red color, 2 to 3 minutes. Remove to a plate.

3. In same wok, heat remaining 2 tablespoons oil over high heat. Add asparagus, scallions, salt, and pepper and stir-fry until asparagus is crisp-tender, 4 to 5 minutes. Return beef to wok.

4. Dissolve cornstarch in beef broth and stir into wok. Cook over high heat, stirring, until sauce boils and thickens, 1 to 2 minutes.

117   CHINESE PEPPER STEAK
Prep: 10 minutes   Cook: 5 to 8 minutes   Serves: 4

1 **pound flank steak**
2 **tablespoons rice wine vinegar**
2 **tablespoons soy sauce**
1 **garlic clove, minced**
1 **teaspoon minced fresh ginger**

3 **tablespoons vegetable oil**
2 **medium green bell peppers, cut into ½-inch strips**
1 **medium white onion, sliced**
1 **cup beef broth**
¼ **teaspoon black pepper**
2 **teaspoons cornstarch**

1. Cut steak across grain on a slight diagonal into thin strips. In a medium bowl, combine vinegar, soy sauce, garlic, and ginger. Add beef slices and toss to coat.

2. In a wok, heat 1½ tablespoons oil over high heat until hot, swirling to coat sides of pan. Add beef and stir-fry until meat loses its red color, 2 to 3 minutes. Remove to a plate.

3. Heat remaining 1½ tablespoons oil in wok. Add bell peppers and onion and stir-fry over high heat until crisp-tender, 2 to 3 minutes. Return beef to wok. Add beef broth and black pepper. Bring to a boil.

4. Dissolve cornstarch in ¼ cup cold water and stir into wok. Cook over high heat, stirring, until sauce boils and thickens, 1 to 2 minutes.

118   BEEF WITH GREEN BEANS AND SESAME SEEDS

Prep: 10 minutes   Cook: 14 to 18 minutes   Serves: 4

3 tablespoons sesame seeds
3 tablespoons vegetable oil
¼ pound green beans, sliced diagonally into 1-inch pieces
1 medium white onion, cut into 8 wedges
2 garlic cloves, minced

1 pound flank steak, cut on diagonal against grain into ¼-inch-thick strips
½ cup beef broth
2 tablespoons soy sauce
2 tablespoons rice vinegar
2 teaspoons Asian sesame oil
¼ teaspoon pepper

1. Cook sesame seeds in a dry wok over medium heat, tossing until lightly browned and fragrant, about 3 minutes. Remove to a plate.

2. In wok, heat 2 tablespoons vegetable oil over high heat until hot, swirling to coat sides of pan. Add green beans, onion, and garlic. Stir-fry until crisp-tender, 4 to 6 minutes. Remove to a plate.

3. In same wok, heat remaining 1 tablespoon vegetable oil over high heat. Add steak strips. Stir-fry until meat just loses its red color, 2 to 3 minutes. Return vegetables to wok.

4. Add beef broth, soy sauce, vinegar, sesame oil, and pepper. Cook, stirring occasionally, 5 minutes. Sprinkle with toasted sesame seeds and serve.

119   BEEF WITH BUCKWHEAT NOODLES IN SPICY PEANUT SAUCE

Prep: 10 minutes   Cook: 12 to 15 minutes   Serves: 4

1 pound flank steak
1½ tablespoons peanut oil
½ pound Chinese buckwheat noodles
½ cup peanut butter
1 teaspoon sugar
¼ cup soy sauce

½ teaspoon crushed hot red pepper
2 tablespoons Asian sesame oil
2 garlic cloves, minced
4 scallions, chopped
¼ cup toasted sesame seeds

1. Cut steak across grain on diagonal into thin strips. In a wok, heat oil over high heat until hot, swirling to coat sides of pan. Add steak and stir-fry until meat loses its red color, 2 to 3 minutes. Remove to a plate.

2. In a large pot of boiling salted water, cook noodles until tender but still firm, 10 to 12 minutes. Drain and rinse under cold water. Drain well.

3. In a medium bowl, whisk together peanut butter, ¼ cup hot water, sugar, soy sauce, hot red pepper, sesame oil, and garlic until sauce is blended.

4. Place noodles in a large serving bowl. Add steak, scallions, and sesame seeds. Pour sauce over noodles and toss to coat. Serve at room temperature.

120   TWICE-COOKED PORK AND NAPA CABBAGE

Prep: 10 minutes   Cook: 65 to 82 minutes   Serves: 4 to 6

1½ pounds boneless pork loin, trimmed of fat
  6 dried black Chinese mushrooms
  3 tablespoons peanut oil
  2 scallions, sliced
  1 teaspoon minced fresh ginger

  3 cups loosely packed shredded Napa or Chinese cabbage
  2 tablespoons hoisin sauce
  2 tablespoons dry sherry
1½ tablespoons soy sauce
  1 teaspoon rice wine vinegar

1. Place pork and enough water to cover in wok. Bring to a boil. Reduce heat to low and cook, covered, until pork is tender, 60 to 75 minutes. Remove meat to a cutting board. Pour out water; dry wok.

2. Meanwhile, soak mushrooms in ½ cup hot water for 20 minutes. Remove from water and squeeze dry. Cut off stems. Slice caps thinly and reserve. Cut pork into thick slices and then into 1-inch cubes.

3. In wok, heat oil over high heat. Add pork, scallions, and ginger and stir-fry until meat begins to brown, 2 to 3 minutes.

4. Add cabbage and mushrooms. Stir-fry 2 minutes. Add hoisin sauce, sherry, soy sauce, and vinegar. Cook until heated through, 1 to 2 minutes.

121   STIR-FRIED PORK WITH CHINESE CABBAGE AND BUCKWHEAT NOODLES

Prep: 10 minutes   Cook: 20 to 25 minutes   Serves: 6

½ pound Chinese buckwheat noodles
  3 tablespoons corn oil
  1 pound lean boneless pork loin, cut into 2 x ½-inch strips
  4 scallions, sliced
  1 celery rib, sliced
  2 garlic cloves, minced

  1 teaspoon minced fresh ginger
  2 cups shredded Chinese cabbage
  2 tablespoons soy sauce
  2 tablespoons oyster sauce
  2 teaspoons Asian sesame oil
¼ teaspoon pepper

1. In a large pot of boiling salted water, cook noodles until tender but still firm, 10 to 12 minutes. Drain and rinse briefly under cold running water; drain well.

2. In a wok, heat 1 tablespoon corn oil over high heat until hot, swirling to coat sides of pan. Add pork and stir-fry until meat is cooked through with no trace of pink, 3 to 5 minutes. Remove to a plate.

3. In same wok, heat remaining 2 tablespoons corn oil over high heat. Add scallions, celery, garlic, and ginger and stir-fry until celery is crisp-tender, about 3 minutes. Add cabbage and cook, stirring, until cabbage is wilted and just tender, about 3 minutes longer. Return pork to wok. Add noodles.

4. In a bowl, combine soy sauce, oyster sauce, sesame oil, pepper and ¼ cup water. Pour into wok. Cook, tossing, until noodles are hot, 1 to 2 minutes.

122 STICKY SPARERIBS WITH BLACK BEANS
Prep: 10 minutes   Cook: 1⅓ to 1½ hours   Serves: 3 to 4

These ribs are moist and succulent. The secret is to partially cook over low heat, followed by simmering and basting with spicy black bean sauce—all in the wok.

1½ **pounds meaty baby back pork spareribs, cut crosswise 3-inches long**	2 **tablespoons honey**
½ **cup apricot nectar**	2 **tablespoons Chinese fermented black beans, rinsed and drained**
¼ **cup dry white wine**	3 **scallions, chopped**
3 **tablespoons hoisin sauce**	2 **garlic cloves, minced**
3 **tablespoons ketchup**	1 **teaspoon grated orange zest**

1. Place ribs in wok. Add cold water to just cover. Bring to a boil. Reduce heat to a simmer, cover, and cook 30 minutes. Drain and return ribs to wok.

2. In a medium bowl, combine apricot nectar, wine, hoisin sauce, ketchup, honey, black beans, scallions, garlic, and orange zest.

3. Pour mixture over ribs, cover wok, and cook over low heat, stirring to coat ribs with sauce occasionally, until meat is tender, 50 minutes to 1 hour.

123   STIR-FRIED PORK WITH GARLIC

Prep: 10 minutes   Marinate: 30 minutes
Cook: 3 to 5 minutes   Serves: 4

Freeze the pork for about 20 minutes to make slicing it into thin strips easier.

1 **pound boneless pork tenderloin, trimmed of fat, cut into 2 x ⅛-inch strips**	2 **teaspoons cornstarch**
	1 **teaspoon minced fresh ginger**
2 **tablespoons dry sherry**	1 **teaspoon sugar**
1½ **tablespoons soy sauce**	¼ **teaspoon Chinese chili paste**
1 **tablespoon rice wine vinegar**	2½ **tablespoons peanut oil**
	3 **scallions, sliced**
	3 **garlic cloves, sliced**

1. In a bowl, combine pork, sherry, soy sauce, vinegar, cornstarch, ginger, sugar, and chili paste. Toss to mix. Marinate 30 minutes.

2. In a wok, heat oil over high heat, swirling to coat sides of pan. Add pork and stir-fry until cooked through with no trace of pink, 2 to 3 minutes. Add scallions and garlic and stir-fry until fragrant, 1 to 2 minutes.

124   SPICY ORANGE-FLAVORED LAMB

Prep: 10 minutes   Cook: 8 to 12 minutes   Serves: 4 to 6

You'll throw away the phone number of your favorite Chinese restaurant when you taste this easy authentic dish. Serve with rice and simply steamed green beans.

⅓ **cup rice wine vinegar**	¼ **cup orange juice**
2 **garlic cloves, minced**	2 **tablespoons soy sauce**
1 **tablespoon Asian sesame oil**	1 **tablespoon honey**
1 **teaspoon grated orange zest**	2 **teaspoons cornstarch**
½ **teaspoon crushed hot red pepper**	3 **tablespoons vegetable oil**
	4 **scallions, sliced**
1½ **pounds boneless leg of lamb, cut into 1-inch pieces**	

1. In a medium bowl, mix together vinegar, garlic, sesame oil, orange zest, and hot pepper. Add lamb pieces and toss to coat well.

2. In a small bowl, combine orange juice, soy sauce, honey, and cornstarch. Stir to blend and dissolve cornstarch. Set sauce aside.

3. In a wok, heat 2 tablespoons vegetable oil over high heat until hot, swirling to coat sides of pan. Add lamb and stir-fry until browned outside and medium-rare inside, 5 to 7 minutes. Remove to a plate.

4. In same wok, heat remaining 1 tablespoon vegetable oil over medium-high heat. Add scallions and stir-fry until softened, 2 to 3 minutes. Return lamb to wok.

5. Stir reserved sauce and add to wok. Cook over high heat, stirring, until sauce boils and thickens, 1 to 2 minutes.

---

125 HUNAN LAMB
Prep: 10 minutes   Marinate: 1 hour   Cook: 6 to 7 minutes
Serves: 4

1 **egg white**
2 **tablespoons soy sauce**
2 **tablespoons lemon juice**
1 **tablespoon cornstarch**
1 **pound boneless leg of lamb,**
   trimmed of excess fat and
   cut into 2 x ½-inch slices
2 **tablespoons vegetable oil**
4 **scallions, cut into 1-inch**
   pieces

2 **garlic cloves, minced**
3 **tablespoons hoisin sauce**
2 **tablespoons rice wine**
   vinegar
2 **tablespoons Chinese chili**
   paste with garlic
2 **teaspoons Asian sesame oil**

1. In a medium bowl, combine egg white, soy sauce, lemon juice, and cornstarch. Mix to blend well. Add lamb and toss to coat. Marinate at room temperature for 1 hour.

2. In a wok, heat vegetable oil over high heat until hot, swirling to coat sides of pan. Add lamb and stir-fry until browned outside and barely pink inside, 2 to 3 minutes. Remove to a plate.

3. Add scallions and garlic to wok. Cook, stirring, until softened, about 2 minutes. Return lamb to pan.

4. Add hoisin sauce, vinegar, chili paste, and sesame oil. Cook, stirring occasionally, 2 minutes and serve.

126 SPICY EGGPLANT IN THE SZECHUAN STYLE

Prep: 10 minutes   Cook: 4 to 7 minutes   Serves: 4

2 tablespoons soy sauce
2 tablespoons dry sherry
2 tablespoons rice wine
   vinegar
1 teaspoon Chinese chili paste
1 teaspoon Asian sesame oil
1 teaspoon chili pepper oil
½ teaspoon sugar
3 tablespoons peanut oil

1½ pounds Japanese eggplant,
   or purple eggplant,
   peeled, sliced, and cut
   into wedges
2 scallions, sliced
2 garlic cloves, minced
1 teaspoon minced fresh
   ginger

1. In a small bowl, combine soy sauce, sherry, vinegar, chili paste, sesame oil, chili pepper oil, and sugar. Set sauce mixture aside.

2. In a wok, heat peanut oil over high heat. Add eggplant and stir-fry until golden, 2 to 3 minutes. Add scallions, garlic, and ginger. Stir-fry until fragrant, 1 to 2 minutes.

3. Add sauce mixture and cook until heated through, 1 to 2 minutes.

---

127 CHINESE NOODLES WITH STEAK AND VEGETABLES

Prep: 10 minutes   Cook: 11 to 17 minutes   Serves: 4

Chinese noodles are available in different shapes and varieties in Asian markets. Spaghetti can be substituted.

12 ounces Chinese noodles
 3 tablespoons vegetable oil
 1 medium red bell pepper,
    diced
 1 celery rib, sliced
 1 medium carrot, sliced
 1 garlic clove, minced
 ½ pound beef rib steak, cut
    into 2 x ¼-inch strips

½ cup dry sherry
2 tablespoons soy sauce
2 tablespoons rice wine
   vinegar
1 tablespoon Asian sesame oil
1 teaspoon minced fresh
   ginger

1. In a large pot of boiling salted water, cook noodles until tender but still firm, 4 to 6 minutes. Drain and rinse under cold water; drain well.

2. In a wok, heat 2 tablespoons vegetable oil over medium-high heat until hot, swirling to coat sides of pan. Add bell pepper, celery, carrot, and garlic and stir-fry until crisp-tender, 3 to 5 minutes. Remove to a plate.

3. In same wok, heat remaining 1 tablespoon vegetable oil over high heat. Add beef strips and stir-fry until meat loses its red color, 2 to 3 minutes. Return vegetables to wok. Add noodles.

4. In a small bowl, combine sherry, soy sauce, vinegar, sesame oil, and ginger. Add to wok. Cook, tossing noodles to coat with sauce, until hot, 2 to 3 minutes.

128 FRIED RICE WITH VEGETABLES
Prep: 10 minutes   Cook: 8 minutes   Serves: 4

3 tablespoons vegetable oil
1 egg, beaten
1 medium green bell pepper, chopped
3 scallions, sliced
1 celery rib, sliced
2 garlic cloves, minced
½ (10-ounce) package frozen peas, thawed (1 cup)

1 (8-ounce) can sliced water chestnuts, drained
1 teaspoon Worcestershire sauce
⅛ teaspoon hot pepper sauce
2 cups cooked rice, cooled
2 tablespoons soy sauce

1. In a wok, heat 1 tablespoon oil over medium-high heat until hot. Add egg and cook, stirring, until firm, about 2 minutes. Remove to a plate. Cut into small pieces.

2. In same wok, heat remaining 2 tablespoons oil over high heat, swirling to coat sides of pan. Add bell pepper, scallions, celery, and garlic and stir-fry until crisp-tender, about 3 minutes. Add peas, water chestnuts, Worcestershire sauce, and hot sauce. Stir-fry 2 minutes. Add rice, cooked egg, and soy sauce. Stir-fry until hot, about 1 minute. Serve at once.

129 CHICKEN FRIED BROWN RICE
Prep: 10 minutes   Cook: 9 to 10 minutes   Serves: 4

3 tablespoons vegetable oil
1 egg, beaten
3 scallions, chopped
2 garlic cloves, minced
2 cups cooked chicken, cut into ½-inch cubes
1 (8-ounce) can sliced water chestnuts, drained

2 teaspoons Asian sesame oil
1 teaspoon Worcestershire sauce
2 cups cooked brown rice, cooled
¼ cup chicken broth
2 tablespoons soy sauce

1. In a wok, heat 1 tablespoon oil over medium-high heat until hot. Add egg and cook, stirring, until firm, about 2 minutes. Remove to a plate. Cut into small pieces.

2. In same wok, heat remaining 2 tablespoons oil over high heat, swirling to coat sides of pan. Add scallions and garlic and stir-fry until softened and fragrant, 1 to 2 minutes. Add chicken, water chestnuts, sesame oil, and Worcestershire sauce. Stir-fry 2 minutes. Add rice and cooked egg. Stir-fry 2 minutes.

3. Add chicken broth and soy sauce. Cook, stirring, 2 minutes and serve.

Chapter 5

Wokking Around the Mediterranean

The distinctive foods of the sun-blessed countries of the Mediterranean are robust and earthy. In the cuisines of France, Italy, and the Middle East, there is a celebration of flavor. These recipes boast a liberal use of seasonings and spices; they are filled with the temptations of olives, capers, lemons, garlic, tomatoes, dried fruit, and fresh herbs.

While the recipes in this chapter come from different countries and employ different cooking techniques, the wok handles them all successfully. From fast sautés, such as Shrimp Scampi and Chicken Piccata, to long-simmering stews, such as Moroccan Chicken Tagine and Turkey Thighs Gremolata, sparked with parsley and lemon, it proves itself the ideal pot.

Look in this chapter for family suppers and delightful dishes for lively entertaining. Turn to these pages for your friends who relish extra flavor. Set your table with your most colorful dishes, close your eyes, and, if you're lucky, with the first forkful, you may think you can see the sun just setting beyond the Mediterranean.

---

130 CHICKEN PICCATA
Prep: 10 minutes   Cook: 7 to 10 minutes   Serves: 4

½ cup flour
1 teaspoon grated lemon zest
½ teaspoon salt
¼ teaspoon pepper
¼ teaspoon paprika
4 skinless, boneless chicken breast halves (4 to 5 ounces each), pounded to ¼-inch thickness

1 tablespoon butter
1 tablespoon olive oil
½ cup dry white wine
2 tablespoons lemon juice
2 tablespoons chopped parsley

1. In a shallow dish, combine flour, lemon zest, salt, pepper, and paprika. Lightly coat chicken on both sides; shake off excess.

2. In a wok, melt butter in olive oil over medium-high heat, swirling to coat sides of pan. Arrange chicken in wok without overlapping and cook, turning once, and rotating as necessary, until golden on both sides, 6 to 8 minutes. Remove to a plate.

3. Add wine and lemon juice to wok, scraping up browned bits from bottom of pan. Return chicken to wok. Cook until heated through, 1 to 2 minutes. Sprinkle with parsley and serve.

131 CHICKEN PARMESAN
Prep: 10 minutes   Cook: 9 to 12 minutes   Serves: 4

Here's an easy one-pot wok version of everyone's favorite Italian dish. Serve with spaghetti—tossed with olive oil and garlic—and a green salad on the side.

1½ cups dried bread crumbs
½ teaspoon dried oregano
½ teaspoon salt
¼ teaspoon pepper
1 egg
4 skinless, boneless chicken breast halves (4 to 5 ounces each), pounded to ¼-inch thickness

3 to 4 tablespoons olive oil
1 cup prepared spaghetti sauce
1 cup shredded mozzarella cheese (4 ounces)
¼ cup grated Parmesan cheese

1. In a shallow pan, combine bread crumbs, oregano, salt, and pepper. In a shallow bowl, beat egg with 2 tablespoons cold water. Dip chicken in egg and then dredge in seasoned bread crumbs to coat; shake off excess.

2. In a wok, heat 3 tablespoons olive oil over medium-high heat until hot, swirling to coat sides of pan. Arrange chicken pieces in wok without overlapping and fry until golden brown on bottom, 3 to 4 minutes. Turn and cook until brown on other side, 2 to 4 minutes. Add remaining 1 tablespoon oil, if necessary, to prevent sticking.

3. Spoon spaghetti sauce over chicken. Sprinkle on mozzarella and Parmesan cheeses. Reduce heat to medium-low. Cover and cook until cheese melts and sauce is heated through, 3 to 4 minutes.

132 SPICED CHICKEN MARRAKESH
Prep: 10 minutes   Cook: 43 to 52 minutes   Serves: 4

¼ cup olive oil
1 garlic clove, minced
1 teaspoon paprika
1 teaspoon grated lime zest
¼ teaspoon ground cumin
¼ teaspoon ground coriander
4 medium chicken breast halves, with bone (6 to 8 ounces each)

2 medium leeks (white part only) or onions, chopped
1 medium tomato, seeded and chopped
¾ cup orange juice
2 tablespoons lime juice
½ cup plain yogurt

1. In a small dish, combine 2 tablespoons olive oil, garlic, paprika, lime zest, cumin, and coriander. Brush mixture on chicken breasts. Heat wok over ∙ medium-high heat, until hot, swirling to coat sides of pan. Arrange chicken breasts on sides of pan without overlapping and cook, turning, until browned all over, 6 to 8 minutes. Remove to a plate. Drain off fat from wok.

2. In same wok, heat remaining 2 tablespoons oil over medium-high heat. Add leeks and cook, stirring occasionally, 3 minutes. Add tomato and cook, stirring, until vegetables are soft, 3 to 4 minutes.

3. Return chicken to wok. Add orange juice and lime juice. Reduce heat to medium-low, cover, and cook until chicken is fork-tender, 30 to 35 minutes. Remove chicken to a serving plate. Reduce heat to low.

4. Whisk yogurt into sauce in wok and cook, stirring, just until heated through, 1 to 2 minutes; do not boil. Spoon sauce over chicken and serve.

---

133   MOROCCAN CHICKEN TAGINE
Prep: 15 minutes   Cook: 50 to 58 minutes   Serves: 4 to 6

Tagines are richly seasoned North African stews, slowly simmered and named for the dish they are cooked and served in. They can be made with meat, poultry, or fish, usually in combination with vegetables and/or fruit. This version features chicken, garlic, lemon, sweet spices, honey, and nuts. Serve with couscous.

¼ cup slivered almonds	½ teaspoon ground cumin
3½ tablespoons olive oil	½ teaspoon salt
1 (3-pound) chicken, cut up	¼ teaspoon pepper
1 medium onion, chopped	1 cup pitted prunes
2 garlic cloves, minced	¼ cup honey
1 teaspoon cinnamon	1 lemon, cut into thin slices
1 teaspoon ground ginger	

1. In dry wok, cook almonds over medium heat, tossing, until lightly browned and fragrant, about 5 minutes. Transfer toasted almonds to a plate.

2. In wok, heat 2 tablespoons olive oil over medium-high heat until hot, swirling to coat sides of pan. Arrange chicken pieces extending up sides of wok without overlapping and cook, turning, until browned all over, 6 to 8 minutes. With tongs, remove to a plate. Pour off fat from wok.

3. Add remaining 1½ tablespoons olive oil to wok and heat over medium-high heat. Add onion and garlic and cook, stirring occasionally, until softened, 3 to 4 minutes. Add cinnamon, ginger, cumin, salt, and pepper and cook, stirring, 1 minute. Return chicken to wok.

4. Add prunes, honey, lemon slices, and 1 cup water. Bring to a boil, reduce heat to medium-low, cover, and simmer until chicken is tender, 35 to 40 minutes.

5. To serve, arrange chicken on a platter. Pour sauce over chicken and sprinkle toasted almonds on top.

134   CHICKEN WITH OLIVES AND CAPERS
Prep: 10 minutes   Cook: 56 to 60 minutes   Serves: 4

The wonderful flavors of southern France—garlic, tomatoes, olives, and capers—are combined with chicken and simmered until the meat is fork-tender and delicious.

¼ cup olive oil
1 chicken (3 pounds), cut up
1 medium onion, chopped
2 garlic cloves, minced
½ teaspoon dried rosemary
¾ teaspoon salt
¼ teaspoon pepper
1 (28-ounce) can Italian peeled tomatoes, cut up, liquid reserved

2 tablespoons tomato paste
1 cup dry red wine
¼ cup chopped pitted green olives
2 tablespoons capers, drained

1. In a wok, heat 2 tablespoons olive oil over medium-high heat until hot, swirling to coat sides of pan. Arrange chicken pieces in wok without over-lapping and cook, turning, until golden brown all over, 8 to 10 minutes. Remove to a plate. Pour off fat from wok.

2. In same wok, heat remaining 2 tablespoons oil over medium-high heat. Add onion, garlic, rosemary, salt, and pepper and cook, stirring, until soft-ened, 3 to 5 minutes. Return chicken to wok.

3. Add tomatoes, tomato paste, and wine. Bring to a boil. Reduce heat to medium-low, cover, and simmer until chicken is tender, about 40 minutes. Add olives and capers. Cook 5 minutes.

135   CHEESY CHICKEN MARINARA
Prep: 10 minutes   Cook: 10 to 14 minutes   Serves: 4 to 6

¼ cup olive oil
4 skinless, boneless chicken breast halves (4 to 5 ounces each), cut crosswise into ½-inch strips
½ pound mushrooms, sliced
1 medium onion, chopped

2 garlic cloves, minced
1 (16-ounce) jar marinara sauce
1 cup shredded mozzarella cheese (about 4 ounces)
¼ cup grated Parmesan cheese
2 tablespoons chopped parsley

1. In a wok, heat 2 tablespoons oil over high heat until hot, swirling to coat sides of pan. Add chicken strips and stir-fry until cooked through but still juicy, 3 to 4 minutes. Remove to a plate.

2. In same wok, heat remaining 2 tablespoons oil over high heat. Add mushrooms, onion, and garlic. Stir-fry until mushrooms are lightly browned, 3 to 5 minutes. Return chicken to wok.

3. Pour in marinara sauce. Cook until heated through, about 3 minutes. Add mozzarella and Parmesan cheeses. Sprinkle parsley on top. Cover and cook until mozzarella melts, 1 to 2 minutes.

---

136 CHICKEN WITH BASMATI RICE, ALMONDS, AND RAISINS

Prep: 10 minutes   Cook: 30 to 38 minutes   Serves: 4

Basmati rice, which is typically used in Indian recipes, has a rich nutty flavor. It can be found in specialty stores and in some larger supermarkets.

3½ tablespoons peanut oil	½ teaspoon ground coriander
1 pound skinless, boneless chicken breasts, cut crosswise into ½-inch strips	½ teaspoon cinnamon
	¼ teaspoon pepper
	¾ cup Basmati rice
	1 cup chicken broth
1 medium onion, chopped	½ cup tomato sauce
1 garlic clove, crushed	¼ cup slivered almonds
½ teaspoon ground cumin	¼ cup raisins

1. In a wok, heat 2 tablespoons oil over high heat until hot, swirling to coat sides of pan. Add chicken and cook, stirring, until meat is white throughout but still juicy, 3 to 4 minutes. Remove to a plate.

2. In same wok, heat remaining 1½ tablespoons oil over medium-high heat. Add onion and garlic and cook, stirring, until softened, 3 to 4 minutes. Add cumin, coriander, cinnamon, and pepper. Cook, stirring, 1 minute.

3. Add rice and stir to coat, 2 minutes. Add chicken broth, tomato sauce, and 1 cup water. Bring to a boil. Reduce heat to low, cover and cook until rice is tender and most of liquid is absorbed, 20 to 25 minutes. Return chicken to wok. Add almonds and raisins. Cook, stirring occasionally, until heated through, 1 to 2 minutes.

137   BOEUF À LA PROVENÇALE

Prep: 10 minutes   Marinate: 2 hours   Cook: 2⅔ to 3 hours
Serves: 6

Here is an adaptation of a popular beef stew from Provence. In this version, two varieties of mushrooms and shallots are browned along with the marinated beef, which gives the stew a rich, intense flavor. If shiitake mushrooms are not available, just double the amount of white mushrooms.

1¼ cups red wine vinegar
2 tablespoons balsamic
     vinegar
2 garlic cloves, minced
1½ teaspoons chopped fresh
     rosemary or ½ teaspoon
     dried
1 bay leaf
2½ pounds boneless beef
     chuck, cut into 1½-inch
     chunks
3 tablespoons olive oil

¼ pound fresh white
     mushrooms, sliced
¼ pound shiitake mushrooms,
     stems removed, caps
     sliced
3 shallots, chopped
2 cups dry red wine
1 (14-ounce) can beef broth
1 teaspoon grated orange zest
     (optional)
1 teaspoon salt
¼ teaspoon pepper

1. In a large bowl, combine wine vinegar, balsamic vinegar, garlic, rosemary, and bay leaf. Add beef cubes and toss to coat. Marinate at room temperature 2 hours. Drain meat; reserve marinade.

2. In a wok, heat olive oil over over high heat until hot, swirling to coat sides of pan. Add beef cubes, white and shiitake mushrooms, and shallots and cook, stirring often and turning meat, until brown all over, 8 to 10 minutes.

3. Add reserved marinade, wine, beef broth, orange zest, salt, and pepper. Bring to a boil. Reduce heat to medium-low, cover, cook until meat is very tender, 2½ to 2¾ hours.

138 TURKEY THIGHS GREMOLATA
Prep: 15 minutes   Cook: 1 hour 12 to 18 minutes   Serves: 4

3 tablespoons olive oil	1 (14½-ounce) can chicken
3 pounds turkey thighs	broth
2 medium carrots, chopped	1 cup dry white wine
2 medium leeks (white part	½ teaspoon salt
only), washed well and	¼ teaspoon pepper
chopped	¼ cup chopped parsley
1 celery rib, chopped	2 teaspoons grated lemon zest
2 garlic cloves, minced	

1. In a wok, heat 2 tablespoon olive oil over medium-high heat, swirling to coat sides of pan. Add turkey thighs and cook, turning, until brown on both sides, 6 to 8 minutes. Remove to a plate. Pour off fat from wok.

2. Add remaining 1 tablespoon oil to wok. Add carrots, leeks, celery, and 1 garlic clove and cook until crisp-tender, 4 to 5 minutes. Return turkey to wok.

3. Add chicken broth, wine, salt, and pepper. Cover and heat to boiling. Reduce heat to low and simmer 1 hour, or until turkey is tender. Add parsley, lemon zest, and remaining garlic. Simmer 2 minutes and serve.

139 FLANK STEAK ITALIANO WITH OLIVES AND BASIL
Prep: 10 minutes   Marinate: 1 hour   Cook: 10 to 11 minutes
Serves: 4

1 pound flank steak	1 garlic clove, minced
1 (8-ounce) bottle Italian salad	½ cup kalamata olives, halved
dressing	and pitted
2 tablespoons olive oil	2 tablespoons lemon juice
½ pound fresh mushrooms,	¼ cup chopped fresh basil
sliced	½ teaspoon salt
3 scallions, sliced	¼ teaspoon pepper

1. Cut meat across grain on diagonal into thin strips. In a large bowl, combine salad dressing and meat. Marinate at room temperature for 1 hour. Remove meat from bowl; reserve ½ cup marinade.

2. In a wok, heat 1 tablespoon olive oil over medium-high heat until hot, swirling to coat sides of pan. Add steak strips and stir-fry until meat loses its red color, about 4 minutes. Remove to a plate.

3. In same wok, heat remaining 1 tablespoon oil over medium-high heat. Add mushrooms, scallions, garlic, and olives and stir-fry until vegetables are crisp-tender, 3 to 4 minutes. Return meat to wok.

4. Add reserved marinade, lemon juice, basil, salt, and pepper. Cook 3 minutes and serve.

140   HAMBURGERS ITALIANO
Prep: 15 minutes   Cook: 16 to 18 minutes   Serves: 4

1 pound ground chuck (80% lean)	½ cup ricotta cheese
1½ cups prepared spaghetti sauce	¼ cup shredded mozzarella cheese
¼ cup dried bread crumbs	2 tablespoons grated Parmesan cheese
½ teaspoon garlic powder	2 tablespoons chopped parsley
¼ teaspoon pepper	2 tablespoons vegetable oil
½ cup chopped cooked broccoli florets	

1. In a medium bowl, combine ground chuck, ¼ cup spaghetti sauce, bread crumbs, garlic powder, and pepper. Shape into 8 thin (¼-inch) patties.

2. In a small bowl, combine broccoli, ricotta, mozzarella and Parmesan cheeses, and parsley. Stir until filling is well mixed.

3. Place one-fourth of filling on each of 4 patties. Cover with remaining 4 patties. Pinch edges to seal and enclose filling.

4. In a wok, heat oil over medium-high heat until hot, swirling to coat sides of pan. Add stuffed hamburgers and cook, turning once, until brown on both sides, 6 to 8 minutes. Drain off fat. Add remaining 1¼ cups spaghetti sauce. Reduce heat to low. Cover and cook 10 minutes.

141   BEEF BRAISED IN RED WINE WITH FRESH BASIL
Prep: 15 minutes   Cook: 2⅔ hours   Serves: 6

3 tablespoons olive oil	1 (10¾-ounce) can beef broth
2½ to 3 pounds boneless beef chuck roast, trimmed and cut into 1½-inch cubes	1 cup dry red wine
	¼ cup chopped parsley
	1 teaspoon salt
2 medium onions, chopped	¼ teaspoon pepper
2 garlic cloves, crushed	¼ cup chopped fresh basil
1 (14-ounce) can Italian peeled tomatoes	

1. In a wok, heat 1 tablespoon olive oil over high heat until hot, swirling to coat sides of pan. Add beef cubes in one layer and cook, turning, until brown all over, 6 to 8 minutes. Remove to a plate.

2. In same wok, heat remaining 2 tablespoons oil over medium-high heat. Add onions and garlic and cook, stirring occasionally, until onions are soft, 6 to 8 minutes. Return meat to wok.

3. Add tomatoes, beef broth, and red wine. Bring to a boil. Reduce heat to medium-low, cover, and cook 1½ hours. Mix in parsley, salt, and pepper. Cook until meat is tender, about 1 hour longer. Add basil and serve.

142   BRAISED BEEF SHANKS IN RED WINE
Prep: 15 minutes   Cook: 2¼ to 2¾ hours   Serves: 4

3 tablespoons olive oil	1 cup beef broth
2½ to 3 pounds beef shanks	1 (8-ounce) can tomato sauce
1 medium onion, chopped	1 cup dry red wine
2 garlic cloves, minced	¼ cup chopped parsley
2 medium carrots, peeled and	1 teaspoon salt
chopped	¼ teaspoon pepper

1. In a wok, heat 2 tablespoons olive oil over high heat until hot, swirling to coat sides of pan. Add beef shanks and cook, turning, until brown all over, 7 to 10 minutes. With tongs, remove to a plate.

2. Add remaining 1 tablespoon oil to wok. Add onion and cook, stirring often, until softened, about 3 minutes. Add garlic and cook 1 minute longer.

3. Return beef shanks to wok, along with any juices that have accumulated on plate. Add carrots, beef broth, tomato sauce, wine, parsley, salt, and pepper. Bring to a boil; reduce heat to low. Cover and simmer, turning shanks occasionally, until beef is very tender, 2 to 2½ hours.

143   VEAL MADEIRA
Prep: 10 minutes   Cook: 7 to 8 minutes   Serves: 4

½ cup flour	4 tablespoons butter
½ teaspoon dried rosemary	1 tablespoon vegetable oil
½ teaspoon salt	½ cup dry Madeira
¼ teaspoon pepper	½ cup chicken broth
1 pound veal scaloppine,	1 tablespoon lemon juice
pounded to ¼-inch	2 tablespoons chopped
thickness	parsley

1. In a shallow dish, combine flour, rosemary, salt, and pepper. Lightly coat both sides of veal with seasoned flour; shake off excess.

2. In a wok, heat 1 tablespoon butter and oil over high heat until hot, swirling to coat sides of pan. Add veal, arranging scaloppine up sides of wok so they don't overlap. Cook, turning once and rotating as necessary, until brown on both sides, 3 to 4 minutes. Remove to a serving plate. Cover with foil to keep warm.

3. Add Madeira, chicken broth, and lemon juice to wok. Boil over high heat, scraping up browned bits from bottom of pan, until sauce is reduced by half, about 3 minutes. Cut remaining 3 tablespoons butter into bits and whisk into sauce until blended and smooth. Add parsley, pour sauce over veal, and serve.

144 VEAL SCALOPPINE WITH MUSHROOMS AND WHITE WINE

Prep: 10 minutes   Cook: 11 to 15 minutes   Serves: 4

2 tablespoons olive oil
2 tablespoons butter
1 pound veal scaloppine, pounded to ¼-inch thickness
½ pound fresh white mushrooms, sliced
2 shallots, chopped
1 garlic clove, minced
1½ teaspoons chopped fresh thyme, or ½ teaspoon dried

½ cup dry white wine
2 tablespoons lemon juice
2 tablespoons chopped parsley
¼ teaspoon salt
⅛ teaspoon freshly ground pepper

1. In a wok, heat 1 tablespoon olive oil and 1 tablespoon butter over medium-high heat until hot, swirling to coat sides of pan. Arrange scaloppine extending up sides of pan without overlapping and cook, turning once and rotating for even browning, until browned and cooked through, 3 to 4 minutes. Remove to a serving plate. Cover with foil to keep warm.

2. In same wok, heat remaining 1 tablespoon oil and remaining 1 tablespoon butter over medium-high heat. Add mushrooms, shallots, garlic, and thyme and cook, stirring, until most of liquid is evaporated, 6 to 8 minutes.

3. Add wine, lemon juice, parsley, salt, and pepper. Boil, scraping up browned bits from bottom of wok, until liquid is reduced by half, 2 to 3 minutes. Spoon mushrooms and sauce over veal.

145 VEAL WITH SUN-DRIED TOMATO SAUCE

Prep: 15 minutes   Cook: 10 to 13 minutes   Serves: 4

½ cup flour
½ teaspoon salt
¼ teaspoon pepper
1 pound veal scaloppine, pounded to ¼-inch thickness
3½ tablespoons olive oil
1 medium onion, chopped
½ pound fresh mushrooms, sliced

1 garlic clove, minced
½ cup chicken broth
½ cup dry red wine
¼ cup tomato sauce
3 sun-dried tomato halves, cut into thin strips
⅓ cup grated Parmesan cheese

1. In a shallow dish, combine flour, salt, and pepper. Lightly coat both sides of veal with seasoned flour, shaking off excess.

2. In a wok, heat 2 tablespoons olive oil over high heat until hot, swirling to coat sides of pan. Arrange veal up sides of pan without overlapping. Cook, turning and rotating for even cooking, until brown on both sides and cooked through, 3 to 4 minutes. Remove to a plate.

3. In same wok, heat remaining 1½ tablespoons oil over high heat. Add onion, mushrooms, and garlic and stir-fry until crisp-tender, 3 to 4 minutes. Remove to a plate.

4. Add chicken broth, wine, and tomato sauce to wok. Bring to a boil, scraping up any browned bits from bottom of pan. Cook over medium heat, stirring, 3 minutes. Add sun-dried tomatoes. Return veal and vegetables to wok. Cook until heated through, 1 to 2 minutes. Sprinkle with cheese and serve.

146 PORK LOIN NORMANDY STYLE, WITH APPLES AND PRUNES IN APPLE CIDER
Prep: 10 minutes   Cook: 65 to 74 minutes   Serves: 4 to 6

This classic combination of pork, fruit, and cider is found in homes and restaurants throughout France.

3 tablespoons olive oil	1 teaspoon cinnamon
2½ to 3 pounds boneless pork loin roast, well trimmed	½ teaspoon grated nutmeg
1 medium onion, chopped	2 apples, peeled, cored, and thinly sliced
2 garlic cloves, minced	½ cup pitted prunes
2 cups apple cider	½ cup heavy cream
1 cup chicken broth	1 tablespoon Dijon mustard

1. In a wok, heat 1½ tablespoons olive oil over medium-high heat until hot, swirling to coat sides of pan. Add pork loin and cook, turning, until brown all over, 5 to 7 minutes. Remove to a plate.

2. In same wok, heat remaining 1½ tablespoons oil over medium-high heat. Add onion and garlic and cook, stirring, until softened, 3 to 4 minutes. Return meat to wok.

3. Add apple cider, chicken broth, cinnamon, and nutmeg. Bring to a boil. Reduce heat to medium-low, cover and cook, turning occasionally, until meat is almost tender, 40 minutes. Add apples and prunes and cook until pork is tender throughout, 15 to 20 minutes longer. Remove meat to a cutting board and let rest 10 minutes before slicing.

4. In a small bowl, combine cream and mustard. Whisk until blended. Stir into wok. Cook until reduced by half, 2 to 3 minutes. Slice meat and arrange on serving platter. Spoon sauce over meat.

147 MIDDLE EASTERN LAMB AND BULGUR

Prep: 10 minutes   Marinate: 1 hour   Cook: 24 to 29 minutes
Serves: 6 to 8

Bulgur, or parched cracked wheat, is a nutty-tasting grain common in the Middle East and now available in supermarkets across the United States. Here it is steamed in chicken broth and combined with sautéed marinated lamb cubes.

2 pounds boneless leg of
    lamb, trimmed of fat and
    cut into ½-inch cubes
½ cup dry red wine
2 tablespoons soy sauce
3 tablespoons orange juice
2 tablespoons honey
3 garlic cloves, minced

3½ tablespoons olive oil
2 medium onions, chopped
2 cups bulgur
4 cups chicken broth
1 teaspoon dried thyme leaves
½ teaspoon salt
¼ teaspoon pepper

1. In a large bowl, combine lamb cubes, wine, soy sauce, orange juice, honey, and garlic. Toss to coat. Cover with plastic wrap and marinate 1 hour at room temperature.

2. In a wok, heat 2 tablespoons olive oil over high heat until hot, swirling to coat sides of pan. Add lamb in two batches and cook, stirring, until browned all over but still pink and juicy inside, 3 to 5 minutes per batch. Remove to a plate.

3. Add remaining 1½ tablespoons oil to wok and reduce heat to medium high. Add onions and cook, stirring, until softened, 3 to 4 minutes. Add bulgur and cook, stirring, 1 minute to coat with oil.

4. Add chicken broth, thyme, salt, and pepper. Reduce heat to low, cover, and cook 12 minutes, or until most of liquid is absorbed. Return lamb to wok. Cook about 2 minutes to heat through and serve.

148 CURRIED LAMB

Prep: 10 minutes   Cook: 53 to 66 minutes   Serves: 6

3 tablespoons olive oil
2½ to 3 pounds boneless leg of
    lamb, trimmed of fat and
    cut into 1-inch cubes
2 medium onions, chopped
2 garlic cloves, minced
1 tablespoon curry powder
¾ teaspoon ground ginger

½ teaspoon crushed hot red
    pepper, or more to taste
1½ cups beef broth
1 cup tomato puree
½ teaspoon salt
¼ teaspoon pepper
1 cup plain yogurt

1. In a wok, heat 2 tablespoons olive oil over high heat until hot, swirling to coat sides of pan. Add lamb in two batches and cook, stirring occasionally, until browned all over, 4 to 6 minutes per batch. Remove to a plate.

2. Add remaining 1 tablespoon oil to wok and heat over high heat. Add onions and garlic and cook, stirring, until softened, 3 to 4 minutes. Add curry powder, ginger, and hot pepper. Cook, stirring, 1 minute longer. Return lamb to wok.

3. Add beef broth, tomato puree, salt, pepper, and 1½ cups water. Bring to a boil, reduce heat to medium, cover, and cook until lamb is fork-tender, 45 to 55 minutes.

4. Remove from heat and add yogurt. Stir to blend and serve.

---

149 NORTH AFRICAN FISH WITH LEMON, OLIVES, AND CAPERS

Prep: 10 minutes   Cook: 14 to 18 minutes   Serves: 4

½ cup flour
½ teaspoon salt
¼ teaspoon black pepper
4 halibut fillets, cut ¾ inch thick (5 to 6 ounces each)
¼ cup olive oil
1 medium red bell pepper, chopped
1 medium onion, chopped
¼ cup pitted black olives, chopped

2 garlic cloves, minced
¼ cup chopped parsley
1 teaspoon grated lemon zest
1 teaspoon ground cumin
¼ teaspoon ground coriander
¼ teaspoon crushed hot red pepper
¼ cup lemon juice

1. In a shallow dish, combine flour, salt, and black pepper. Lightly coat fish on both sides, shaking off excess.

2. In a wok, heat 2 tablespoons olive oil over medium-high heat until hot, swirling to coat sides of pan. Add bell pepper and onion and cook, stirring, until softened, 3 to 5 minutes.

3. Add olives, garlic, parsley, lemon zest, cumin, coriander, and hot red pepper. Cook, stirring, 2 minutes. Remove to a plate.

4. In same wok, heat remaining 2 tablespoons oil over medium-high heat. Arrange fish fillets in pan without overlapping and cook, turning once, until golden on both sides, and just opaque in center, 6 to 8 minutes. Remove halibut to a platter. Return vegetables to wok. Add lemon juice. Cook, stirring, until heated through, 1 to 2 minutes. Spoon vegetables and any pan juices over fish and serve.

150   FRESH TUNA STEAKS WITH CAPERS

Prep: 10 minutes   Cook: 14 to 17 minutes   Serves: 4

½ cup dried bread crumbs
1 teaspoon lemon pepper
   seasoning
½ teaspoon ground cumin
2 tablespoons Dijon mustard
4 fresh tuna steaks, 6 ounces
   each
3 tablespoons olive oil

2 scallions, chopped
¼ cup clam juice
¼ cup dry white wine
1 tablespoon lime juice
¼ cup pitted chopped black
   olives, preferably
   Kalamata
2 tablespoons capers, drained

1. In a shallow dish, combine bread crumbs, lemon pepper seasoning, and cumin. Brush mustard on both sides of tuna. Dip fish into seasoned bread crumbs.

2. In a wok, heat 2 tablespoons olive oil over medium-high heat, swirling to coat sides of pan. Arrange tuna steaks in wok and cook, turning once, until lightly browned outside and opaque in center, 6 to 8 minutes. Remove to a serving platter, and cover with foil to keep warm.

3. In same wok, heat remaining 1 tablespoon oil over medium-high heat. Add scallions. Cook until softened, 2 to 3 minutes.

4. Add clam juice, wine, and lime juice. Bring to a boil, scraping up any brown bits from bottom of pan. Cook, stirring, until sauce is reduced slightly, about 3 minutes. Add olives and capers. Pour sauce over fish and serve.

151   FLOUNDER À LA PROVENÇALE

Prep: 5 minutes   Cook: 23 to 26 minutes   Serves: 4

2 tablespoons olive oil
4 shallots, chopped
2 garlic cloves, minced
¼ cup chopped pitted black
   olives
1 cup canned crushed
   tomatoes

½ cup clam juice
¼ cup dry white wine
1 teaspoon dried oregano
½ teaspoon salt
¼ teaspoon pepper
4 flounder fillets (about 6
   ounces each)

1. In a wok, heat olive oil over medium-high heat until hot, swirling to coat sides of pan. Add shallots and garlic and cook until softened, 1 to 2 minutes.

2. Add olives, tomatoes, clam juice, wine, oregano, salt, and pepper. Bring to a boil; reduce heat to medium-low. Cook until sauce is reduced slightly, 7 to 10 minutes

3. Add flounder to sauce in wok. Simmer until just opaque throughout, 5 to 7 minutes.

152   SHARK MIDDLE EASTERN STYLE
Prep: 10 minutes   Cook: 18 to 24 minutes   Serves: 4

¼ cup olive oil
4 shark steaks, 8 ounces each,
    skin removed
1 small eggplant, peeled and
    cut into ½-inch cubes
1 small zucchini, cut into
    ½-inch cubes
1 small onion, chopped
2 garlic cloves, minced

1 large ripe tomato, peeled,
    seeded, and chopped
½ cup tomato sauce
½ cup chicken broth
1 teaspoon paprika
½ teaspoon ground cumin
½ teaspoon salt
¼ teaspoon pepper

1. In a wok, heat 2 tablespoons olive oil over medium-high heat until hot, swirling to coat sides of pan. Arrange shark steaks extending up sides of pan and cook, turning once, until opaque in center and cooked through, 8 to 10 minutes. Remove to a plate.

2. In same wok, heat remaining 2 tablespoons oil over medium-high heat. Add eggplant, zucchini, onion, and garlic and cook, stirring, until crisp-tender, 3 to 5 minutes. Add tomato and cook, stirring, until vegetables are soft, 3 to 4 minutes.

3. Add tomato sauce, chicken broth, paprika, cumin, salt, and pepper. Boil until sauce thickens slightly, 3 to 4 minutes.

4. Return fish to wok. Cook until heated through, about 1 minute.

153   SHRIMP WITH BULGUR, CHICK-PEAS, AND OLIVES
Prep: 15 minutes   Cook: 13 to 15 minutes   Serves: 6 to 8

3 tablespoons olive oil
1½ pounds medium shrimp,
    shelled and deveined
4 scallions, chopped
1 celery rib, chopped
2 garlic cloves, chopped
1½ cups bulgur (cracked wheat)
3 cups chicken broth

1 (16-ounce) can chick-peas
    (garbanzo beans),
    drained
¾ cup pitted black olives
⅓ cup chopped parsley
½ teaspoon salt
¼ teaspoon pepper

1. In a wok, heat olive oil over medium-high heat until hot, swirling to coat sides of pan. Add shrimp, scallions, celery, and garlic. Stir-fry until shrimp are pink and curled, 2 to 3 minutes.

2. Add bulgur and stir to coat. Add chicken broth and bring to a boil. Reduce heat to low, cover, and cook until most of liquid is absorbed, about 10 minutes.

3. Add chick-peas, olives, parsley, salt, and pepper. Stir to combine. Cook until heated through, 1 to 2 minutes.

154 MEDITERRANEAN TUNA AND EGGPLANT RAGOUT
Prep: 10 minutes   Cook: 22 to 26 minutes   Serves: 4

¼ cup olive oil
4 tuna steaks, 8 ounces each
1 small eggplant, peeled and cut into ½-inch cubes
1 small onion, chopped
1 celery rib, chopped
2 garlic cloves, minced
1 (14-ounce) can Italian peeled tomatoes, broken up

¼ cup red wine vinegar
¼ cup chopped pitted black olives
2 tablespoons chopped fresh basil (optional)
2 tablespoons chopped Italian flat-leaf parsley
¼ teaspoon pepper
1 tablespoon capers, drained

1. In a wok, heat 2 tablespoons olive oil over medium-high heat, swirling oil with a spatula to coat sides of pan. Add tuna steaks, arranging them up sides of pan without overlapping. Cook, turning once, until opaque in center and cooked through, 7 to 9 minutes. Remove to a plate.

2. In same wok, heat remaining 2 tablespoons oil over medium-high heat. Add eggplant, onion, celery, and garlic and cook, stirring, until softened, 4 to 5 minutes.

3. Add tomatoes, vinegar, olives, basil, parsley, and pepper. Reduce heat to medium, cover, and cook 10 minutes. Return tuna to wok. Add capers. Spoon vegetables and sauce over fish. Cook until heated through, 1 to 2 minutes.

155 SHRIMP AND RICE PILAF
Prep: 15 minutes   Cook: 23 to 27 minutes   Serves: 6

2 tablespoons olive oil
2 tablespoons butter
1½ pounds medium shrimp, shelled and deveined
4 scallions, sliced
1 garlic clove, minced
¼ cup pitted black olives, chopped

1 cup long-grain white rice
2 cups chicken broth
1 teaspoon dried oregano
½ teaspoon salt
¼ teaspoon pepper

1. In a wok, heat 1 tablespoon olive oil and 1 tablespoon butter over medium-high heat until hot, swirling to coat sides of pan. Add shrimp and stir-fry until shrimp are pink and curled, 2 to 3 minutes. Remove to a plate.

2. In same wok, heat remaining 1 tablespoon oil and 1 tablespoon butter over medium-high heat. Add scallions and garlic and stir-fry until scallions are softened, 2 to 3 minutes. Add olives.

3. Add rice and stir to coat, 1 minute. Add chicken broth, oregano, salt, and pepper. Bring to a boil. Reduce heat to low. Cover and cook until rice is tender, 18 to 20 minutes. Return shrimp to wok. Fluff rice with a fork.

156 SHRIMP SCAMPI
Prep: 15 minutes   Cook: 8 to 10 minutes   Serves: 4

2 tablespoons olive oil	1 garlic clove, minced
2 tablespoons butter	¼ cup dry white wine
1 cup bread cubes, crust removed	1 tablespoon lemon juice
	¼ teaspoon pepper
1½ pounds medium shrimp, peeled and deveined	2 tablespoons chopped parsley

1. In a wok, heat 1 tablespoon olive oil and 1 tablespoon butter over medium-high heat until hot, swirling to coat sides of pan. Add bread cubes. Cook, tossing, until golden brown, 3 to 4 minutes. Remove and drain on paper towels.

2. In same wok, heat remaining 1 tablespoon oil and 1 tablespoon butter over medium-high heat. Add shrimp and stir-fry until shrimp are pink and curled, 2 to 3 minutes. Add garlic. Stir-fry 1 minute.

3. Add wine, lemon juice, pepper, and parsley. Cook 2 minutes. Remove to a serving platter. Sprinkle croutons over shrimp and serve at once.

157 BRAISED EGGPLANT, POTATOES, AND LEEKS WITH SUN-DRIED TOMATOES
Prep: 10 minutes   Cook: 22 to 30 minutes   Serves: 4

This is a terrific combination of vegetables that could easily suffice as a vegetarian entree. Note the relatively small amount of oil used in this eggplant-based dish.

3 tablespoons olive oil	1½ cups chicken broth
1 small eggplant, peeled and cut crosswise into thin slices	1 teaspoon dried oregano
	½ teaspoon salt
1 medium leek (white part only), chopped	¼ teaspoon pepper
2 medium potatoes, peeled and cut into thin slices	3 sun-dried tomatoes packed in oil, drained and coarsely chopped
2 garlic cloves, minced	2 tablespoons chopped parsley

1. In a wok, heat olive oil over medium-high heat until hot, swirling to coat sides of pan. Add eggplant, leek, potatoes, and garlic. Cook, stirring, until potatoes are translucent, 6 to 8 minutes.

2. Add chicken broth, oregano, salt, and pepper. Bring to a boil. Reduce heat to medium-low, cover, and cook until vegetables are very soft and most of liquid is absorbed, 15 to 20 minutes. Stir in sun-dried tomatoes and parsley. Cook until heated through, 1 to 2 minutes.

158 RISOTTO WITH SMOKED HAM AND PEPPERS

Prep: 5 minutes   Cook: 34 to 36 minutes   Serves: 4

Risotto is a wonderful Italian rice dish, creamy and luxurious. Be sure to buy Arborio rice for this recipe. It can be found at many supermarkets among the other rices on the shelf and in specialty food shops.

1 tablespoon butter	1 cup Arborio rice
1 tablespoon olive oil	½ pound smoked ham, cut
2 medium leeks (white part only), chopped	into ½-inch pieces
	½ teaspoon salt
½ medium red bell pepper, chopped	¼ teaspoon pepper
	⅓ cup dry white wine
½ medium green bell pepper, chopped	3 to 3½ cups hot chicken broth
	⅓ cup grated Parmesan cheese

1. In a wok, melt butter in olive oil over medium-high heat. Add leeks and red and green bell peppers and cook, stirring, until leeks are softened but not browned, 5 to 6 minutes. Add rice and stir to coat. Cook, stirring, until translucent, 1 to 2 minutes. Add smoked ham, salt, and pepper.

2. Pour in wine and ½ cup chicken broth. Cook, stirring frequently, until most of liquid is absorbed, 3 to 5 minutes. Continue adding broth, ½ cup at a time as it is absorbed, cooking and stirring until rice is just tender and sauce is creamy in consistency, about 25 minutes. Add cheese. Stir gently to combine. Serve immediately.

159 FRIED CALZONE
Prep: 30 minutes   Cook: 9 to 15 minutes   Serves: 6

Taste testers at home put their stamps of approval on this pizza-parlor favorite.

¾ pound ricotta cheese
6 ounces mozzarella cheese, shredded (1½ cups)
¼ cup grated Parmesan cheese
1 egg
2 tablespoons chopped parsley
1 teaspoon dried oregano

½ teaspoon salt
¼ teaspoon pepper
1 pound frozen bread dough, thawed
½ cup prepared spaghetti sauce
   Vegetable oil, for frying

1. In a medium bowl, combine ricotta, mozzarella, Parmesan cheese, egg, parsley, oregano, salt, and pepper; mix thoroughly. Set cheese filling aside.

2. On a lightly floured board, roll out bread dough to a 20 x 15-inch rectangle. Cut dough into 12 (5-inch) squares. Cover lightly with waxed paper to keep dough from drying out.

3. Place 2 teaspoons of spaghetti sauce and 2 tablespoons of cheese filling on each dough square. Fold squares in half diagonally to form triangles, completely enclosing filling. Crimp edges to seal.

4. In a wok, heat 3 inches of oil over medium-high heat until temperature measures 350°F on a deep-frying thermometer. Fry 4 calzone at a time until golden on bottom, 2 to 3 minutes. Turn and fry until golden on other side, 1 to 2 minutes. Repeat procedure 2 times, replacing oil in wok, if needed, to maintain level at 3 inches. Drain fried turnovers on paper towels. Serve hot.

Chapter 6

Wokking to Applause

Set the table with your best linens. Get out the crystal and pick fresh flowers from your garden or order them from your local florist. Tonight is a special dinner party. Sometimes we just want to splurge on a meal: the occasion may call for it—a promotion, birthday, or graduation—or perhaps we're just in the mood to entertain our favorite friends.

What can we serve? The wok to the rescue! The wok is ideal for an elegant sauté, such as Turkey Paillards with Pesto Cream Sauce, Fresh Tuna with Artichokes and Mushrooms in Madeira Cream Sauce, or Veal and Macadamia Nuts in Pineapple-Lime Sauce.

Sauces are quickly assembled at the last minute by combining cream with wine or broth and a dash of fresh herbs or Dijon mustard. Boil over moderately high or high heat until thickened slightly, and that's it! Another idea is to deglaze the bottom of the wok with juice, broth, or wine and then add a splash of cream. Season to taste and pour over the entree.

Accompaniments could include a simple starch and vegetable or one of the more interesting side dishes in Chapter 8, such as Wild Rice with Vegetables in Wine or Two-Pepper Orzo Pilaf. Some dressed-up vegetables are Shiitake Mushrooms and Zucchini in Red Wine, Caramelized Onions, or Snow Peas and Carrots in Grapefruit-Orange Sauce. Pair simpler dishes with more complex side dishes and vice-versa.

A VIP meal should include a fabulous dessert. Borrowing from the dessert chapter, I suggest Peaches with Brandied Custard Sauce, Sautéed Apples in Butterscotch Sauce, or Cocoa Fudge Pudding Cake. The important thing to remember is to enjoy your own party. *Bon appétit!*

160 FRESH TUNA WITH ARTICHOKES AND MUSHROOMS IN MADEIRA CREAM SAUCE

Prep: 10 minutes   Cook: 15 to 20 minutes   Serves: 6

Anyone who has tasted fresh tuna knows what a treat the meaty fish can be. Here is a spectacular way of preparing it for your favorite friends.

2 tablespoons butter
1 (8-ounce) jar marinated
   artichoke hearts in oil,
   coarsely chopped,
   marinade reserved
1 medium leek (white part
   only) or onion, chopped
½ pound fresh mushrooms,
   sliced

2 pounds tuna steaks, ¾ inch
   thick, cut into 1-inch
   chunks
½ cup dry Madeira
⅓ cup heavy cream
2 tablespoons chopped
   parsley

1. In a wok, heat butter and artichoke marinade over medium-high heat until hot. Add leek and mushrooms and cook, stirring, until mushrooms are tender, 4 to 6 minutes.

2. Add tuna and cook, stirring occasionally, until fish is just barely opaque throughout, 4 to 6 minutes. Remove to a bowl.

3. Add Madeira to wok and bring to a boil, scraping up any brown bits from bottom of pan. Boil until liquid is reduced by almost half, about 3 minutes. Add cream and cook until slightly thickened, 2 to 3 minutes longer. Return tuna and mushrooms to wok and add artichoke hearts. Cook, stirring gently, 2 minutes. Sprinkle with chopped parsley. Serve at once.

161 MAHI-MAHI WITH GRAND MARNIER

Prep: 10 minutes   Cook: 22 to 27 minutes   Serves: 4

Mahi-mahi is a medium-firm, mildly flavored whitefish. As its popularity soars, it can be found in an increasing number of fish stores and supermarkets across the country. Here is an unusual, elegant way of preparing the fillets. I like to serve it with simple accompaniments, such as steamed rice and buttered asparagus.

½ cup flour
½ teaspoon salt
¼ teaspoon pepper
1½ pounds mahi mahi fillets,
   1 inch thick
3 tablespoons olive oil

1 small onion, chopped
1 garlic clove, minced
½ cup orange juice
¼ cup Grand Marnier
¼ cup dry white wine
1 teaspoon grated orange zest

1. In a shallow dish, combine flour, salt, and pepper. Dredge fish fillets in seasoned flour to lightly coat both sides. Shake off excess.

2. In a wok, heat 2 tablespoons olive oil over medium-high heat until hot, swirling to coat sides of pan. Arrange fillets extending up sides of pan and cook, turning once and rotating to cook evenly, until golden brown on both sides, 6 to 8 minutes. Remove to a plate.

3. In same wok, heat remaining 1 tablespoon oil over medium-high heat. Add onion and garlic and cook, stirring often and scraping up browned bits from bottom of pan, until soft, 3 to 4 minutes. Return fish to wok.

4. Add orange juice, Grand Marnier, wine, and orange zest. Bring to a boil. Reduce heat to medium, cover, and simmer until fish is opaque and cooked through, about 10 minutes. Remove fish to a serving plate and cover with foil to keep warm. Raise heat to high. Boil until sauce thickens, 3 to 5 minutes. Spoon sauce over fish and serve at once.

---

162 SHRIMP À LA PROVENÇALE
Prep: 15 minutes   Cook: 9 to 11 minutes   Serves 4 to 6

¼ cup olive oil
4 garlic cloves, minced
2 pounds large shrimp,
    shelled and deveined
¾ cup dry white wine
1 (28-ounce) can Italian peeled
    tomatoes, drained and
    chopped
¼ cup chopped pitted black
    olives

2 teaspoons capers
1½ tablespoons chopped
    parsley
1 tablespoon chopped fresh
    basil (optional)
¼ teaspoon dried thyme leaves
¼ teaspoon salt
¼ teaspoon pepper

1. In a wok, heat olive oil over medium-high heat until hot, swirling to coat sides of pan. Add garlic and cook, stirring, 30 seconds. Add shrimp and cook, tossing, until shrimp are pink and curled, 3 to 4 minutes. Remove to a serving platter.

2. Raise heat to high. Add wine. Boil until reduced by half, 2 to 3 minutes.

3. Add tomatoes, olives, capers, parsley, basil, thyme, salt, and pepper. Cook, stirring, 3 minutes. Pour sauce over shrimp and serve.

163   CHICKEN PAILLARDS WITH PORT WINE SAUCE

Prep: 10 minutes   Cook: 13 to 20 minutes   Serves: 4

½ cup flour
1½ teaspoons fresh thyme or
　　½ teaspoon dried
½ teaspoon salt
¼ teaspoon pepper
4 skinless, boneless chicken
　　breast halves (4 to 5
　　ounces each), pounded to
　　¼-inch thickness

2 tablespoons vegetable oil
2 tablespoons butter
1 medium onion, minced
1 medium carrot, minced
1 celery rib, minced
1 cup port
½ cup chicken broth
1½ teaspoons cornstarch

1. In a shallow dish, combine flour, thyme, salt, and pepper. Dredge chicken in seasoned flour to lightly coat both sides; shake off excess.

2. In a wok, heat 1 tablespoon oil and 1 tablespoon butter over medium-high heat until hot, swirling to coat sides of pan. Add chicken, arranging breasts up side of pan without overlapping, and cook, turning once and rotating as needed for even browning, until golden on both sides, 6 to 8 minutes. Remove to a plate. Tent with foil to keep warm.

3. In same wok, heat remaining 1 tablespoon oil and 1 tablespoon butter over medium-high heat. Add onion, carrot, and celery. Cook, stirring, until onion and celery are softened, 3 to 5 minutes. Add port and boil until reduced by one-third, 3 to 5 minutes. Add half of chicken broth.

4. Dissolve cornstarch in remaining ¼ cup broth and stir into wok. Bring to a boil and cook, stirring, until sauce is smooth and thickened, 1 to 2 minutes. Season with additional salt and pepper to taste. Pour sauce over chicken paillards and serve.

164   CHICKEN THIGHS WITH BROWN RICE–APRICOT PILAF

Prep: 10 minutes   Cook: 49 to 59 minutes   Serves: 4 to 6

3 tablespoons olive oil
6 boneless chicken thighs,
　　about 2 pounds total
1 small onion, minced
1 small celery rib, minced
¼ pound fresh mushrooms,
　　chopped

1 cup brown rice
½ teaspoon salt
¼ teaspoon pepper
2½ cups chicken broth
½ cup apricot nectar
¼ pound dried apricots,
　　coarsely chopped

1. In a wok, heat 1½ tablespoons olive oil over medium-high heat until hot, swirling to coat sides of pan. Arrange chicken thighs in pan and cook, turning, until browned all over, 5 to 7 minutes. With tongs, remove to a plate. Pour off fat from wok.

2. In same wok, heat remaining 1½ tablespoons oil over medium-high heat until hot. Add onion, celery, and mushrooms and cook, stirring, until soft, 3 to 5 minutes. Add rice, salt. and pepper and cook, stirring to coat, 1 to 2 minutes. Return chicken to wok.

3. Add chicken broth, apricot nectar, and apricots. Bring to a boil. Reduce heat to low. Cover and cook until chicken and rice are tender, 40 to 45 minutes.

---

165   CHICKEN ROLL-UPS WITH SUN-DRIED TOMATOES AND MUSHROOMS

Prep: 20 minutes   Cook: 30 to 41 minutes   Serves 6: to 8

½ cup chopped cooked
    broccoli
6 ounces shredded Jarlsberg
    cheese (1½ cups)
3 sun-dried tomatoes packed
    in oil, drained and
    chopped
¼ cup chopped parsley
½ teaspoon salt
¼ teaspoon pepper
1 egg
2 cups dried bread crumbs

8 skinless, boneless chicken
    breast halves (about 2
    pounds total), pounded
    ¼ inch thick
6 tablespoons vegetable oil
¼ pound fresh mushrooms,
    chopped
1 medium onion, chopped
1 (10-ounce) can mushroom
    gravy
1 cup dry red wine

1. In a bowl, combine broccoli, cheese, sun-dried tomatoes, parsley, salt, and pepper. Mix filling well.

2. In a shallow bowl, beat egg until blended. Place bread crumbs on a plate. Lay chicken flat. Place 2 tablespoons filling on each piece. Roll up, folding sides in to enclose filling. Dip each roll in beaten egg and then dredge in bread crumbs to coat.

3. In a wok, heat 2 tablespoons oil over medium-high heat until hot, swirling to coat sides of pan. Add mushrooms and onion and cook, stirring, until softened, 3 to 5 minutes. Remove to a plate.

4. In same wok, heat 2 more tablespoons oil over medium-high heat. Add 4 chicken roll-ups and cook, turning, until browned all over, 6 to 8 minutes. Remove to a plate. Repeat procedure with remaining 2 tablespoons oil and 4 chicken roll-ups. Return chicken roll-ups and vegetables to wok.

5. Add mushroom gravy and wine. Reduce heat to medium-low and cook until sauce is reduced and chicken is cooked through and fork-tender, 15 to 20 minutes.

166   CHICKEN WITH RASPBERRY GLAZE
Prep: 5 minutes   Cook: 11 to 15 minutes   Serves: 4

4 skinless, boneless chicken
   breast halves (4 to 5
   ounces each), pounded
   ¼ inch thick
½ teaspoon salt
¼ teaspoon pepper
3 tablespoons butter

6 scallions, chopped
⅓ cup raspberry vinegar
½ cup chicken broth
⅓ cup heavy cream
1 tablespoon Dijon mustard
1 cup fresh or frozen
   raspberries

1. Season chicken with salt and pepper. In a wok, melt 2 tablespoons butter over medium-high heat. Swirl with a spatula to coat sides of pan. Add chicken, arranging pieces up the sides without overlapping, and cook, turning once, until lightly browned on both sides, 6 to 8 minutes. Remove to a plate.

2. In same wok, melt remaining 1 tablespoon butter over medium-high heat. Add scallions and cook, stirring, until soft and fragrant, 1 to 2 minutes. Stir in vinegar, chicken broth, cream, and mustard. Bring to a boil, reduce heat to medium, and boil until sauce thickens slightly, 2 to 3 minutes. Return chicken to wok.

3. Add raspberries. Stir gently. Cook until just heated through, about 1 minute. To serve, arrange chicken on a platter. Pour raspberries and sauce over chicken.

167   TURKEY SCALLOPS WITH MARSALA AND BALSAMIC VINEGAR
Prep: 10 minutes   Cook: 13 to 17 minutes   Serves: 4 to 6

With its lean nutritional profile, turkey is becoming increasingly popular as an alternative light meat. And the many cuts of the bird now available in supermarket meat cases lend themselves to a great variety of cooking techniques and seasonings. Here thin slices of boneless breast, or cutlets, are used in place of expensive veal scaloppine.

½   cup flour
½   teaspoon salt
¼   teaspoon pepper
1½ pounds thinly sliced turkey
    breast (cutlets), pounded
    to ¼-inch thickness
2   tablespoons butter
2   tablespoons olive oil

½   pound fresh mushrooms,
    sliced
1   teaspoon dried rosemary
⅔   cup dry Marsala wine
⅓   cup chicken broth
2   tablespoons balsamic
    vinegar
2   tablespoons chopped
    parsley

1. In a shallow dish, combine flour, salt and pepper. Dredge turkey in seasoned flour to coat both sides; shake off excess.

2. In a wok, melt 1 tablespoon butter in 1 tablespoon olive oil over medium-high heat until hot, swirling to coat sides of pan. Add turkey, arranging slices up side of wok without overlapping. Cook, turning once and rotating, until golden brown on both sides and cooked through, 6 to 8 minutes. Remove to a platter. Cover with foil to keep warm.

3. In same wok, heat remaining 1 tablespoon each butter and oil over high heat. Add mushrooms and rosemary and cook, stirring often, until mushrooms are lightly browned, 3 to 4 minutes. Add wine and boil, scraping up any brown bits from bottom of pan, until reduced by half, about 2 minutes. Add chicken broth and vinegar. Boil 2 minutes longer.

4. Spoon mushrooms and sauce over turkey. Garnish with chopped parsley and serve.

---

168   TURKEY PAILLARDS WITH PESTO CREAM SAUCE

Prep: 10 minutes   Cook: 7 to 10 minutes   Serves: 4

Paillards are thin slices of meat or poultry that are cooked very quickly, sealing in natural juices.

½ **cup flour**	2 **tablespoons olive oil**
½ **teaspoon salt**	1 **(8-ounce) jar prepared pesto**
¼ **teaspoon pepper**	**sauce**
1½ **pounds skinless, boneless**	½ **cup sour cream**
turkey cutlets, pounded	¼ **cup grated Parmesan cheese**
to ¼-inch thickness	

1. In a shallow dish, combine flour, salt, and pepper. Dredge turkey in seasoned flour, turning to lightly coat both sides; shake off excess.

2. In a wok, heat the olive oil over medium-high heat until hot, swirling to coat sides of pan. Add turkey, arranging cutlets up sides of pan without overlapping, and cook, turning once and rotating, until golden on both sides, 6 to 8 minutes. Remove to a plate. Cover with foil to keep warm.

3. Add pesto sauce and ¼ cup water to wok. Cook until hot, 1 to 2 minutes. Turn off heat. Stir in sour cream. Pour sauce over turkey. Sprinkle Parmesan cheese over top.

169 HAPPY NEW YEAR BRISKET

Prep: 10 minutes   Cook: 3¼ to 3¾ hours   Serves: 6 to 8

This is my cousin Carol's recipe, which she traditionally serves at her New Year's Eve party. Leftovers, if there are any, are even better the next day. In fact, I recommend that you cook the meat in advance and reheat it before serving.

3 pounds brisket of beef, first-cut section	1 (7-ounce) bottle beer
1 teaspoon garlic powder	½ (6-ounce) bottle chili sauce
1 teaspoon salt	1 teaspoon Gravy Master
¼ teaspoon pepper	1 teaspoon dried dill
3 tablespoons olive oil	4 medium carrots, sliced
10 scallions, sliced	½ inch thick

1. Place brisket in a shallow dish. Season all over with garlic powder, salt, and pepper.

2. In a wok, heat 2 tablespoons oil over high heat until hot, swirling to coat sides of pan. Add scallions and cook, stirring, until softened, 2 to 4 minutes. Push to edges of wok. Add remaining 1 tablespoon oil to center of wok and heat until hot. Add brisket. Cook, turning, until nicely browned all over, 8 to 12 minutes.

3. Spoon scallions over meat. Add beer, chili sauce, Gravy Master, and enough hot water to barely cover meat. Bring to a boil; reduce heat to medium-low. Cover and cook 2 hours. Add dill and carrots. Continue cooking until meat is tender, 1 to 1½ hours longer.

170 SAUERBRATEN

Prep: 10 minutes   Marinate: overnight   Cook: 3¼ to 4¼ hours   Serves: 6 to 8

1 large onion, quartered	2 bay leaves, halved
2 celery ribs, quartered	1 teaspoon dried sage
2 carrots, cut into 1-inch pieces	1 teaspoon dried rosemary
1 cup dry red wine	4 pounds rump roast
1 cup red wine vinegar	2 tablespoons vegetable oil
2 garlic cloves, crushed	2 cups beef broth
2 teaspoons black peppercorns	10 gingersnaps, coarsely crumbled
1 teaspoon salt	

1. In a large bowl, combine onion, celery, carrots, wine, vinegar, garlic, peppercorns, salt, bay leaves, sage, and rosemary. Add meat and turn to coat all surfaces. Cover with plastic wrap and marinate in refrigerator overnight, turning once or twice.

2. Remove meat from marinade. Strain liquid and reserve. Pat meat dry.

3. In a wok, heat oil over medium-high heat until hot, swirling to coat sides of pan. Add meat and cook, turning, until brown all over, 10 to 12 minutes. Add reserved marinade, beef broth, and gingersnaps. Bring to a boil; reduce heat to low. Cover and cook until meat is tender, 3 to 4 hours. Remove meat to a cutting board. Let stand 10 minutes before slicing.

4. Meanwhile, boil liquid over high heat until slightly reduced and thickened, 3 to 5 minutes. Carve meat against grain crosswise on a diagonal. Arrange on a platter and ladle some of gravy over meat. Pass remaining gravy on the side.

---

171 ROLLED STUFFED FLANK STEAK WITH RED WINE SAUCE

Prep: 25 minutes   Cook: 1²/₃ to 2¼ hours   Serves: 6

3 tablespoons vegetable oil	½ teaspoon salt
1 medium leek (white part only) or 1 onion, chopped	¼ teaspoon pepper
1 celery rib, chopped	1 (14½-ounce) can beef broth
1½ pounds flank steak	1 cup dry red wine
1 cup dry bread crumbs	½ cup tomato sauce
1 egg	1 tablespoon cornstarch
½ teaspoon dried marjoram or oregano	

1. In a wok, heat 2 tablespoons oil over medium-high heat until hot. Add leek and celery and cook, stirring, until soft, about 3 minutes. Remove to a bowl to cool.

2. Split flank steak horizontally almost in half, without cutting completely through. Open meat up like a book and pound to ¼-inch thickness. Set aside.

3. In a medium bowl, combine cooked leek and celery with bread crumbs, egg, marjoram, salt, and pepper. Spread over flank steak, leaving a 1½-inch border on all sides. Roll up meat to enclose filling, starting at a long side and tucking in short ends. Tie firmly with white kitchen string to hold shape.

4. In same wok, heat remaining 1 tablespoon oil over high heat, swirling to coat sides of pan. Add rolled flank steak and cook, turning, until browned all over, 5 to 7 minutes. Add beef broth, wine, and tomato sauce and bring to a boil. Reduce heat to medium-low, cover, and cook until meat is tender, 1½ to 2 hours. Remove steak roll to a cutting board and let rest 15 minutes before slicing.

5. Dissolve cornstarch in ¼ cup cold water and stir into sauce in wok. Cook over high heat, stirring, until sauce boils and thickens, 1 to 2 minutes. Cut meat across grain into 1-inch slices and arrange on a serving platter. Pass sauce separately.

172 TARRAGON VEAL CHOPS WITH TOMATO-CREAM SAUCE

Prep: 10 minutes   Cook: 14 to 19 minutes   Serves: 6

Veal chops are always a luxurious treat, and this light tomato-cream sauce, fragrant with tarragon, makes them especially appropriate for company. I like to serve this dish with roasted potatoes and green beans tossed in butter and fresh lemon juice.

½ cup flour
½ teaspoon salt
¼ teaspoon pepper
2 tablespoons chopped fresh
   tarragon or 1 teaspoon
   dried
6 loin veal chops, cut 1 inch
   thick (about 3 pounds)
3 tablespoons olive oil

2 shallots, minced
1 garlic clove, crushed
   through a press
⅓ cup dry white wine
1 (14-ounce) can Italian peeled
   tomatoes, drained and
   coarsely chopped
½ cup heavy cream

1. In a shallow dish, combine flour, salt, pepper, and half of tarragon. Mix well. Dredge veal chops in seasoned flour to coat lightly on both sides; shake off excess.

2. In a wok, heat 2 tablespoons olive oil over high heat until hot, swirling to coat sides of pan. Add veal, arranging chops extending up sides of wok without overlapping. Cook, turning once and rotating chops, until lightly browned on both sides, 4 to 6 minutes. With tongs, remove chops to a plate.

3. In same wok, heat remaining 1 tablespoon oil over medium-high heat. Add shallots and garlic, and cook, stirring, until softened and fragrant, about 1 minute. Add wine and boil until reduced by half, 1 to 2 minutes.

4. Add tomatoes to wok. Return veal chops to pan. Cover and simmer, turning occasionally, until veal is cooked through but still juicy, 5 to 7 minutes. Remove meat to a serving platter and cover with foil to keep warm.

5. Add cream and remaining tarragon to wok. Boil over high heat, stirring, until sauce is reduced and slightly thickened, about 3 minutes. Season with additional salt and pepper to taste. Pour sauce over veal chops and serve.

173 VEAL AND MACADAMIA NUTS IN PINEAPPLE-LIME SAUCE

Prep: 10 minutes   Cook: 8 to 11 minutes   Serves: 4

Here is a taste of Hawaii, stateside. The contrast of macadamias and pineapple—crunchy and soft, salty and sweet—is irresistible.

½ cup cornstarch
½ teaspoon salt
¼ teaspoon pepper
1 pound veal scallops, pounded to ¼-inch thickness
3 tablespoons vegetable oil
3 scallions, chopped

½ cup unsweetened pineapple juice
2 tablespoons lime juice
2 tablespoons honey
1 teaspoon grated lime zest
¼ cup coarsely chopped macadamia nuts

1. In a shallow dish, combine cornstarch, salt, and pepper. Dredge veal in seasoned cornstarch to lightly coat both sides. Shake off excess.

2. In a wok, heat 2 tablespoons oil over medium-high heat until hot, swirling to coat sides of pan. Arrange veal scallops so they extend up sides of wok without overlapping. Cook, turning once and rotating as necessary, until brown on both sides, 3 to 4 minutes. Remove to a plate.

3. In same wok, heat remaining 1 tablespoon oil over medium-high heat. Add scallions and cook, stirring, until softened, 3 to 4 minutes. Remove to plate with veal.

4. Add pineapple juice, lime juice, honey, and lime zest to wok. Boil until thick and syrupy, 2 to 3 minutes. Return veal and scallions to wok. Top with macadamia nuts and serve.

174   PORK CALVADOS
Prep: 5 minutes   Cook: 12 to 16 minutes   Serves: 4

½ cup flour
½ teaspoon salt
¼ teaspoon pepper
1½ pounds thinly sliced
    boneless loin pork chops
    (tenders), ¼ inch thick
3½ tablespoons butter

1 tablespoon olive oil
1 tart-sweet cooking apple,
    peeled, cored, and sliced
1 tablespoon sugar
½ teaspoon cinnamon
½ cup Calvados or applejack
½ cup heavy cream

1. In a shallow dish, combine flour, salt, and pepper. Lightly coat pork on both sides; shake off excess.

2. In a wok, heat 1½ tablespoons butter in olive oil over medium-high heat until hot, swirling to coat sides of pan. Arrange chops extending up sides without overlapping. Cook until golden brown on both sides and cooked through, 5 to 7 minutes. Remove to a plate.

3. In same wok, melt remaining 2 tablespoons butter over medium-high heat. Add apple, sugar, and cinnamon and cook, stirring, until apple is tender but still firm, 3 to 4 minutes.

4. Add Calvados. Cook 2 minutes. Add cream and return pork to wok. Cook, stirring, until sauce is slightly thickened, 2 to 3 minutes.

175   PORK ROAST IN CRANBERRY PORT WINE SAUCE
Prep: 5 minutes   Cook: 2¼ hours   Serves: 4 to 6

2 tablespoons vegetable oil
3 pounds boneless pork loin
    roast
3 scallions, chopped
1 (8-ounce) can whole
    cranberry sauce
½ cup beef broth

½ cup cranberry juice
½ cup orange juice
½ cup port
1 teaspoon grated orange zest
1 teaspoon cinnamon
1 tablespoon cornstarch

1. In a wok, heat oil over medium-high heat until hot, swirling to coat sides of pan. Add pork and cook, turning, until brown all over, 8 to 10 minutes. Add scallions. Cook until softened, 2 to 3 minutes.

2. Add cranberry sauce, beef broth, cranberry juice, orange juice, port, orange zest, and cinnamon. Bring to a boil. Reduce heat to medium-low, cover, and cook until meat is tender, about 2 hours. Remove roast to a carving board.

3. Dissolve cornstarch in ¼ cup cold water and stir into wok. Cook, stirring, until sauce boils and thickens, 1 to 2 minutes. Carve roast and serve with sauce.

176 PORK MARSALA WITH MUSHROOMS AND GARLICKY BALSAMIC VINEGAR SAUCE

Prep: 10 minutes   Cook: 48 to 57 minutes   Serves: 4

½ cup flour
1 teaspoon dried thyme leaves
½ teaspoon salt
¼ teaspoon pepper
4 loin pork chops, cut ¾ inch thick
¼ cup olive oil

½ pound fresh mushrooms, sliced
3 garlic cloves, crushed
½ cup chicken broth
½ cup Marsala
3 tablespoons balsamic vinegar

1. In a shallow dish, combine flour, thyme, salt, and pepper. Dredge pork chops in seasoned flour to coat lightly on both sides; shake off excess.

2. In a wok, heat 2 tablespoons olive oil over medium-high heat until hot, swirling to coat sides of pan. Arrange chops extending up sides of pan without overlapping and cook, turning once, until brown on both sides, 5 to 7 minutes. Remove to a plate.

3. In same wok, heat remaining 2 tablespoons oil over medium-high heat. Add mushrooms and garlic and cook, stirring, until tender, 3 to 5 minutes. Return chops to wok.

4. Add chicken broth, Marsala, and balsamic vinegar. Reduce heat to low, cover, and cook until pork is tender, 40 to 45 minutes.

Chapter 7

Pasta in the Wok

If a poll were taken to determine which food was the most popular with the American public, pasta would definitely be right up there. It's quick to cook, adaptable to a wealth of sauces, cheeses, and vegetables, and it comes in a myriad of varieties.

General directions for cooking pasta are as follows: Bring a large pot of salted water to a full boil. Add the pasta. Return the water to a boil, stirring occasionally to prevent sticking. Be sure to drain the pasta well so it doesn't dilute the sauce. Fresh pasta cooks much faster than dry, so don't walk far from the pot. One pound of most fresh pasta cooks in 1 to 3 minutes, depending on the shape and width. One pound of dried pasta cooks in approximately 10 to 12 minutes, again depending upon shape and thickness. Keep tasting, starting about a minute before you think it's done to prevent overcooking. The pasta should be *al dente,* tender but with a pleasingly firm resistance when you chew.

Pasta and sauce should complement each other. Certain sauces pair up best with tubular pastas, such as penne or elbows in Macaroni and Cheese and in Penne with Salsa Cream Sauce. Other toppings work well with strands of fettuccine or spaghetti, as in Four-Cheese Pasta, Spinach Fettuccine with Spinach and Feta, and Wokked Spaghetti and "Gravy." Orzo, a rice-shaped pasta, is featured in Cod and Orzo Pilaf with Feta Cheese.

177   WOKKED SPAGHETTI AND "GRAVY"
Prep: 10 minutes   Cook: 28 to 37 minutes   Serves: 4

In South Philly, Italians call spaghetti sauce gravy. Cooking pasta in a wok definitely isn't traditional, but it works! One night, the large pot used for spaghetti was filled with sweet and sour meatballs, so I had to cook the pasta and sauce in the wok.

1 **pound thin spaghetti**	1 **teaspoon dried oregano**
3 **tablespoons olive oil**	1 **teaspoon dried basil**
1 **medium onion, chopped**	2 **teaspoons sugar**
2 **garlic cloves, minced**	1 **teaspoon salt**
1 **(28-ounce) can crushed**	¼ **teaspoon black pepper**
tomatoes	⅛ **teaspoon crushed hot red**
1 **(6-ounce) can tomato paste**	**pepper**
¼ **cup chopped Italian flat-leaf**	**Grated Romano cheese**
parsley	

1. In a wok filled with boiling salted water, cook spaghetti until tender but still firm, 9 to 11 minutes. Drain and rinse under cold running water; drain well. Place in a deep bowl. Wipe out wok.

2. In same wok, heat olive oil over medium-high heat until hot. Add onion and garlic and cook, stirring, until soft, 4 to 6 minutes.

3. Add crushed tomatoes, tomato paste, parsley, oregano, basil, sugar, salt, black pepper, hot pepper, and 1 cup water. Bring to a boil. Partially cover, reduce heat to medium, and cook until reduced by one-third, 15 to 20 minutes. Add spaghetti to wok and toss with sauce to heat through. Serve at once, with a sprinkling of grated Romano cheese.

178   ZITI PRIMAVERA WITH GOAT CHEESE AND PESTO
Prep: 10 minutes   Cook: 16 to 20 minutes   Serves: 4 to 6

2 **tablespoons olive oil**	1 **pound ziti**
1 **medium onion, sliced**	8 **ounces goat cheese,**
1 **medium zucchini, sliced**	**crumbled**
1 **large tomato, coarsely**	1 **(4-ounce) jar pesto sauce**
chopped	¼ **cup grated Parmesan cheese**

1. In a wok, heat olive oil over medium-high heat until hot, swirling to coat sides of pan. Add onion and zucchini. Cook, stirring occasionally, until onion is softened, 4 to 6 minutes. Add tomato. Cook 2 minutes.

2. Meanwhile, in a large pot of boiling salted water, cook ziti until tender but still firm, 10 to 12 minutes. Drain and rinse under cold running water; drain well.

3. Add pasta to vegetables in wok. Add goat cheese, pesto, and Parmesan cheese. Toss well to combine. Serve hot or at room temperature.

179 FETTUCCINE WITH RICOTTA AND VEGETABLES PROVENÇALE

Prep: 10 minutes   Cook: 8 to 14 minutes   Serves: 4

1 pound fresh fettuccine
1 (6-ounce) jar marinated artichoke hearts, coarsely chopped, marinade reserved
2 tablespoons butter
1 small onion, chopped
1 small green bell pepper, chopped
1 small red bell pepper, chopped
1 small yellow bell pepper, chopped

3 garlic cloves, minced
1 cup dry white wine
⅓ cup pitted black olives, chopped
1 cup ricotta cheese
2 tablespoons chopped fresh basil or parsley
½ teaspoon dried oregano
   Salt and freshly ground pepper

1. In a large pot of boiling salted water, cook fettuccine until tender but still firm, 2 to 4 minutes. Drain and rinse under cold running water; drain well.

2. In a wok, heat artichoke marinade and butter over medium-high heat. Add onion, bell peppers, and garlic. Cook, stirring, until soft, 3 to 5 minutes. Add wine, olives, and artichokes. Cook, stirring, until sauce is slightly reduced, 3 to 5 minutes.

3. Add ricotta, basil, oregano, salt, and pepper. Stir to mix well. Add fettuccine and toss to combine.

---

180 MACARONI AND CHEESE

Prep: 5 minutes   Cook: 13 to 16 minutes   Serves: 4

1 (8-ounce) box elbow macaroni
3 cups milk
1 teaspoon dry mustard
¼ teaspoon Worcestershire sauce

2 cups grated Cheddar cheese (8 ounces)
½ teaspoon salt
¼ teaspoon pepper
1 cup fresh bread crumbs
4 tablespoons butter, melted

1. In a large pot of boiling salted water, cook macaroni until tender but still firm, about 10 minutes. Drain and rinse under cold running water; drain well.

2. In a wok, combine milk, mustard, and Worcestershire sauce. Bring to a boil over medium heat. Add cheese, salt, and pepper. Cook, stirring, until cheese melts, 1 to 2 minutes. Add macaroni and stir to coat well with cheese sauce. Cook, stirring, until most of liquid is absorbed, 2 to 4 minutes.

3. In a bowl, combine bread crumbs and melted butter. Sprinkle over top of macaroni and cheese and serve.

181 ZITI WITH ASPARAGUS AND MUSHROOMS
Prep: 10 minutes   Cook: 16 to 21 minutes   Serves: 4 to 6

The cooking water from the pasta is used in this sauce both as a liquid and as a thickener—an authentic Italian trick.

1 pound ziti	½ teaspoon dried tarragon
3 tablespoons olive oil	½ teaspoon salt
2 garlic cloves, minced	¼ teaspoon pepper
¾ pound mushrooms, sliced	⅛ teaspoon cayenne
2 teaspoons lemon juice	½ cup grated Parmesan cheese
¾ pound fresh asparagus, cut diagonally into ½-inch slices	

1. In a large pot of boiling salted water, cook ziti until tender but still firm, 10 to 12 minutes. Measure out ½ cup cooking liquid and set aside. Drain pasta into a colander.

2. Meanwhile, in a wok, heat olive oil over high heat until hot, swirling to coat sides of pan. Add garlic and mushrooms and stir-fry until mushrooms exude most of their juices, 3 to 5 minutes. Toss with lemon juice. Add asparagus, tarragon, salt, pepper, and cayenne. Stir-fry until asparagus is crisp-tender, 2 to 3 minutes.

3. Add reserved cooking liquid to vegetables in wok. Add ziti and half of Parmesan cheese and cook, tossing, about 30 seconds, until cheese is melted and pasta is heated through. Turn into a serving bowl and sprinkle remaining Parmesan over top. Serve at once.

182 FOUR-CHEESE PASTA
Prep: 10 minutes   Cook: 7 to 12 minutes   Serves: 4 to 6

3 tablespoons butter	1 pound fresh fettuccine
1 small onion, minced	1 cup shredded fontina cheese (about 4 ounces)
½ cup heavy cream	1 cup ricotta cheese
½ teaspoon grated nutmeg	½ cup crumbled Gorgonzola cheese
½ teaspoon salt	½ cup grated Parmesan cheese
¼ teaspoon freshly ground pepper	

1. In a wok, melt butter over medium heat. Add onion and cook, stirring, until softened, 3 to 4 minutes. Add cream, nutmeg, salt, and pepper. Boil 1 to 2 minutes to reduce slightly.

2. Meanwhile, in a large pot of boiling salted water, cook fettuccine until tender but still firm, 2 to 4 minutes. Drain into a colander.

3. Add fontina, ricotta, and Gorgonzola cheeses to cream in wok. Cook over medium heat, stirring, until melted and smooth, 1 to 2 minutes. Add pasta and half of Parmesan cheese and toss to coat. Season with additional freshly ground pepper to taste. Turn into a serving bowl and sprinkle remaining cheese over top. Serve at once.

183 PASTA SHELLS WITH EGGPLANT, OLIVES, AND CAPERS

Prep: 10 minutes   Cook: 24 to 26 minutes   Serves: 4 to 6

3 tablespoons olive oil
1 medium eggplant, peeled and cut into ½-inch cubes
3 scallions, chopped
1 medium red bell pepper, chopped
2 garlic cloves, minced
1 cup chicken broth
1 cup canned crushed tomatoes

¼ cup chopped pitted black olives, preferably Kalamata
2 tablespoons capers
1 teaspoon dried basil
½ teaspoon salt
¼ teaspoon pepper
2 cups small pasta shells
⅓ cup grated Parmesan cheese

1. In a wok, heat olive oil over medium-high heat until hot, swirling to coat sides of pan. Add eggplant, scallions, bell pepper, and garlic. Cook, stirring, until softened, 4 to 6 minutes.

2. Add chicken broth, tomatoes, olives, capers, basil, salt, and pepper. Boil until liquid has reduced by half, about 20 minutes. Remove from heat and reserve.

3. Meanwhile, in a large pot of boiling salted water, cook pasta until tender but still firm to the bite, 10 to 12 minutes. Drain and rinse under cold running water; drain well.

4. Add pasta to tomato-eggplant mixture in wok. Toss well to combine. Sprinkle with cheese. Serve warm or at room temperature.

184 SPINACH FETTUCCINE WITH SPINACH AND FETA

Prep: 10 minutes   Cook: 9 to 13 minutes   Serves: 4

1 **pound fresh spinach fettuccine**
2 **tablespoons olive oil**
3 **scallions, chopped**
1 **(10-ounce) box frozen spinach, thawed and drained well**
½ **pound ricotta cheese**

½ **pound feta cheese, crumbled**
½ **teaspoon grated nutmeg**
¼ **teaspoon pepper**
¼ **cup chopped parsley**
2 **tablespoons chopped fresh dill or 1½ teaspoons dried**

1. In a large pot of boiling salted water, cook fettuccine until tender but still firm, 2 to 4 minutes. Drain and rinse under cold water; drain well.

2. In a wok, heat olive oil over medium-high heat until hot, swirling to coat sides of pan. Add scallions and spinach and cook until wilted, 3 to 4 minutes. Add ricotta, feta cheese, nutmeg, and pepper. Cook, stirring, until cheeses are creamy and smooth, about 3 minutes.

3. Add fettuccine, parsley, and dill. Cook, tossing to coat, 1 to 2 minutes, to heat through.

185 TORTELLINI WITH SUN-DRIED TOMATOES

Prep: 5 minutes   Cook: 9 to 12 minutes   Serves: 4

1 **pound cheese-filled spinach tortellini**
2 **tablespoons butter**
1 **tablespoon olive oil**
1 **medium onion, chopped**
2 **garlic cloves, minced**
⅓ **cup sun-dried tomatoes, packed in oil, drained and chopped**

¼ **teaspoon salt**
¼ **teaspoon freshly ground pepper**
¾ **cup heavy cream**
½ **cup grated Parmesan cheese**

1. In a large pot of boiling salted water, cook tortellini until tender but still firm, 8 to 10 minutes. Drain into a colander and rinse under cold running water; drain well.

2. Meanwhile, in a wok, melt butter in olive oil over medium-high heat. Add onion and garlic and cook, stirring often, until soft, 3 to 4 minutes. Add sun-dried tomatoes, salt, and pepper, and cook, stirring, 1 minute.

3. Add cream and boil until reduced by one-third, about 3 minutes. Add tortellini and toss to coat. Cook until heated through, 1 to 2 minutes. Sprinkle on Parmesan cheese, toss, and serve.

186 ROTINI WITH PLUM TOMATOES AND MUSHROOMS

Prep: 15 minutes   Cook: 23 to 28 minutes   Serves: 4 to 6

3 tablespoons olive oil
1 medium onion, chopped
2 garlic cloves, minced
½ pound fresh mushrooms, sliced
8 fresh plum tomatoes, peeled, seeded, and chopped, or 1 (14-ounce) can Italian peeled tomatoes, drained and chopped

¼ cup chopped Italian flat-leaf parsley
¼ cup chopped fresh basil or 1½ teaspoons dried
½ teaspoon salt
¼ teaspoon black pepper
¼ teaspoon crushed hot red pepper
1 pound rotini or fusilli
½ cup grated Parmesan cheese

1. In a wok, heat oil over high heat, swirling to coat sides of pan. Add onion and cook, stirring, 2 minutes. Add garlic and mushrooms and cook, stirring often, until onion is soft and mushrooms are lightly browned, 3 to 4 minutes.

2. Add tomatoes, parsley, basil, salt, black pepper, and hot pepper. Reduce heat to medium. Cook, stirring occasionally, until sauce is slightly thickened, 8 to 10 minutes.

3. Meantime, in a large pot of boiling salted water, cook rotini until tender but still firm, 10 to 12 minutes. Drain and rinse under cold running water; drain well.

4. Place pasta in a large serving bowl. Pour sauce over pasta and toss. Sprinkle Parmesan cheese over top.

187   SPAGHETTI WITH RED MEAT SAUCE

Prep: 10 minutes   Cook: 33 to 42 minutes   Serves: 4

2 tablespoons olive oil
1 medium onion, chopped
1 medium carrot, chopped
1 celery rib with leaves,
      chopped
1 garlic clove, minced
1 pound ground chuck (80%
      lean)
1 (28-ounce) can crushed
      tomatoes

1 (6-ounce) can tomato paste
¼ cup chopped parsley
¼ cup chopped fresh basil or
      1 teaspoon dried
½ teaspoon salt
¼ teaspoon pepper
1 pound spaghetti

1. In a wok, heat olive oil over high heat until hot, swirling to coat sides of pan. Add onion, carrot, celery, and garlic and stir-fry until softened, 3 to 5 minutes. Add ground chuck and cook, stirring, until meat loses its red color, 3 to 5 minutes longer.

2. Add tomatoes, tomato paste, parsley, basil, salt, pepper, and 1 cup water. Bring to a boil. Reduce heat to medium-low and cook, covered, until reduced slightly, 25 to 30 minutes.

3. Meanwhile, in a large pot of boiling salted water, cook spaghetti until tender but still firm, about 10 minutes. Drain well. Place spaghetti in a large deep serving bowl. Pour sauce over pasta, toss, and serve.

188   PENNE WITH SALSA CREAM SAUCE

Prep: 5 minutes   Cook: 16 to 19 minutes   Serves: 4

1 pound penne
2 tablespoons olive oil
1 large onion, chopped
¼ teaspoon crushed hot red
      pepper
1 (12-ounce) jar salsa

1 (8-ounce) can tomato sauce
½ cup heavy cream
¼ cup chopped pitted green
      olives
¼ cup chopped cilantro or
      parsley

1. In a large pot of boiling salted water, cook pasta until tender but still firm, 10 to 12 minutes. Drain and rinse under cold water; drain well.

2. In a wok, heat olive oil over medium-high heat until hot. Add onion and cook, stirring, until softened, about 3 minutes.

3. Add hot pepper, salsa, tomato sauce, cream, and olives. Cook 2 minutes. Add penne and cilantro and cook, tossing, until heated through, 1 to 2 minutes.

189 STUFFED SHELLS MARINARA WITH RICOTTA AND MUSHROOMS

Prep: 10 minutes   Cook: 23 to 26 minutes   Serves: 4

12 ounces large pasta shells
2 tablespoons olive oil
¼ pound fresh mushrooms, chopped
1 egg, beaten
½ pound ricotta cheese
¼ pound shredded mozzarella cheese (about 1 cup)

1 teaspoon dried basil
½ teaspoon salt
¼ teaspoon pepper
2 cups prepared marinara sauce

1. In a large pot of boiling salted water, cook shells until tender but still firm, 10 to 12 minutes. Drain and rinse under cold running water; drain well.

2. In a wok, heat olive oil over medium-high heat until hot, swirling to coat sides of pan. Add mushrooms and cook until most of liquid is absorbed, 3 to 4 minutes. Remove to a bowl to cool slightly. Mix egg, ricotta and mozzarella cheeses, basil, salt, and pepper with mushrooms. Fill shells lightly with cheese mixture.

3. Pour marinara sauce into wok and heat over medium heat. Place filled shells over sauce. Reduce heat to low. Cover and cook 10 minutes.

190 SPAGHETTI CHICKEN

Prep: 10 minutes   Cook: 14 to 18 minutes   Serves: 4

3 tablespoons vegetable oil
1 pound skinless, boneless chicken breasts, cut crosswise into ½-inch cubes
1 large yellow bell pepper, chopped
3 scallions, sliced

2 garlic cloves, minced
3 cups cooked spaghetti, about 4 ounces
1 cup chicken broth
½ cup dry red wine
¾ teaspoon salt
¼ teaspoon pepper
2 teaspoons cornstarch

1. In a wok, heat 1 tablespoon oil over high heat until hot, swirling to coat sides of pan. Add chicken and stir-fry until meat is white throughout but still juicy, 3 to 4 minutes. Remove to a plate.

2. In same wok, heat remaining 2 tablespoons oil over high heat. Add bell pepper, scallions, and garlic and stir-fry until pepper is soft, 3 to 5 minutes.

3. Return chicken to wok. Add spaghetti. Cook 2 minutes, stirring. Add chicken broth, wine, salt, and pepper. Cook 5 minutes.

4. Dissolve cornstarch in ¼ cup cold water and stir into wok. Cook over high heat, stirring until sauce boils and thickens, 1 to 2 minutes.

191   LINGUINE WITH SMOKED MOZZARELLA AND BACON

Prep: 7 minutes   Cook: 18 to 21 minutes   Serves: 4

1   pound linguine
½   pound bacon, diced
1   cup heavy cream
½   pound smoked mozzarella, shredded (about 2 cups)

½   teaspoon coarsely cracked pepper
⅓   cup grated Parmesan cheese
¼   cup chopped Italian flat-leaf parsley

1. In a large pot of boiling salted water, cook linguine until tender but still firm, about 10 minutes. Drain and rinse under cold running water; drain well.

2. Meanwhile, in a wok, cook bacon over medium heat until crisp, 4 to 6 minutes. Drain on paper towels. Wipe out wok.

3. In wok, bring cream to a boil over high heat. Boil 2 minutes. Reduce heat to medium. Add mozzarella and pepper. Cook, stirring, until cheese melts, 1 to 2 minutes.

4. Add pasta and bacon to sauce in wok. Cook, tossing to coat, 1 minute. Transfer to a large serving bowl. Sprinkle grated Parmesan and parsley on top and serve.

192   CHICKEN AND ZUCCHINI WITH NOODLES

Prep: 10 minutes   Cook: 17 to 23 minutes   Serves: 4

2   cups fine egg noodles (4 ounces)
3   tablespoons olive oil
1   pound skinless, boneless chicken breasts, cut crosswise into ¼-inch strips

2   medium zucchini, sliced
1   small onion, chopped
1   garlic clove, minced
1   (8-ounce) can tomato sauce
1   cup dry white wine
½   teaspoon salt
¼   teaspoon pepper

1. In a large pot of boiling salted water, cook noodles until just tender, 5 to 6 minutes. Drain and rinse under cold running water; drain well.

2. In a wok, heat 1 tablespoon olive oil over medium-high heat until hot, swirling to coat sides of pan. Add chicken and stir-fry until meat is white throughout but still juicy, 3 to 5 minutes. Remove to a plate.

3. In same wok, heat remaining 2 tablespoons oil over medium-high heat. Add zucchini, onion, and garlic and stir-fry until crisp-tender, 3 to 5 minutes. Add tomato sauce, wine, salt, pepper, and ½ cup water. Cook 5 minutes.

4. Return chicken to wok. Add cooked egg noodles. Toss to combine. Cook until heated through, 1 to 2 minutes. Serve at once.

193   PENNE WITH SPINACH MEAT SAUCE
Prep: 5 minutes   Cook: 39 to 43 minutes   Serves: 6

 1 tablespoon olive oil
1½ pounds ground chuck (80%
       lean)
 1 large onion, chopped
 2 garlic cloves, minced
 1 (28-ounce) can Italian peeled
       tomatoes, coarsely
       chopped, juices reserved
 1 teaspoon dried basil
 1 teaspoon dried oregano
 ½ teaspoon salt
 ¼ teaspoon pepper
 1 pound penne or other
       tubular pasta
 1 (10-ounce) package frozen
       chopped spinach, thawed
       and drained
 ⅓ cup grated Romano cheese

1. In a wok, heat olive oil over high heat until hot, swirling to coat sides of pan. Add ground chuck, onion, and garlic and cook, stirring, until onions are soft and meat loses its red color, 4 to 6 minutes.

2. Add tomatoes with their juice, basil, oregano, salt, and pepper. Simmer, partially covered, 20 minutes.

3. Meanwhile, in a large pot of boiling salted water, cook pasta until tender but still firm, 10 to 12 minutes; drain.

4. Add spinach to meat sauce in wok. Cook 5 minutes. Stir in pasta and toss well to combine. Sprinkle on cheese and serve.

194   FUSILLI WITH SHRIMP AND FETA CHEESE
Prep: 10 minutes   Cook: 17 to 19 minutes   Serves: 4

12 ounces fusilli (corkscrew
       pasta)
 2 tablespoons olive oil
 1 small onion, minced
 1 garlic clove, crushed
 ¾ pound medium shrimp,
       shelled and deveined
 ¼ cup chopped pitted black
       olives
 ½ cup bottled clam juice
 2 tablespoons lemon juice
 ½ pound feta cheese,
       crumbled
 1 tablespoon minced fresh
       oregano or 1 teaspoon
       dried
 ¼ teaspoon pepper

1. In a large pot of boiling salted water, cook fusilli until tender but still firm, about 10 minutes. Drain well and keep warm.

2. Meanwhile, in a wok, heat olive oil over high heat until hot. Add onion and garlic and cook, stirring, until softened, 2 to 3 minutes. Add shrimp and cook, stirring, until they are pink and curled, 2 to 3 minutes longer.

3. Add olives, clam juice, and lemon juice. Reduce heat to medium-high and cook 2 minutes to reduce slightly. Add feta cheese, oregano, and pepper. Cook, stirring, until cheese melts, about 1 minute.

4. Add hot pasta and toss to mix. Turn into a large pasta bowl and serve.

195 PASTA SHELLS WITH FRESH SALMON AND WILD MUSHROOMS

Prep: 10 minutes   Cook: 22 to 27 minutes   Serves: 4 to 6

1 pound medium pasta shells	¼ teaspoon pepper
¼ cup olive oil	½ pound salmon fillet, skin
3 shallots, minced	removed, cut into ¾-inch
½ pound fresh shiitake	pieces
mushrooms, stemmed	½ cup dry white wine
and sliced	½ cup heavy cream
2 ripe plum tomatoes, diced	¼ cup grated Parmesan cheese
½ teaspoon salt	2 tablespoon chopped parsley

1. In a large pot of boiling salted water, cook shells until tender but still firm, 10 to 12 minutes. Drain into a colander and rinse under cold, running water; drain well.

2. In a wok, heat 2 tablespoons olive oil over medium-high heat until hot. Add shallots and shiitake mushrooms. Cook, stirring, until mushrooms are tender, 3 to 5 minutes. Add tomatoes and cook 1 minute. Season with ¼ teaspoon salt and ⅛ teaspoon pepper. Remove to a bowl.

3. In same wok, heat remaining 2 tablespoons oil over medium-high heat until hot. Add salmon and cook, turning, until opaque throughout, 3 to 4 minutes. Remove to bowl with vegetables.

4. Add wine to wok and boil over high heat until reduced by half, about 2 minutes. Add cream and remaining salt and pepper. Cook, stirring, 2 minutes longer. Return salmon and vegetables to wok. Cook 1 minute. Add pasta and half of cheese. Toss to coat. Sprinkle with parsley and remaining Parmesan cheese on top and serve at once.

196 FETTUCCINE WITH SALMON AND ARTICHOKES

Prep: 5 minutes   Cook: 10 to 16 minutes   Serves: 4

1 pound fresh fettuccine	1 (7½-ounce) can sockeye
1 (6-ounce) jar marinated	salmon, bones removed,
artichoke hearts, coarsely	drained, and flaked
chopped, marinade	1 cup heavy cream
reserved	½ teaspoon salt
6 scallions, chopped	¼ teaspoon pepper
1 garlic clove, minced	

1. In a large pot of boiling salted water, cook fettuccine until tender but still firm, 2 to 3 minutes. Rinse under cold water; drain well.

2. In a wok, heat artichoke marinade over medium heat until hot. Add scallions and garlic and cook, stirring, until soft, 2 to 4 minutes. Add artichokes and salmon and cook, stirring, until heated through, 1 to 2 minutes.

3. Add cream, salt, and pepper and boil until reduced by half, 3 to 4 minutes. Add fettuccini and cook, tossing to coat, 1 minute.

197   TUNA PASTA PROVENÇALE
Prep: 10 minutes   Cook: 15 to 21 minutes   Serves: 6

1 pound small pasta shells	⅓ cup chopped pitted black
2 tablespoons olive oil	olives
1 medium sweet onion,	½ teaspoon pepper
chopped	½ cup plain yogurt
1 medium red bell pepper,	½ cup mayonnaise
chopped	1 tablespoon anchovy paste
1 (14-ounce) can tuna, drained	2 tablespoons capers, drained
and flaked	

1. In a large pot of boiling salted water, cook shells until tender but still firm, 8 to 10 minutes. Drain and rinse under cold running water; drain well.

2. In a wok, heat olive oil over medium-high heat until hot. Add onion and bell pepper and cook, stirring, until softened, 4 to 6 minutes. Add tuna, olives, and pepper. Cook, stirring, until tuna is hot, 1 to 2 minutes. Stir in shells.

3. In a bowl, mix yogurt, mayonnaise, and anchovy paste. Add to wok. Cook over low heat, tossing, until mixture is heated through, 1 to 2 minutes. Stir in capers. Cook 1 minute.

198   PASTA WITH TUNA AND WHITE BEANS
Prep: 5 minutes   Cook: 12 to 16 minutes   Serves: 4

8 ounces small pasta shells	¼ cup brine-cured imported
3 tablespoons olive oil	black olives, such as
4 scallions, chopped	Niçoise, halved and
1 garlic clove, minced	pitted
2 (7-ounce) cans light tuna	¼ cup chopped parsley
packed in oil, undrained	1 tablespoon lemon juice
1 (16-ounce) can white kidney	½ teaspoon freshly ground
beans, rinsed and drained	pepper

1. In a large pot of boiling salted water, cook shells until tender but still firm, 8 to 10 minutes. Drain and rinse under cold running water; drain well.

2. In a wok, heat olive oil over high heat until hot. Add scallions and garlic and cook, stirring, until softened and fragrant, 1 to 2 minutes.

3. Add tuna with its oil, beans, olives, parsley, lemon juice, and pepper. Cook, stirring, 2 minutes. Add pasta to wok. Cook, tossing, until heated through, 1 to 2 minutes.

199   FETTUCCINE FLORENTINE
Prep: 15 minutes   Cook: 14 to 22 minutes   Serves: 4 to 6

In culinary jargon, "Florentine" always means spinach. Here a full pound of the healthful leaf is mellowed with cream and Parmesan cheese, enlivened with Canadian bacon, and bolstered with the meatiness of fresh mushrooms for a sublime pasta that will serve 6 as an appetizer and 4 as a main course.

¼ cup olive oil
½ pound Canadian-style
  bacon, cut into ½-inch
  dice
½ pound fresh mushrooms,
  sliced
4 scallions, chopped
2 garlic cloves, minced

1 pound fresh spinach leaves,
  rinsed well, drained, and
  coarsely chopped
1 cup heavy cream
½ teaspoon freshly ground
  pepper
1 pound fresh fettuccine
½ cup grated Parmesan cheese

1. In a wok, heat 1 tablespoon olive oil over medium-high heat until hot, swirling to coat sides of pan. Add bacon and cook, stirring occasionally, until browned all over, 4 to 6 minutes. Remove bacon to a plate.

2. In same wok, heat remaining 3 tablespoons oil over high heat. Add mushrooms, scallions, and garlic. Stir-fry until mushrooms are lightly browned, 3 to 5 minutes. Reduce heat to medium-high. Add spinach and stir-fry until wilted, 2 to 3 minutes. Add cream and and pepper and return bacon to pan. Boil until sauce is slightly reduced, 3 to 4 minutes.

3. Meanwhile, in a large pot of boiling salted water, cook fettuccine until just tender, 2 to 3 minutes. Drain well. Add pasta to sauce along with half of grated cheese. Toss to combine. Transfer to a large serving bowl and sprinkle remaining grated cheese over top. Serve at once.

200 PASTA WITH TUNA, BROCCOLI, ARTICHOKES, AND OLIVES

Prep: 10 minutes   Cook: 18 to 22 minutes   Serves: 4

12 ounces rigatoni
1 (8-ounce) jar marinated
   artichoke hearts, halved
   or quartered, marinade
   reserved
1 cup broccoli florets
1 medium carrot, sliced
2 garlic cloves, minced
⅓ cup black olives, preferably
   Kalamata, pitted and
   chopped

2 tablespoons chopped
   pimiento
1 (7-ounce) can light tuna
   packed in oil, oil reserved
   Freshly ground pepper
¼ cup grated Parmesan cheese

1. In a large pot of boiling salted water, cook rigatoni until tender but still firm, 10 to 12 minutes. Drain and rinse under cold running water; drain well.

2. In a wok, heat artichoke marinade over medium heat. Add broccoli, carrot, and garlic. Cook, stirring, until crisp-tender, 4 to 5 minutes.

3. Add olives, pimiento, tuna with its oil, artichoke hearts, and pepper. Cook, stirring often, 3 minutes. Add pasta to wok and toss to coat. Cook until rigatoni is heated through, 1 to 2 minutes. Sprinkle Parmesan cheese on top and serve.

201 FUSILLI WITH SCALLOPS AND SNOW PEAS

Prep: 10 minutes   Cook: 20 to 25 minutes   Serves: 6

3 tablespoons vegetable oil
1 small red bell pepper,
   chopped
3 scallions, chopped
1 garlic clove, minced
12 ounces fusilli or penne
2 cups clam juice
1 cup dry white wine

1 pound bay scallops
¼ pound snow peas, stemmed
   and stringed
⅓ cup chopped pitted black
   olives
¼ cup chopped parsley
2 tablespoons capers, drained
¼ teaspoon pepper

1. In a wok, heat oil over medium-high heat until hot. Add bell pepper, scallions, and garlic and cook, stirring, until crisp-tender, 3 to 4 minutes. Add fusilli and cook, stirring to coat, 1 minute.

2. Add clam juice and wine. Bring to a boil. Reduce heat to medium-low and cook until pasta is tender but still firm, 12 to 14 minutes.

3. Add scallops and snow peas. Cook, stirring, until scallops are opaque, 2 to 3 minutes. Stir in olives, parsley, capers, and pepper. Cook until most of liquid is absorbed, 2 to 3 minutes.

202   COD AND ORZO PILAF WITH FETA CHEESE

Prep: 10 minutes   Cook: 18 to 24 minutes   Serves: 4

3 tablespoon olive oil
1 pound cod fillets, ¾ inch
    thick, cut into 1-inch
    cubes
1 medium onion, chopped
1 garlic clove, minced
1½ cups orzo (rice-shaped pasta)
2 tablespoons tomato paste

1 teaspoon dried oregano
¼ teaspoon pepper
2 cups chicken broth
1 cup dry white wine
2 tablespoons lemon juice
1 cup crumbled feta cheese
    (4 ounces)

1. In a wok, heat 2 tablespoons olive oil over medium-high heat until hot, swirling to coat sides of pan. Add fish cubes and cook, stirring, until lightly browned, 3 to 5 minutes. Remove to a plate.

2. In same wok, heat remaining 1 tablespoon oil over medium-high heat. Add onion and garlic and cook, stirring, until softened, 3 to 4 minutes. Add orzo, tomato paste, oregano, and pepper. Cook, stirring to coat, 1 minute.

3. Add chicken broth, wine, and lemon juice. Bring to a boil. Reduce heat to medium-low, cover, and cook until orzo is tender and most of liquid is absorbed, 10 to 12 minutes. Return fish to wok. Stir in feta cheese and cook until heated through, 1 to 2 minutes.

Chapter 8

Wok-Cooked Vegetables, Rice, and Grains

Most of us are trying to add more vegetables and grains to our daily diets, and the wok can provide plenty of encouragement. In this one large pot, you can stir-fry, boil, steam, sauté, stew, even fry all your favorite vegetables, using whatever technique will best preserve the texture and flavor you desire.

Variety is the key. Vegetable-Stuffed Peppers, filled with rice, assorted vegetables, mushrooms, and cheese, make a substantial vegetarian main course. Recipes like Potatoes and Leeks with Rosemary, Mexican Rice with Corn and Peas, and Sauté of Summer Vegetables, flecked with fresh basil, offer an appealing assortment of side dishes. Others, such as Winter Root Vegetable Fritters and Israeli Eggplant Salad, make fine first courses.

Rices and grains cook well in the covered wok. As a rule of thumb, long-grain white rice cooks in 2 cups liquid (usually water or stock) to each 1 cup rice for 18 to 20 minutes. Brown and wild rice take 40 to 45 minutes in 2½ cups liquid for each 1 cup rice. Add rice to boiling liquid, cover, and reduce heat to lowest setting possible to avoid sticking and scorching. When done, fluff with a fork.

---

203 CORN CAKES
Prep: 5 minutes   Cook: 15 to 18 minutes   Serves: 4 to 6

2 cups corn kernels—fresh, frozen, or canned	1 teaspoon baking powder
2 eggs, lightly beaten	½ teaspoon salt
¼ cup milk	¼ teaspoon white pepper
2 tablespoons flour	½ cup plus 1 tablespoon corn oil

1. In a large bowl, combine corn, eggs, milk, flour, baking powder, salt, and pepper. Mix to blend well.

2. In a wok, heat 3 tablespoons oil over medium-high heat until hot, swirling to coat sides of pan. Drop in about one-third of batter by tablespoons. Fry until golden on bottom, 3 to 4 minutes. Turn and brown on other side, about 2 minutes. Remove with a slotted spatula and drain on paper towels. Repeat procedure 2 times with remaining corn batter, using additional oil, if needed.

204 ISRAELI EGGPLANT SALAD

Prep: 10 minutes   Cook: 9 to 13 minutes   Chill: 2 hours   Serves: 6

This authentic Israeli salad comes from my friend and coworker Ariela. She suggests serving it with hummus and pita bread, or as a side dish for meat or chicken.

Juice of 2 lemons
2 tablespoons distilled white vinegar
2 tablespoons tomato paste
2 tablespoons chopped cilantro or parsley
2 teaspoons sugar
¾ teaspoon salt
¼ teaspoon pepper

6 tablespoons olive oil
2 medium eggplants, peeled and cut into 2 x ½-inch strips
2 medium red bell peppers, cut into ½-inch strips
1 large onion, chopped
4 garlic cloves, crushed

1. In a bowl, combine lemon juice, vinegar, tomato paste, cilantro, sugar, salt, and pepper. Whisk to blend well. Set lemon dressing aside.

2. In a wok, heat 3 tablespoons olive oil over medium-high heat until hot, swirling to coat sides of pan. Add eggplant and cook, stirring, until softened, 3 to 5 minutes. Push eggplant to sides of wok.

3. Add remaining 3 tablespoons oil to center of wok and heat until hot. Add bell peppers, onion, and garlic. Cook, stirring, 2 minutes. Mix vegetables with eggplant and continue to cook, stirring, until soft, 4 to 6 minutes. Remove to a bowl.

4. Pour lemon dressing over vegetables and toss. Cover and refrigerate 2 to 3 hours, until chilled, before serving.

205 SAUTÉED MUSHROOMS WITH PARSLEY AND LEMON

Prep: 10 minutes   Cook: 5 to 8 minutes   Serves: 3 to 4

3 tablespoons olive oil
¾ pound fresh mushrooms, sliced
1 medium onion, sliced
1 garlic clove, minced
¼ cup dry white wine

1 tablespoon lemon juice
½ teaspoon salt
¼ teaspoon pepper
¼ cup chopped parsley
1 teaspoon grated lemon zest

1. In a wok, heat olive oil over high heat until hot, swirling to coat sides of pan. Add mushrooms, onion, and garlic and cook, stirring, until onion is soft and mushrooms are lightly browned, 4 to 6 minutes.

2. Add wine and lemon juice and cook, stirring, until most of liquid is absorbed, 1 to 2 minutes. Add salt, pepper, parsley, and lemon zest; toss and serve.

206 WILTED CABBAGE WITH WALNUTS, APPLES, AND GOAT CHEESE

Prep: 10 minutes   Cook: 12 to 16 minutes   Serves: 4 to 6

2½ tablespoons vegetable oil
1 small head of green
   cabbage, shredded
1 medium apple, peeled,
   cored, and shredded
½ cup chopped walnuts
⅓ cup apple juice
2 tablespoons balsamic
   vinegar

1½ teaspoons walnut oil
½ teaspoon salt
¼ teaspoon pepper
¼ teaspoon grated nutmeg
1 (5-ounce) log goat cheese,
   cut into ½-inch slices

1. In a wok, heat vegetable oil over medium heat until hot, swirling to coat sides of pan. Add cabbage and apple, and cook, stirring, until soft, 6 to 8 minutes. Add walnuts. Cook, stirring, 2 minutes.

2. Add apple juice, balsamic vinegar, walnut oil, salt, pepper, and nutmeg. Cook until most of the liquid is absorbed, 2 to 3 minutes.

3. Arrange goat cheese slices over cabbage mixture. Cover and cook until cheese softens and begins to melt, 2 to 3 minutes.

207 MUSHROOMS ROMANO

Prep: 10 minutes   Cook: 6 to 9 minutes   Serves: 4

3 tablespoons olive oil
1 pound fresh mushrooms,
   quartered
2 shallots or 1 small onion,
   sliced
2 garlic cloves, minced
¾ cup Italian-seasoned bread
   crumbs

⅓ cup grated Romano cheese
2 tablespoons chopped
   parsley
1 teaspoon dried oregano
½ teaspoon salt
¼ teaspoon pepper

1. In a wok, heat olive oil over medium-high heat until hot, swirling to coat sides of pan. Add mushrooms, shallots, and garlic. Cook, stirring often, until mushrooms are tender, 4 to 6 minutes. Add ¼ cup water and cook, stirring, 1 minute.

2. Add bread crumbs, cheese, parsley, oregano, salt, and pepper. Cook, tossing, until mixture is hot and cheese has melted, 1 to 2 minutes.

208   SHIITAKE MUSHROOMS AND ZUCCHINI IN RED WINE
Prep: 10 minutes   Cook: 5 to 7 minutes   Serves: 4

2 tablespoons olive oil	2 shallots, chopped
½ pound shiitake mushrooms, stems removed, caps sliced	1 garlic clove, minced
	½ cup dry red wine
	1 tablespoon fresh thyme
1 medium zucchini, halved lengthwise, cut into ¼-inch slices	leaves or 1 teaspoon dried
	½ teaspoon salt
	¼ teaspoon pepper

1. In a wok, heat olive oil over high heat until hot, swirling to coat sides of pan. Add mushrooms, zucchini, shallots, and garlic. Cook, stirring, until zucchini is crisp-tender and mushrooms are softened, 3 to 4 minutes.

2. Add wine, thyme, salt, and pepper. Boil until liquid is reduced by half, 2 to 3 minutes.

209   CARAMELIZED ONIONS
Prep: 10 minutes   Cook: 19 to 22 minutes   Serves: 4

7 tablespoons butter	2 tablespoons sugar
1 cup fresh bread crumbs	¼ cup sweet vermouth
¼ cup chopped parsley	¼ cup beef broth
1 (20-ounce) package frozen whole onions, thawed	¼ teaspoon pepper

1. In a wok, melt 4 tablespoons butter over medium heat until hot. Add bread crumbs and cook, stirring, until golden, 2 to 3 minutes. Add parsley. Cook 1 minute longer. Remove to a bowl.

2. In same wok, melt remaining 3 tablespoons butter over medium heat. Add onions and cook, turning to coat all surfaces, until just tender and lightly browned, 6 to 8 minutes. Sprinkle sugar over onions and cook, stirring, 5 minutes.

3. Add vermouth, beef broth, and pepper. Cook, stirring, until most of liquid has evaporated, about 5 minutes. Place in a serving bowl and top with buttered bread crumbs.

210   FRIED ONION RINGS
Prep: 10 minutes   Cook: 2 to 4 minutes per batch   Serves: 6

¾ cup flour
½ teaspoon salt
½ teaspoon baking soda
 1 egg, beaten
¾ cup buttermilk

2½ cups vegetable oil, for frying
 2 Spanish onions, cut into
     ¼-inch slices and
     separated into rings

1. In a bowl, combine flour, salt, and baking soda. Whisk gently or stir to mix. Add egg and buttermilk and whisk until batter is blended.

2. In a wok, heat oil over medium-high heat until temperature measures 350°F on a deep-frying thermometer.

3. Dip onion rings in buttermilk batter, allowing excess to drain off, and gently lower into wok in batches without crowding. Fry until golden on one side, 1 to 2 minutes. Turn and cook until golden on other side, 1 to 2 minutes. Remove and drain well on paper towels. Fry remaining onion rings, adding additional oil, if necessary, to maintain depth.

211   SAVORY BLACK-EYED PEAS
Prep: 10 minutes   Cook: 51 to 53 minutes   Serves: 4

These dried beans take much less time to cook than many other varieties, and they require no presoaking, so you can decide to make them at the last minute. They go especially well with pork chops, spareribs, or ham.

 2 tablespoons vegetable oil
 1 medium onion, finely
     chopped
 1 medium carrot, finely
     chopped
 1 stalk celery, finely chopped
 1 garlic clove, minced

½ pound dried black-eyed
     peas
 1 (14½-ounce) can chicken
     broth
 1 teaspoon salt
¼ teaspoon pepper
 1 bay leaf

1. In a wok, heat oil over medium-high heat until hot. Add onion, carrot, celery, and garlic and cook, stirring, until soft, 6 to 8 minutes.

2. Add black-eyed peas, chicken broth, salt, pepper, bay leaf, and 1 cup water. Bring to a boil. Reduce heat to low, cover, and cook until peas are tender but not mushy, about 45 minutes. Remove bay leaf before serving.

212 TWO-PEPPER ORZO PILAF

Prep: 5 minutes   Cook: 14 to 18 minutes   Serves: 4 to 6

2 tablespoons olive oil
1 tablespoon butter
1 medium purple onion, chopped
1 medium red bell pepper, chopped
1 medium yellow bell pepper, chopped

1 garlic clove, minced
1 cup orzo (rice-shaped pasta)
2 cups chicken broth
½ teaspoon salt
¼ teaspoon pepper
¼ cup chopped Italian flat-leaf parsley

1. In a wok, heat olive oil and butter over medium-high heat until hot. Add onion, red and yellow bell peppers, and garlic. Cook, stirring, until softened, 3 to 5 minutes.

2. Add orzo and cook, stirring to coat, 1 minute. Add chicken broth, salt, and pepper. Bring to a boil. Reduce heat to low, cover, and cook until orzo is tender, 10 to 12 minutes. Add parsley. Fluff with a fork and serve.

213 VEGETABLE-STUFFED PEPPERS

Prep: 15 minutes   Cook: 22 to 23 minutes   Serves: 4 to 6

3 tablespoons olive oil
1 small onion, minced
¼ pound fresh mushrooms, finely chopped
1 carrot, finely chopped
1 garlic clove, crushed
½ cup fresh broccoli florets, finely chopped
¼ cup chopped parsley
½ teaspoon salt

¼ teaspoon pepper
2 cups cooked rice
½ cup shredded mozzarella cheese
¼ cup grated Parmesan cheese
4 medium green bell peppers, split in half lengthwise, seeded, and cored
1 cup chicken broth
½ cup tomato sauce

1. In a wok, heat olive oil over medium-high heat until hot, swirling to coat sides of pan. Add onion, mushrooms, carrot, and garlic. Cook, stirring, until softened, 3 to 4 minutes. Add broccoli, parsley, salt, and pepper. Cook 2 minutes. Add rice, mozzarella, and Parmesan cheese. Cook, stirring, 2 minutes. Remove to a bowl. Rinse and dry wok.

2. Fill bell pepper halves with vegetable-rice mixture.

3. In wok, bring chicken broth and tomato sauce to a boil over high heat. Place filled peppers in wok, cut sides up. Reduce heat to medium-low, cover, and cook until peppers are tender, about 15 minutes.

214 POTATO PANCAKES
Prep: 10 minutes   Cook: 15 to 18 minutes   Serves: 4 to 6

4 medium white potatoes,
    peeled and grated
1 small onion, grated
2 eggs, lightly beaten
2 tablespoons flour

1 teaspoon baking powder
½ teaspoon salt
¼ teaspoon pepper
¼ cup plus 2 tablespoons
    vegetable oil

1. In a large bowl, combine grated potatoes, onion, eggs, flour, baking powder, salt, and pepper. Stir until mixed.

2. In a wok, heat 2 tablespoons oil over medium-high heat until hot, swirling to coat sides of pan. Drop in about one-third of mixture by tablespoons. Fry until golden on bottom, 3 to 4 minutes. Turn and brown on other side, 2 minutes. Remove from wok and drain on paper towels. Repeat procedure 2 times with remaining potato mixture and oil. Place pancakes on serving platter and serve at once.

215 POTATOES AU GRATIN
Prep: 10 minutes   Cook: 23 to 29 minutes   Serves: 4

A great accompaniment for poultry, pork, lamb, or beef. Lightly stirring in the cheese enables it to melt quicker and more evenly.

2 tablespoons vegetable oil
3 medium russet potatoes,
    peeled and cut into
    ½-inch cubes
1 medium onion, chopped
1 cup chicken broth

1 cup dry white wine
½ teaspoon salt
¼ teaspoon pepper
1 cup grated extra-sharp
    cheddar cheese (4 ounces)

1. In a wok, heat oil over medium-high heat. Add potatoes and onion and cook, stirring, until potatoes are translucent, 4 to 6 minutes.

2. Add chicken broth, wine, salt, and pepper and cook, covered, until potatoes are tender and most of liquid is absorbed, 17 to 20 minutes.

3. Add cheese; stir briefly. Cover and cook until cheese melts, 2 to 3 minutes.

216   RATATOUILLE
Prep: 10 minutes   Cook: 19 to 24 minutes   Serves: 4 to 6

From Provence comes a classic recipe highlighting summer's bounty of fresh vegetables—eggplant, zucchini, tomatoes, and bell peppers, seasoned with basil and parsley. This wonderful medley can be served warm or cool.

5 tablespoons olive oil	1 medium zucchini, halved
2 small eggplants, peeled and	lengthwise and sliced
cut into ¾-inch cubes	2 medium ripe tomatoes,
1 large onion, chopped	peeled, seeded, and diced
2 garlic cloves, minced	¼ cup chopped parsley
1 medium red bell pepper,	¼ cup chopped fresh basil or
diced	1 teaspoon dried
1 medium green bell pepper,	¾ teaspoon salt
diced	½ teaspoon pepper

1. In a wok, heat 3 tablespoons olive oil over high heat until hot, swirling to coat sides of pan. Add eggplant and cook, stirring, until soft, 4 to 6 minutes. Remove to a bowl.

2. In same wok, heat remaining 2 tablespoons oil over medium-high heat. Add onion and cook until softened, 2 to 3 minutes. Add garlic, red and green bell peppers, zucchini, and tomatoes and cook, stirring often, until vegetables are tender, 3 to 5 minutes.

3. Return eggplant to wok. Stir in parsley, basil, salt, and pepper. Reduce heat to medium-low, cover, and cook 10 minutes.

217   POTATOES, CARROTS, AND SPINACH
Prep: 10 minutes   Cook: 16 to 20 minutes   Serves: 4

3 tablespoons olive oil	1 pound fresh spinach leaves,
2 medium russet potatoes,	rinsed, drained, and
peeled and sliced	coarsely chopped
1 medium onion, sliced	¼ teaspoon grated nutmeg
2 medium carrots, thinly	1½ cups chicken broth
sliced	½ teaspoon salt
1 garlic clove, minced	¼ teaspoon pepper

1. In a wok, heat olive oil over medium-high heat until hot. Add potatoes and onion, and cook, stirring, until translucent, 4 to 6 minutes. Add carrots and garlic and cook 2 minutes. Add spinach and nutmeg. Cook, stirring, until spinach begins to wilt, about 2 minutes longer.

2. Add chicken broth, salt, and pepper. Bring to a boil over high heat. Reduce heat to medium, cover, and cook until potatoes and carrots are tender and most of liquid is absorbed, 8 to 10 minutes.

218   MEXICAN RICE WITH CORN AND PEAS
Prep: 10 minutes   Cook: 25 to 29 minutes   Serves: 4

2 tablespoons olive oil
1 medium onion, chopped
1 medium red or green bell
   pepper, chopped
1 garlic clove, minced
2 fresh hot green chiles,
   seeded and minced
2 cups long-grain rice
1 (16-ounce) can crushed
   tomatoes

1 (14½-ounce) can chicken
   broth
½ teaspoon salt
¼ teaspoon pepper
¼ teaspoon saffron threads
1 (10-ounce) package frozen
   peas, thawed
1 (10-ounce) package frozen
   corn, thawed

1. In a wok, heat olive oil over medium-high heat until hot. Add onion, bell pepper, garlic, and chiles. Cook, stirring, until softened, 3 to 4 minutes. Add rice and cook, stirring, until lightly colored, about 2 minutes.

2. Add tomatoes, chicken broth, salt, pepper, and saffron. Bring to a boil; reduce heat to low. Cover and cook until rice is tender and most of liquid is absorbed, 18 to 20 minutes.

3. Stir in peas and corn. Cook until vegetables are heated through and just tender, 2 to 3 minutes.

219   POTATOES AND LEEKS WITH ROSEMARY
Prep: 10 minutes   Cook: 30 to 37 minutes   Serves: 6

This vegetable is elegant enough for company and easy to assemble for family meals. Try pairing it with lamb or chicken.

2 tablespoons olive oil
1 tablespoon butter
2 pounds russet potatoes,
   peeled and thinly sliced
1 large leek (white part only),
   chopped
1 cup chicken broth

1 cup dry white wine
1 tablespoon chopped fresh
   rosemary or 1 teaspoon
   dried
¾ teaspoon salt
¼ teaspoon pepper

1. In a wok, heat olive oil and butter over medium-high heat until hot, swirling to coat sides of pan. Add potatoes and leek and cook, stirring and turning potato slices until they turn translucent, 6 to 8 minutes.

2. Add chicken broth, wine, rosemary, salt, and pepper. Bring to a boil. Reduce heat to medium-low, cover, and cook until potatoes are tender, 20 to 25 minutes.

3. Uncover and cook, stirring occasionally, until most of liquid is absorbed, about 4 minutes.

220   CHEESY RED BEANS AND RICE
Prep: 10 minutes   Cook: 8 to 12 minutes   Serves: 4

3 tablespoons olive oil
1 large onion, chopped
1 celery rib, chopped
1 medium green bell pepper,
   chopped
1 garlic clove, minced
1 teaspoon chili powder
½ teaspoon ground cumin
½ teaspoon salt

¼ teaspoon pepper
⅛ teaspoon hot pepper sauce
1 (16-ounce) can red kidney
   beans
2 cups cooked rice
1 cup grated extra-sharp
   Cheddar cheese
   (4 ounces)

1. In a wok, heat olive oil over medium-high heat until hot. Add onion, celery, bell pepper, and garlic. Cook, stirring often, until soft, 5 to 7 minutes. Add chili powder, cumin, salt, pepper, and hot sauce. Cook, stirring, 1 minute.

2. Add kidney beans and rice. Cook, stirring, until heated through, 1 to 2 minutes. Sprinkle on cheese. Reduce heat to medium-low. Cover and cook until cheese melts, 1 to 2 minutes longer.

221   GREEN RICE WITH PECANS
Prep: 10 minutes   Cook: 21 to 25 minutes   Serves: 4

2 tablespoons vegetable oil
1 tablespoon butter
1 small onion, chopped
1 celery rib, chopped
1 small green bell pepper,
   chopped
1½ cups long-grain white rice

2 tablespoons prepared pesto
3 cups chicken stock or
   canned broth
¼ teaspoon pepper
¼ cup chopped parsley
½ cup pecans

1. In a wok, heat oil and butter over medium-high heat until hot. Add onion, celery, and bell pepper and cook, stirring, until crisp-tender, 3 to 5 minutes. Add rice and pesto and stir to coat.

2. Add chicken broth and pepper. Bring to a boil. Reduce heat to low, cover, and cook until rice is tender and liquid is absorbed, 18 to 20 minutes. Fluff with a fork. Stir in parsley and pecans and serve.

222   TOMATO RICE AND BLACK BEANS

Prep: 5 minutes   Cook: 24 to 28 minutes   Serves: 4

2 tablespoons olive oil
1 small onion, chopped
1 garlic clove, crushed
1 cup long-grain white rice
2 cups chicken broth
1 (14½-ounce) can stewed
    tomatoes with peppers

1 (4-ounce) can green chiles,
    chopped
1 serrano pepper, minced
1 teaspoon ground cumin
½ teaspoon salt
¼ teaspoon pepper
1 (16-ounce) can black beans

1. In a wok, heat olive oil over medium-high heat until hot. Add onion and garlic and cook, stirring, until soft, 3 to 4 minutes. Add rice and cook, stirring, to coat, 2 minutes.

2. Add chicken broth, stewed tomatoes, chiles, serrano pepper, cumin, salt, and pepper. Bring to a boil. Reduce heat to low, cover, and cook until rice is tender and most of liquid is absorbed, 18 to 20 minutes.

3. Add beans. Stir to combine. Cook 1 minute to heat through.

---

223   BARLEY AND WILD RICE PILAF

Prep: 10 minutes   Cook: 49 to 55 minutes   Serves: 6

Usually made with rice, this pilaf goes against the grain by combining barley and wild rice. The cooking times have to be compatible so they finish at the same time. This is a combination with great texture.

3 tablespoons vegetable oil
1 medium onion, chopped
¼ pound fresh mushrooms,
    chopped
1 small carrot, grated
1 cup medium barley
1 cup wild rice

¼ cup pitted black olives,
    chopped
5 cups boiling chicken broth
2 tablespoons soy sauce
1 tablespoon lemon juice
½ cup toasted almonds, sliced

1. In a wok, heat oil over medium-high heat until hot. Add onion, mushrooms, and carrot and cook, stirring, until onion and carrot are softened, 3 to 4 minutes.

2. Add barley and wild rice and stir to coat. Cook, stirring, 1 minute.

3. Stir in olives, chicken broth, soy sauce, and lemon juice. Bring to a boil. Reduce heat to low, cover, and cook until barley and rice are tender, 45 to 50 minutes. Fluff with a fork. Sprinkle almonds on top and serve.

224   WILD RICE WITH VEGETABLES IN WINE

Prep: 10 minutes   Cook: 44 to 51 minutes   Serves: 4

3 tablespoons olive oil
2 medium leeks (white part only), rinsed well and chopped
2 carrots, chopped
1 celery rib, sliced
½ pound fresh mushrooms, sliced

1 cup wild rice
¾ teaspoon dried thyme leaves
½ teaspoon salt
¼ teaspoon pepper
3 cups chicken broth
1 cup dry white wine

1. In a wok, heat olive oil over high heat until hot, swirling to coat sides of pan. Add leeks, carrots, celery, and mushrooms and cook, stirring, until tender, 4 to 6 minutes. Add wild rice, thyme, salt, and pepper. Cook, stirring, until rice is coated, 2 minutes.

2. Add chicken broth and wine. Bring to a boil. Reduce heat to low and cook, covered, until rice is tender and most of liquid is absorbed, 40 to 45 minutes.

225   CHEESY SCALLIONS, LEEKS, AND ONIONS

Prep: 10 minutes   Cook: 11 to 14 minutes   Serves: 6

3 tablespoons olive oil
6 scallions, sliced
2 medium leeks (white part only) rinsed well and chopped
2 large onions, sliced
2 garlic cloves, minced
½ cup heavy cream
¼ cup Madeira

¼ cup beef broth
½ teaspoon salt
¼ teaspoon pepper
¼ teaspoon grated nutmeg
¾ cup shredded Swiss cheese (6 ounces)
¼ cup grated Parmesan cheese
3 tablespoons butter, melted

1. In a wok, heat olive oil over medium-high heat. Add scallions, leeks, onions, and garlic. Cook, stirring, until soft, 5 to 7 minutes. Remove to a bowl.

2. Add cream, Madeira, beef broth, salt, pepper, and nutmeg. Boil, scraping up any browned bits from bottom of wok, until liquid is reduced by almost half, 4 to 5 minutes. Return vegetables to wok.

3. Sprinkle Swiss and Parmesan cheeses over vegetables. Drizzle butter over cheeses. Reduce heat to low, cover, and cook until cheese melts, 2 to 3 minutes.

226 SNOW PEAS AND CARROTS IN GRAPEFRUIT-ORANGE SAUCE

Prep: 10 minutes   Cook: 8 to 10 minutes   Serves: 4

3 tablespoons vegetable oil
3 medium carrots, sliced
    diagonally into ½-inch
    pieces
¼ pound snow peas, stemmed
    and stringed
3 scallions, sliced

½ cup grapefruit juice
¼ cup Grand Marnier
1 teaspoon grated orange zest
½ teaspoon cinnamon
3 tablespoons butter, cut into
    pieces
1 cup grapefruit sections

1. In a wok, heat oil over medium-high heat until hot. Add carrots and cook, stirring 2 minutes. Add snow peas and scallions and cook, stirring, until crisp-tender, 3 to 4 minutes. Remove vegetables to a serving bowl.

2. Add grapefruit juice, Grand Marnier, orange zest, and cinnamon. Raise heat to high and boil until reduced by half, 2 to 4 minutes.

3. Whisk in butter, a few pieces at a time, until thoroughly incorporated and sauce is smooth, 1 to 2 minutes. Add grapefruit sections, pour over vegetables, and serve.

227 SAUTÉED SPINACH WITH WHITE BEANS AND GARLIC

Prep: 10 minutes   Cook: 4 to 5 minutes   Serves: 4

A recipe from restaurateurs Jean and Vivian Fiorentino, who serve this delicious dish with lamb, in the French manner.

2 tablespoons olive oil
4 garlic cloves, slivered
½ pound fresh spinach,
    stemmed, rinsed, and
    dried
1 (8-ounce) can cannellini
    (white kidney beans),
    drained

½ teaspoon salt
¼ teaspoon pepper
¼ teaspoon grated nutmeg

1. In a wok, heat olive oil over medium-high heat until hot, swirling to coat sides of pan. Add garlic and cook, stirring, until golden and fragrant, 1 minute.

2. Add spinach and beans. Cook, stirring, until spinach is just wilted, 2 to 3 minutes. Season with salt, pepper, and nutmeg. Cook 1 minute longer and serve.

228 SWEET POTATO PANCAKES WITH SWEETENED SOUR CREAM
Prep: 10 minutes   Cook: 15 to 18 minutes   Serves: 4 to 6

1 cup sour cream	1 teaspoon baking powder
¼ cup packed brown sugar	2 tablespoons grated lemon
4 medium sweet potatoes	zest
(2 pounds), peeled	2 teaspoons grated fresh
2 eggs, beaten	ginger
2 tablespoons flour	½ teaspoon salt
	6 tablespoons vegetable oil

1. In a small bowl, mix sour cream and 2 tablespoons brown sugar. Set aside.

2. Grate sweet potatoes, using large holes of a hand grater or shredding disc in a food processor. In a large mixing bowl, combine remaining 2 table-spoons brown sugar, grated sweet potatoes, eggs, flour, baking powder, lemon zest, ginger, and salt. Beat until well blended.

3. In a wok, heat 2 tablespoons oil over medium-high heat until hot, swirl-ing to coat sides of pan. Drop in about one-third of sweet potato mixture by tablespoons. Fry until golden on bottom, 3 to 4 minutes. Turn and brown on other side, 2 minutes. Remove from pan and drain on paper towels. Repeat procedure 2 times with remaining potato mixture and oil. Place pan-cakes on serving platter. Serve with sweetened sour cream.

229 MAPLE SYRUP SWEETS 'N' WHITES
Prep: 10 minutes   Cook: 36 to 44 minutes   Serves: 6 to 8

½ cup chopped walnuts	2 cups heavy cream
3 tablespoons vegetable oil	¾ cup packed brown sugar
3 medium sweet potatoes,	½ cup maple syrup
peeled and thinly sliced	2 tablespoons butter
3 medium all-purpose	
potatoes, peeled and	
thinly sliced	

1. In dry wok, cook walnuts over medium heat, tossing, until fragrant and lightly toasted, about 3 minutes. Remove to a plate and set aside.

2. In same wok, heat oil over medium-high heat until hot, swirling to coat sides of pan. Add sweet and white potato slices and cook, turning, until white potatoes begin to turn translucent, 6 to 8 minutes. Remove to a plate.

3. Add cream, brown sugar, maple syrup, and butter to wok. Cook over medium-high heat, stirring, until mixture comes to a boil, 2 to 3 minutes.

4. Add potatoes and turn gently to coat. Reduce heat to medium-low, cover, and simmer until potatoes are tender and most of sauce is absorbed, 25 to 30 minutes. Place in a serving bowl and sprinkle toasted walnuts on top.

230 CANDIED SWEET POTATOES AND SQUASH

Prep: 10 minutes   Cook: 13 to 16 minutes   Serves: 6

When there's not an inch of room left in your oven on Thanksgiving, try this fabulous way of preparing candied sweet potatoes in a single pot—the wok—right on top of the stove.

1 medium acorn squash	⅓ cup packed brown sugar
3 medium sweet potatoes, peeled and cut into ½-inch slices	¼ cup molasses
	1 teaspoon cinnamon
	½ teaspoon grated nutmeg
6 tablespoons unsalted butter	

1. Cut squash in half lengthwise. Scoop out seeds. Cut each half crosswise into ½-inch slices. Peel slices.

2. In a wok, combine squash and sweet potato slices. Add enough cold water to cover. Bring to a boil over high heat. Reduce heat to medium, cover, and cook until vegetables are tender, 10 to 12 minutes. Drain well. Wipe out wok.

3. Melt butter in wok over medium-high heat. Add brown sugar, molasses, cinnamon, and nutmeg. Cook, stirring, until brown sugar dissolves, about 2 minutes. Add sweet potatoes and squash. Stir gently to coat. Cover and cook until hot and bubbly, 1 to 2 minutes.

231 DWAYNE'S CANDIED YAMS

Prep: 10 minutes   Cook: 41 to 44 minutes   Serves: 4 to 6

My friend Dwayne could not get his aunt to reveal the exact recipe for these potatoes, so he developed his own interpretation of this favorite holiday dish—and it's a winner.

1½ pounds medium yams or sweet potatoes, peeled, halved lengthwise, and cut crosswise into ⅛-inch slices	¼ cup packed brown sugar
	¼ cup corn syrup
	1 teaspoon cinnamon
	½ teaspoon ground ginger
	½ teaspoon grated nutmeg
4 tablespoons butter	

1. In a large saucepan of boiling water, cook yams over medium heat until almost tender, 10 to 12 minutes; drain well.

2. In a wok, cook butter and brown sugar over medium heat, stirring, until sugar dissolves, about 2 minutes. Add corn syrup, cinnamon, ginger, and nutmeg. Cook, stirring, 1 minute.

3. Add cooked yams and spoon some of sauce over them. Reduce heat to low, cover, and cook until yams are very soft, about 30 minutes.

232   SAUTÉ OF SUMMER VEGETABLES

Prep: 15 minutes   Cook: 7 to 10 minutes   Serves: 4

3 tablespoons olive oil
1 medium onion, cut into
    ½-inch dice
1 medium red bell pepper, cut
    into ½-inch dice
1 medium green bell pepper,
    cut into ½-inch dice
1 medium zucchini, thinly
    sliced

2 garlic cloves, minced
2 medium tomatoes, peeled
    and cut into ½-inch dice
¼ cup chopped fresh basil
    (optional)
¼ cup chopped parsley
½ teaspoon salt
¼ teaspoon pepper

1. In a wok, heat olive oil over medium-high heat until hot. Add onion and cook, stirring, 2 minutes. Add red and green bell peppers, zucchini, and garlic and stir-fry until crisp-tender, 3 to 5 minutes.

2. Add tomatoes and stir-fry until tomatoes begin to soften, 2 to 3 minutes. Add basil and parsley and season with salt and pepper. Toss and serve.

233   STIR-FRIED VEGETABLES WITH BROKEN NOODLES

Prep: 10 minutes   Cook: 10 to 13 minutes   Serves: 4

3 tablespoons vegetable oil
2 medium carrots, sliced
1 medium green bell pepper,
    cut into 1½-inch strips
½ pound fresh asparagus, cut
    into 1-inch lengths
3 scallions, sliced

1 garlic clove, minced
1 teaspoon salt
½ teaspoon pepper
2 cups vermicelli, broken into
    1-inch pieces
2 cups chicken broth

1. In a wok, heat 2 tablespoons oil over high heat until hot. Add carrots and green pepper and stir-fry 2 minutes. Add asparagus, scallions, and garlic. Stir-fry until vegetables are crisp-tender, 3 to 4 minutes. Season with half of salt and pepper. Cook 2 minutes. Remove to a plate.

2. In same wok, heat remaining 1 tablespoon oil over medium-high heat. Add vermicelli and stir to coat. Add broth and remaining salt and pepper. Bring to a boil; reduce heat to low, cover, and cook until most of liquid is absorbed and pasta is tender, 4 to 6 minutes. Return vegetables to wok. Cook 1 minute to heat through.

234   WINTER ROOT VEGETABLE FRITTERS

Prep: 10 minutes   Cook: 15 to 18 minutes   Serves: 4

2 medium carrots, grated	1 teaspoon baking powder
1 white turnip, grated	1 teaspoon sugar
1 parsnip, grated	¼ teaspoon grated nutmeg
2 eggs, lightly beaten	¼ teaspoon salt
3 tablespoons flour	9 tablespoons vegetable oil

1. In a large mixing bowl, combine carrots, turnip, parsnip, eggs, flour, baking powder, sugar, nutmeg, and salt. Mix until combined.

2. In a wok, heat 3 tablespoons oil over medium-high heat until hot, swirling to coat sides of pan. Carefully drop about one-third of mixture in by tablespoons without crowding. Fry until golden on bottom, 3 to 4 minutes. Turn and cook until brown on other side, about 2 minutes. Remove from wok with slotted spatula and drain on paper towels. Repeat procedure 2 times with remaining vegetable mixture and oil. Serve fritters while still hot.

235   VEGETABLE MEDLEY

Prep: 20 minutes   Cook: 8 to 10 minutes   Serves: 6

¼ cup olive oil	⅓ cup chicken broth
2 medium carrots, sliced	¼ cup pitted black olives,
1 medium red bell pepper, cut	sliced
into thin strips	¼ cup chopped cilantro or
1 medium onion, chopped	parsley
1 garlic clove, minced	Freshly ground pepper
2 pounds small new potatoes, cooked and drained	
½ pound fresh asparagus, cut diagonally into ½-inch slices	

1. In a wok, heat 2 tablespoons olive oil over medium-high heat until hot. Add carrots, bell pepper, onion, and garlic and stir-fry until crisp-tender, 3 to 5 minutes. Remove to a plate.

2. In same wok, heat remaining 2 tablespoons oil over medium-high heat. Add potatoes and asparagus and stir-fry 3 minutes. Return cooked vegetables to wok. Add chicken broth. Cook 2 minutes.

3. Add olives, cilantro, and pepper and serve.

236 MEDITERRANEAN VEGETABLE BULGUR

Prep: 10 minutes   Cook: 16 to 17 minutes   Serves: 4

2 tablespoons olive oil
4 scallions, chopped
1 medium carrot, chopped
1 medium green bell pepper, chopped
¼ cup chopped pitted black olives
1 garlic clove, minced
1 cup bulgur (cracked wheat)
1 medium tomato, chopped
½ cup canned chick-peas (garbanzo beans), rinsed and drained

½ cup plain nonfat yogurt
½ cup chopped parsley
¼ cup chopped fresh mint (optional)
1 tablespoon lemon juice
1 teaspoon ground cumin
½ teaspoon salt
¼ teaspoon pepper

1. In a wok, heat olive oil over medium-high heat until hot. Add scallions, carrot, bell pepper, olives, and garlic. Cook, stirring, until crisp-tender, 3 to 5 minutes.

2. Add bulgur and 2 cups water to vegetables in wok. Bring to a boil. Reduce heat to low, cover, and cook until liquid is absorbed, about 10 minutes. Add tomato and chick-peas. Cook, stirring, 2 minutes. Remove from heat.

3. In a small bowl, combine yogurt, parsley, mint, lemon juice, cumin, salt, and pepper. Add to bulgur. Stir to combine.

Chapter 9

Wok Stews and Braised Meats

These are the homey, comfort dishes to turn to when the weather becomes cooler and appetites grow heartier. While some of these big tastes require longer cooking, the time the cook spends in the kitchen is still kept to a minimum.

These dishes are a boon for busy cooks—and who isn't a busy cook these days?—because once the ingredients are put up, they simmer away by themselves with little or no attention. Even for slow-cooking stews and braised meats, the wok is an ideal utensil. It can be used almost everywhere a recipe calls for a large heavy pot with a lid.

Stews and braises are both forms of moist-heat cooking; stews usually have more liquid. Aromatic vegetables, herbs, spices, and sometimes wine are added to enhance flavor. Sometimes the meat is marinated before it is browned, to increase flavor and help tenderize tougher cuts.

Recipes using ingredients with high acidity, such as wine, vinegar, lemon juice, or tomatoes, are best cooked in a spun steel, stainless steel, or very well-seasoned wok to avoid a possible unpleasant-tasting reaction between the metal and the food.

Many of the recipes in this chapter, such as Chicken with Spanish Rice, Turkey Goulash, and Beef Stroganoff are one-pot meals. Any number—Ale-Sauced Chili, Orange Beef Curry, Soda-Sauced BBQ Chicken—doubled in volume would make great party fare.

237   DEVIKA'S CHICKEN CURRY

Prep: 15 minutes   Marinate: 1 hour   Cook: 40 to 45 minutes
Serves: 4 to 6

8 large chicken thighs, skin
   removed (about 4 pounds
   total)
1½ cups plain yogurt
4 teaspoons curry powder
3 tablespoons vegetable oil
2 bay leaves
4 whole cloves
2 cinnamon sticks

4 medium onions, sliced
3 garlic cloves, crushed
   1-inch piece fresh ginger,
   peeled and minced
½ teaspoon cayenne, or more
   to taste
2 tablespoons grated coconut
¼ cup tomato paste

1. Place chicken in a shallow dish. Prick with a fork. In a small bowl, combine ½ cup yogurt and 3 teaspoons (1 tablespoon) curry powder. Brush over chicken pieces. Marinate at room temperature for 1 hour.

2. In a wok, heat oil over medium heat until hot. Add bay leaves, cloves, and cinnamon sticks. Cook until fragrant, about 1 minute. Add onions and cook, stirring often, until softened, about 3 minutes. Add garlic, ginger, remaining 1 teaspoon curry powder, cayenne, and coconut. Cook, stirring, 1 to 2 minutes.

3. Add chicken, turning to coat with sauce. Cover and cook, turning occasionally, until meat is fork tender. 35 to 40 minutes.

238   APRICOT CHICKEN

Prep: 10 minutes   Cook: 43 to 51 minutes   Serves: 4

1 cup apricot nectar
½ cup apricot preserves
1 envelope dry onion soup
   mix
3 tablespoons vegetable oil
4 chicken breast halves with
   bone (about 8 ounces
   each)

1 small onion, chopped
¾ cup coarsely chopped dried
   apricots
¼ cup golden raisins

1. In a medium bowl, combine apricot nectar, apricot preserves, onion soup mix, and 1 cup water. Stir until well blended.

2. In a wok, heat 2 tablespoons oil over medium-high heat until hot, swirling to coat sides of pan. Arrange chicken extending up sides of pan and cook, turning once, until golden brown on both sides, 5 to 7 minutes. With tongs, transfer chicken to a plate.

3. Add remaining 1 tablespoon oil to fat in wok and heat over medium-high heat. Add onion and cook, stirring, until softened, 3 to 4 minutes. Return chicken to wok.

4. Add apricot nectar mixture. Bring to a boil. Reduce heat to medium-low, cover, and cook until chicken is tender and white throughout but still juicy, 30 to 35 minutes. Stir in apricots and golden raisins. Cook 5 minutes.

---

239 STUFFED CHICKEN THIGHS WITH CRANBERRY SAUCE

Prep: 30 minutes   Cook: 68 to 75 minutes   Serves: 4

4 skinless, boneless chicken thighs	1 egg
3½ tablespoons vegetable oil	½ teaspoon salt
1 medium onion, chopped	¼ teaspoon pepper
1 medium celery rib, chopped	1 cup orange juice
1 cup fresh bread crumbs	¼ cup dry sherry
2 tablespoons chopped parsley	⅓ cup sugar
½ teaspoon celery seed	¾ cup fresh or frozen cranberries
	2 teaspoons cornstarch

1. With a paring knife, cut a pocket in each chicken thigh. Refrigerate thighs until needed.

2. In a wok, heat 1½ tablespoons oil over medium-high heat until hot. Add onion and celery and cook until softened, 3 to 5 minutes. Remove to a medium bowl and let cool.

3. To onion-celery mixture, add bread crumbs, parsley, celery seed, egg, salt, and pepper. Mix filling well. Stuff pockets of each chicken thigh with filling. Close with toothpicks.

4. In same wok, heat remaining 2 tablespoons oil over medium-high heat, swirling to coat sides of pan. Add stuffed chicken thighs and cook, turning, until browned all over, 6 to 8 minutes. Drain off fat from wok. Add orange juice and sherry. Bring to a boil. Reduce heat to low, cover, and cook until chicken is tender, about 50 minutes. Remove thighs to a plate.

5. Add sugar to sauce and stir to dissolve. Cook 2 minutes. Add cranberries, cover, and boil over medium heat until cranberries pop, 6 to 8 minutes.

6. Dissolve cornstarch in ¼ cup cold water and stir into wok. Cook over high heat, stirring, until sauce boils and thickens, 1 to 2 minutes. Return chicken to wok. Cook until heated through, 2 minutes. Remove toothpicks before serving.

240   CHICKEN WITH WALNUTS AND PINEAPPLE

Prep: 5 minutes   Cook: 56 to 65 minutes   Serves: 4

3   tablespoons vegetable oil
1   chicken (3 pounds), cut up
1   medium onion, cut into
     ½-inch dice
1   medium green bell pepper,
     cut into ½-inch dice
1   cup chicken broth
1   (10-ounce) jar pineapple
     preserves

1   (8-ounce) can unsweetened
     pineapple chunks, juice
     reserved
2   tablespoons soy sauce
¼   teaspoon pepper
½   cup walnut halves

1. In a wok, heat 2 tablespoons oil over medium-high heat until hot, swirling to coat sides of pan. Arrange chicken pieces extending up sides of pan and cook, turning, until golden brown all over, 8 to 10 minutes. With tongs, remove chicken to a plate. Pour off fat from wok.

2. In same wok, heat remaining 1 tablespoon oil over medium-high heat. Add onion and bell pepper and stir-fry until softened, 3 to 5 minutes. Return chicken to wok.

3. In a medium bowl, combine chicken broth, pineapple preserves, reserved pineapple juice, soy sauce, and pepper. Whisk until blended. Pour over chicken. Reduce heat to medium-low, cover, and cook, basting occasionally, until chicken is fork-tender and juices from thigh run clear when pierced near bone, 45 to 50 minutes. Add walnuts and serve.

241   CHICKEN IN MELLOW MUSTARD SAUCE

Prep: 10 minutes   Cook: 55 to 65 minutes   Serves: 4 to 6

2½   pounds assorted chicken
      pieces
⅓   cup Dijon mustard
3   tablespoons olive oil
2   tablespoons butter
1   small onion, chopped

2   tablespoons flour
1   cup chicken broth
1   cup dry white wine
1   teaspoon dried tarragon
½   teaspoon salt
¼   teaspoon pepper

1. Rinse chicken and pat dry. Brush chicken pieces with mustard. In a wok, heat 2 tablespoons olive oil and 1 tablespoon butter over medium-high heat until hot, swirling to coat sides of pan. Add chicken and cook until browned all over, 8 to 10 minutes. Remove chicken to a plate and cover with foil to keep warm. Pour off fat from pan.

2. In same wok, heat remaining 1 tablespoon each oil and butter over medium-high heat. Add onion and cook until softened but not browned, 3 to 4 minutes. Add flour and cook, stirring, 2 minutes.

3. Whisk in chicken broth, wine, tarragon, salt, and pepper. Bring to a boil, scraping up any browned bits from bottom of wok. Return chicken to wok. Reduce heat to medium-low, cover, and cook until chicken is tender and juices run clear, 40 to 45 minutes.

242 CHICKEN WITH CHERRIES
Prep: 10 minutes   Cook: 38 to 44 minutes   Serves: 4

3½ tablespoons vegetable oil
2 medium onions, chopped
1 garlic clove, minced
4 medium chicken breast
   halves, with bone
1 (16-ounce) can dark, sweet
   pitted cherries, drained,
   with juice reserved

¾ cup long-grain white rice
½ teaspoon salt
¼ teaspoon pepper
1 (8-ounce) can sliced water
   chestnuts, drained

1. In a wok, heat 2 tablespoon oil over medium-high heat, until hot. Add onions and garlic. Cook, stirring often, until softened, 3 to 5 minutes. With a slotted spoon, remove to a plate.

2. In same wok, heat remaining 1½ tablespoons oil over high heat, swirling to coat sides of pan. Arrange chicken pieces extending up sides of pan and cook, turning, until brown on both sides, 4 to 6 minutes. Remove to plate with onions.

3. Pour reserved cherry juice into a glass measuring cup. Add enough water to make 2 cups liquid. Add to wok and bring to a boil. Add rice, salt, and pepper. Reduce heat to medium-low. Return chicken and onions to wok, cover and cook, turning occasionally, until chicken is tender and cooked through, about 25 minutes.

4. Add water chestnuts and cherries. Cook, stirring, until heated through, 1 to 2 minutes.

243   CHICKEN MARENGO
Prep: 10 minutes   Cook: 1 hour to 77 minutes   Serves: 4

½ cup flour
½ teaspoon dried thyme leaves
½ teaspoon salt
¼ teaspoon pepper
1 chicken (3 pounds), cut up
¼ cup olive oil
1 medium onion, chopped
½ pound fresh mushrooms, sliced

1 garlic clove, minced
1 (28-ounce) can tomato puree
½ cup sauterne or other sweet white wine
½ cup chicken broth
¼ cup chopped parsley
1 (10-ounce) package frozen whole onions, thawed

1. In a shallow dish, combine flour, thyme, salt, and pepper. Dredge chicken pieces in seasoned flour to lightly coat; shake off excess.

2. In a wok, heat 2 tablespoons olive oil over medium-high heat until hot, swirling to coat sides of pan. Add chicken and cook, turning and rotating, until browned all over, 8 to 10 minutes. Remove to a plate. Pour off fat from pan.

3. In same wok, heat remaining 2 tablespoon oil over medium-high heat. Add onion, mushrooms, and garlic and cook, stirring, until onion is softened and mushrooms are tender, about 5 minutes. Return chicken to wok.

4. Add tomato puree, sauterne, chicken broth, and parsley. Reduce heat to medium-low, cover, and cook until chicken is fork-tender, 45 to 50 minutes. Add onions and cook until heated through, 3 to 4 minutes.

244   SWEET AND SOUR CHICKEN
Prep: 10 minutes   Cook: 54 to 62 minutes   Serves: 4

3½ tablespoons vegetable oil
2 celery ribs, chopped
1 medium onion, chopped
2 pounds chicken breasts, bone in
1 (18-ounce) bottle ketchup

1 (8-ounce) can whole cranberry sauce
1 tablespoon lemon juice
1 teaspoon grated lemon zest
½ teaspoon salt
¼ teaspoon pepper

1. In a wok, heat 2 tablespoons oil over high heat until hot, swirling to coat sides of pan. Add celery and onion and cook, stirring, until soft, 3 to 4 minutes. Remove to a plate.

2. In same wok, heat remaining 1½ tablespoons oil over medium-high heat. Arrange chicken pieces extending up sides of pan and cook, turning, until browned all over, 6 to 8 minutes. Return vegetables to wok.

3. In a medium bowl, combine ketchup, cranberry sauce, lemon juice, lemon zest, salt, and pepper. Pour over chicken and cook until chicken is tender, 45 to 50 minutes, turning occasionally.

245 HONEY BARBECUE SAUCED CHICKEN

Prep: 10 minutes   Cook: 48 to 56 minutes   Serves: 6

3 pounds assorted chicken
  pieces
1 cup prepared barbecue
  sauce
½ cup chicken broth
½ cup orange juice
2 tablespoons soy sauce

2 tablespoons honey
1 teaspoon orange zest
2 tablespoons vegetable oil
1 medium red bell pepper,
  chopped
2 medium leeks (white part
  only), chopped

1. Rinse chicken pieces and pat dry. In a medium bowl, combine barbecue sauce, chicken broth, orange juice, soy sauce, honey, and orange zest. Whisk until sauce is well blended.

2. In a wok, heat oil over medium-high heat until hot. Add bell pepper and leeks and stir-fry until softened, 3 to 5 minutes. Arrange chicken pieces on top of vegetables in wok.

3. Pour sauce over chicken and vegetables. Raise heat to high and bring to a boil. Reduce heat to medium, cover, and cook 20 minutes. Turn chicken over. Cook, covered, until chicken is tender, 20 to 25 minutes longer. Remove chicken to a serving bowl and cover to keep warm.

4. Raise heat to high and boil until sauce thickens, 4 to 5 minutes. Pour sauce over chicken and serve.

246 CHICKEN THIGHS IN CHEESY BROCCOLI SAUCE

Prep: 5 minutes   Cook: 45 to 53 minutes   Serves: 4

¼ cup vegetable oil
2 pounds chicken thighs
2 medium carrots, chopped
1 medium onion, chopped
1 small green bell pepper,
  chopped
1 garlic clove, minced

1 (10¾-ounce) can broccoli
  and cheese soup
¾ cup chicken broth
¾ cup half-and-half
½ teaspoon salt
¼ teaspoon pepper

1. In a wok, heat 2 tablespoons oil over medium-high heat until hot, swirling to coat sides of pan. Add chicken and cook, turning, until browned all over, 5 to 7 minutes. Remove chicken to a plate. Pour off fat from wok.

2. In same wok, heat remaining 2 tablespoons oil over medium-high heat. Add carrots, onion, bell pepper, and garlic and stir-fry until softened, 5 to 6 minutes. Return chicken to wok.

3. In a medium bowl, whisk together soup, chicken broth, half-and-half, salt, and pepper. Pour over chicken and vegetables. Bring to a boil. Reduce heat to medium-low, cover, and cook until chicken is tender, 35 to 40 minutes.

247   CHICKEN AND EGGPLANT STEW
Prep: 10 minutes   Cook: 48 to 57 minutes   Serves: 4

3 tablespoons olive oil	2 garlic cloves, minced
6 chicken thighs, about 2 pounds	1 (14-ounce) can Italian peeled tomatoes, with their juice
1 medium eggplant, peeled and cut into ½-inch cubes	1 cup dry Marsala wine
1 large onion, chopped	1 teaspoon dried thyme leaves
1 large green bell pepper, chopped	1 teaspoon salt
	¼ teaspoon pepper

1. In a wok, heat 1 tablespoon olive oil over high heat until hot, swirling to coat sides of pan. Arrange chicken thighs in wok and cook, turning, until browned all over, 4 to 6 minutes. Remove to a plate. Pour off chicken fat.

2. In same wok, heat remaining 2 tablespoons oil over high heat. Add eggplant, onion, bell pepper, and garlic. Stir-fry until vegetables are soft, 4 to 6 minutes.

3. Return chicken to wok. Add tomatoes with their juice, Marsala, thyme, salt, and pepper. Bring to a boil. Reduce heat to medium, cover, and cook until chicken is tender and sauce has reduced slightly, 40 to 45 minutes.

248   BRAISED CHICKEN THIGHS WITH POTATOES, CARROTS, AND DILL
Prep: 10 minutes   Cook: 58 to 65 minutes   Serves: 6

Here is a homey one-pot dish that is perfect for Sunday supper. Any favorite herb can be substituted for the dill, but be sure to halve the amount.

¼ cup vegetable oil	3 carrots, peeled and cut into 1-inch pieces
6 large chicken thighs, 2½ to 3 pounds total	¼ cup chopped parsley
5 scallions, sliced	2 tablespoons chopped fresh dill or 2 teaspoons dried
1 cup white wine	½ teaspoon salt
1 cup chicken broth	¼ teaspoon pepper
2 russet potatoes, peeled and cut into 8 wedges each	

1. In a wok, heat 2 tablespoons oil over medium-high heat until hot, swirling to coat sides of pan. Arrange chicken pieces extending up sides of pan and cook, turning, until browned on both sides, 6 to 8 minutes. Remove to a plate.

2. In same wok, heat remaining 2 tablespoons oil over medium-high heat. Add scallions and cook until softened, about 2 minutes. Return chicken to wok. Add wine and chicken broth, cover, and cook 20 minutes.

3. Add potatoes, carrots, parsley, dill, salt, and pepper to wok. Cover and cook until chicken and vegetables are tender, 30 to 35 minutes.

249   SODA-SAUCED BBQ CHICKEN
Prep: 10 minutes   Cook: 54 to 62 minutes   Serves: 4

This tangy sauce works equally well with ribs—beef and pork. The secret ingredient is cola.

¼ cup vegetable oil	⅓ cup packed brown sugar
1 chicken (3 pounds), cut up	1 tablespoon Worcestershire
1 medium onion, chopped	sauce
2 garlic cloves, minced	1 teaspoon dry mustard
1½ cups ketchup	½ teaspoon hot pepper sauce
½ cup carbonated cola drink	½ teaspoon salt
⅓ cup red wine vinegar	¼ teaspoon pepper

1. In a wok, heat 2 tablespoons oil over high heat until hot, swirling to coat sides of pan. Arrange chicken pieces extending up sides of pan and cook, turning, until golden brown all over, 6 to 8 minutes. Remove to a plate. Pour out chicken fat.

2. In same wok, heat remaining 2 tablespoons oil over high heat until hot. Add onion and garlic. Cook, stirring, until softened, 3 to 4 minutes. Return chicken to wok.

3. In a medium bowl, combine ketchup, cola, vinegar, brown sugar, Worcestershire sauce, mustard, hot sauce, salt, and pepper. Whisk to blend well. Pour over chicken. Reduce heat to medium-low, cover, and cook, basting occasionally, until chicken is tender and juices from thigh run clear when pricked near bone, 45 to 50 minutes.

250   CHICKEN AND SAUSAGE MEAL-IN-A-WOK
Prep: 5 minutes   Cook: 56 to 69 minutes   Serves: 6

1 pound sweet Italian sausage	1 (28-ounce) bottle barbecue
1 chicken (3 pounds), cut up	sauce with onions
2 pounds small red-skinned	½ teaspoon fennel seeds
potatoes	¼ teaspoon pepper
1 (20-ounce) bag frozen whole	1 (8-ounce) can whole-kernel
onions	corn, drained

1. Prick sausage in several places with a fork. In a wok, cook sausage over medium heat, turning, until browned all over, 5 to 7 minutes. Remove from wok and drain on paper towels. Slice sausage into 1-inch pieces. Wipe out any fat from wok. Return sausage to wok.

2. Add chicken, potatoes, onions, barbecue sauce, fennel, and pepper. Bring to a boil. Reduce heat to medium-low, cover, and cook, turning occasionally, until chicken is tender, 50 minutes to 1 hour. Add corn and cook until heated through, 1 to 2 minutes.

251 CHICKEN THIGHS COOKED IN CHILI SAUCE

Prep: 5 minutes   Cook: 50 to 57 minutes   Serves: 6

3½ tablespoons vegetable oil
6 large chicken thighs (about 3 pounds total)
1 medium red bell pepper, chopped

1 (16-ounce) jar chili sauce
¼ cup dry red wine
1 teaspoon grated lemon zest

1. In a wok, heat 2½ tablespoons oil over medium-high heat until hot, swirling to coat sides of pan. Add chicken and cook, turning, until browned on both sides, 6 to 8 minutes. Remove to a plate. Pour off chicken fat.

2. In same wok, heat remaining 1 tablespoon oil over medium-high heat. Add bell pepper and cook, stirring often, until softened, about 4 minutes. Return chicken to wok.

3. Add chili sauce, wine, and lemon zest. Reduce heat to medium-low, cover, and cook until chicken is tender and juices run clear, 40 to 45 minutes.

252 CHICKEN WITH SPANISH RICE

Prep: 5 minutes   Cook: 27 to 32 minutes   Serves: 4

I like one-pot, or in this case, one-wok, meals. After an initial separate cooking, the ingredients are all combined and simmer happily together.

3 tablespoons olive oil
1 medium onion, chopped
1 celery rib, chopped
1 medium green bell pepper, chopped
1 garlic clove, minced
1 pound skinless, boneless chicken breasts, cut into 1-inch pieces

1 (14-ounce) can Italian peeled tomatoes, with juices
¾ cup chicken broth
1 cup long-grain white rice
1 teaspoon chili powder
1 teaspoon ground cumin
¼ teaspoon pepper
¼ teaspoon hot pepper sauce

1. In a wok, heat 1½ tablespoons olive oil over medium-high heat until hot. Add onion, celery, bell pepper, and garlic. Cook, stirring, until softened, 5 to 6 minutes. With a slotted spoon, remove to a plate.

2. In same wok, heat remaining 1½ tablespoons oil over medium-high heat, swirling to coat sides of pan. Add chicken and cook, stirring, until golden brown but still juicy, 4 to 6 minutes. Return vegetables to wok.

3. Add tomatoes, chicken broth, rice, chili powder, cumin, pepper, and hot sauce. Bring to a boil. Reduce heat to low, cover, and cook until rice is tender and most of liquid is absorbed, 18 to 20 minutes.

253   CHICKEN WITH WILD RICE, APPLES, AND WALNUTS

Prep: 10 minutes   Cook: 51 to 58 minutes   Serves: 6

3½ tablespoons vegetable oil
1½ pounds skinless, boneless
    chicken breasts, cut into
    ½-inch cubes
1 medium red onion, chopped
1 Granny Smith apple, cored,
    and cut into ½-inch cubes

½ cup walnut halves
½ cup golden raisins
4 cups chicken broth
1 cup wild rice
3 tablespoons red wine
    vinegar

1. In a wok, heat 2 tablespoons oil over medium-high heat until hot, swirling to coat sides of pan. Add chicken and cook, stirring, until meat is white throughout but still juicy, 3 to 4 minutes. Remove to a plate.

2. In same wok, heat remaining 1½ tablespoons oil over medium-high heat. Add red onion and cook until softened, 4 to 5 minutes. Add apple, walnuts, and raisins. Cook, stirring, 2 minutes. Remove to plate with chicken.

3. In same wok, heat chicken broth to boiling over high heat. Add rice. Reduce heat to low. Cook, covered, until rice is tender, 40 to 45 minutes.

4. Return chicken and vegetables to wok. Stir in vinegar. Cook 2 minutes, or until heated through.

254   CHICKEN PAPRIKASH WITH NOODLES

Prep: 10 minutes   Cook: 72 to 85 minutes   Serves: 4

8 ounces egg noodles
5 tablespoons butter
1 chicken (3 pounds), cut up
3 medium onions, sliced
2 tablespoons imported
    sweet paprika

½ teaspoon salt
¼ teaspoon pepper
½ cup chicken broth
2 tablespoons lemon juice
1 cup sour cream

1. In a large pot of boiling salted water, cook noodles until tender but still firm, 10 to 12 minutes. Drain and rinse under cold water; drain well.

2. In a wok, melt 2 tablespoons butter over medium heat, swirling to coat sides of pan. Arrange chicken pieces extending up sides of wok and cook, turning, until golden brown all over, 8 to 10 minutes. Remove chicken to a plate. Pour out fat.

3. In same wok, melt remaining 3 tablespoons butter over medium heat. Add onions and cook, stirring, until soft, 6 to 8 minutes. Add paprika, salt, and pepper. Cook, stirring, 1 to 2 minutes. Return chicken to wok. Add chicken broth and lemon juice. Cover and cook until chicken is tender and juices from thigh run clear when pierced near bone, 45 to 50 minutes.

4. Add noodles. Reduce heat to low. Stir in sour cream. Cook, tossing noodles, until just heated through, 2 to 3 minutes.

255 CHICKEN AND WILD RICE WITH MADEIRA AND MUSHROOMS

Prep: 10 minutes   Soak: 20 minutes   Cook: 50 to 56 minutes
Serves: 4

4 dried porcini or other
   imported mushrooms
1 cup Madeira
2 tablespoons vegetable oil
1 medium onion, chopped
½ carrot, chopped
1 cup wild rice, rinsed 3 times,
   drained well

2 cups chicken broth
2 cups cooked chicken, cut
   into ½-inch cubes
2 tablespoons soy sauce
¼ teaspoon freshly ground
   black pepper

1. In a small bowl, soak mushrooms in Madeira for 20 minutes. Strain liquid through sieve; reserve. Slice off stems and discard; chop reconstituted mushrooms coarsely. Set aside.

2. In a wok, heat oil over high heat until hot. Add onion and carrot and cook until softened, 3 to 4 minutes.

3. Add wild rice and chopped mushrooms. Cook, stirring to coat, 2 minutes. Add chicken broth, reserved mushroom soaking liquid, and 1 cup water. Bring to a boil. Reduce heat to low, cover, and cook until rice is tender, 45 to 50 minutes. Turn off heat. Let sit, covered, 5 minutes.

4. Add chicken, soy sauce, and pepper. Fluff with a fork.

256 CHICKEN AND SMOKED TURKEY IN TOMATO-OLIVE SAUCE

Prep: 10 minutes   Cook: 39 to 47 minutes   Serves: 6

2 tablespoons olive oil
6 large chicken thighs (about
   2½ pounds total)
1 medium red bell pepper, cut
   into thin strips
1 medium green bell pepper,
   cut into thin strips
1 medium onion, chopped
1 garlic clove, minced
½ cup chicken broth

2 tablespoons red wine
   vinegar
¼ pound cooked smoked
   turkey breast, cut into
   ½-inch dice
½ cup tomato sauce
2 tablespoons tomato paste
¼ cup sliced pitted green
   olives
¼ teaspoon pepper

1. In a wok, heat olive oil over medium-high heat until hot, swirling to coat sides of pan. Add chicken and cook, turning, until browned on both sides, 6 to 8 minutes. Remove to a plate. Pour out all but 2 tablespoons fat.

2. Add red and green bell peppers, onion, and garlic to wok. Cook over medium-high heat, stirring, until onion is softened and peppers are crisp-tender, 3 to 4 minutes.

3. Add chicken broth and vinegar. Bring to a boil, scraping up browned bits from bottom of wok. Return chicken to wok. Add smoked turkey, tomato sauce, tomato paste, olives, and pepper. Bring to a boil; reduce heat to medium-low. Cover and cook until chicken is tender, 30 to 35 minutes.

257   CHICKEN IN RED SAUCE
Prep: 5 minutes   Cook: 52 to 62 minutes   Serves: 4

3 tablespoons vegetable oil	¼ cup red wine vinegar
1 medium onion, chopped	¼ cup orange juice
1 medium red bell pepper, chopped	1 teaspoon dried thyme
	½ teaspoon salt
2 garlic cloves, crushed	¼ teaspoon pepper
1 chicken (3 pounds), cut up	2 teaspoons cornstarch
1 (8-ounce) can tomato sauce	
½ cup ketchup	

1. In a wok, heat 2 tablespoons oil over medium-high heat until hot, swirling to coat sides of pan. Add onion, bell pepper, and garlic. Cook until softened, 3 to 5 minutes. Remove to a plate.

2. In same wok, heat remaining 1 tablespoon oil over medium-high heat. Arrange chicken pieces extending up sides of pan. Cook, turning, until browned on all surfaces, 8 to 10 minutes. Return vegetables to wok.

3. Add tomato sauce, ketchup, vinegar, orange juice, thyme, salt, and pepper. Bring to a boil. Reduce heat to medium-low. Cook, covered, until chicken is tender and juices run clear, 40 to 45 minutes. Remove chicken and vegetables to a serving bowl.

4. Dissolve cornstarch in ¼ cup cold water. Add to wok. Cook, stirring, until sauce boils and thickens, 1 to 2 minutes. Pour over chicken and vegetables and serve.

258   CREAMY CHICKEN STEW
Prep: 10 minutes   Cook: 22 to 24 minutes   Serves: 4

3 tablespoons vegetable oil
1 pound skinless, boneless
chicken breasts, cut into
1-inch cubes
1 medium onion, chopped
2 medium carrots, sliced
3 medium potatoes, peeled
and cut into ½-inch cubes
½ pound green beans, cut into
1-inch pieces

1 (10¾-ounce) can cream of
potato soup
1 (10¾-ounce) can chicken
broth
2 teaspoons Worcestershire
sauce
¼ teaspoon freshly ground
pepper

1. In a wok, heat 1 tablespoon oil over medium-high heat until hot, swirling to coat sides of pan. Add chicken and stir-fry until meat is white throughout but still juicy, 3 to 4 minutes. Remove to a plate.

2. In same wok, heat remaining 2 tablespoons oil over medium-high heat. Add onion and carrots. Cook, stirring, until crisp-tender, 4 to 5 minutes.

3. Return chicken to wok. Add potatoes, green beans, cream of potato soup, chicken broth, Worcestershire sauce, and pepper. Cook over medium heat until potatoes and beans are tender, about 15 minutes.

259   CHICKEN CHILI
Prep: 10 minutes   Cook: 35 to 37 minutes   Serves: 4

2 tablespoons olive oil
2 medium onions, chopped
2 garlic cloves, crushed
2 teaspoons ground cumin
1 teaspoon dried oregano
1 teaspoon salt
¼ teaspoon crushed hot red
pepper
1 (4-ounce) can chopped green
chiles

1 (16-ounce) can Italian
crushed tomatoes
1 cup chicken broth
1 (16-ounce) can cannellini
(white kidney beans),
liquid reserved
1¼ pounds skinless, boneless
chicken breasts, cubed

1. In a wok, heat olive oil over medium-high heat until hot. Add onions and stir-fry until beginning to brown, 4 to 6 minutes. Add garlic, cumin, oregano, salt, and hot pepper. Cook, stirring, 1 minute.

2. Add chiles, tomatoes, chicken broth, beans with their liquid, and chicken. Bring to a boil; reduce heat to medium. Cover and cook until liquid is reduced by one-third, about 30 minutes.

260   CHICKEN WITH LEEKS AND APPLES
Prep: 10 minutes   Cook: 43 to 53 minutes   Serves: 4

Chicken and fruit go well together, as this dish proves. I like to serve it with couscous or wild rice and buttered broccoli. If leeks are not available, or if they are too expensive, feel free to substitute a couple of onions in step 1.

2 tablespoons olive oil
2½ to 3 pounds chicken pieces
2 medium leeks (white and
    tender green), chopped
1 garlic clove, minced
¼ cup orange marmalade

2 cups apple juice
1 cup chicken broth
2 tart cooking apples, such as
    Granny Smith, cored and
    thinly sliced
1 teaspoon cinnamon

1. In a wok, heat olive oil over medium-high heat until hot, swirling to coat sides of pan. Add chicken, arranging pieces extending up sides of wok. Cook, turning, until browned all over, 7 to 10 minutes. Remove to a plate. Pour off all but 2 tablespoons fat from wok.

2. Add leeks and garlic and cook, stirring, until soft, 3 to 5 minutes. Return chicken to wok, along with any juices that have accumulated on plate. Add marmalade, apple juice, and chicken broth. Bring to a boil; reduce heat to medium-low. Cover and cook until chicken is just white near bone, 30 to 35 minutes.

3. Add apples and cinnamon. Raise heat to high. Boil uncovered, stirring occasionally, until sauce is slightly thickened and chicken and apples are tender, about 3 minutes.

261 BRAISED CHICKEN WITH LEEKS, MUSHROOMS, AND TARRAGON

Prep: 10 minutes   Cook: 52 to 60 minutes   Serves: 4

Serve this savory stew with plenty of mashed potatoes and crusty bread to soak up the sauce.

2 tablespoons olive oil
1 chicken (3 pounds), cut up
2 medium leeks (white and tender green), chopped
½ pound cremini (Italian brown) mushrooms, quartered

2 garlic cloves, minced
2 cups chicken broth
1½ tablespoons chopped fresh tarragon or 1 teaspoon dried
½ teaspoon salt
¼ teaspoon pepper

1. In a wok, heat olive oil over medium-high heat until hot, swirling to coat sides of pan. Add chicken, arranging pieces up sides of wok. Cook, turning, until golden brown all over, 7 to 10 minutes. With tongs, remove chicken to a plate. Pour off all but 2 tablespoons fat from wok.

2. Add leeks, mushrooms, and garlic to fat in wok. Cook, stirring, until mushrooms are tender, 4 to 5 minutes. Return chicken to pan.

3. Add chicken broth, tarragon, salt, and pepper. Bring to a boil; reduce heat to medium-low. Cover and cook, turning occassionally, until chicken is very tender, 40 to 45 minutes.

262 AMERICAN MIXED GRILL

Prep: 10 minutes   Cook: 1¾ to 2 hours   Serves: 4 to 6

Three meats—chicken, veal, and beef—give the effect of a mixed grill, even though the dish is a savory stew. I like to serve it with steamed green beans and oven-roasted potatoes and carrots. Be sure to ask your butcher to cut the shanks into pieces for you.

3½ tablespoons olive oil
2 chicken breast halves, bone in (about 8 ounces each), cut in half crosswise
1½ pounds veal shanks, cut into 1-inch lengths
1½ pounds beef shanks, cut into 1-inch lengths
2 medium onions, chopped
1 medium red bell pepper, diced

1 celery rib, diced
1 garlic clove, crushed through a press
½ cup brine-cured olives, such as Gaeta, halved and pitted
1½ cups dry red wine
1 cup chicken broth
1 bay leaf
1 teaspoon dried thyme leaves
¼ teaspoon pepper

1. In a wok, heat 1½ tablespoons olive oil over high heat until hot, swirling to coat sides of pan. Arrange chicken, veal, and beef up sides of pan without overlapping and cook, turning and rotating, until browned all over, 7 to 10 minutes. Remove to a plate. Pour off fat.

2. In same wok, heat remaining 2 tablespoons oil over medium-high heat. Add onions, bell pepper, celery, and garlic. Cook, stirring, until onions are soft, 4 to 6 minutes.

3. Return meats to wok, along with any juices that have accumulated on plate. Add olives, wine, broth, bay leaf, thyme, and pepper. Bring to a boil; reduce heat to medium-low. Cover and cook until shanks are tender, 1½ to 1¾ hours. Remove and discard bay leaf before serving.

---

263   GINGERED TURKEY AND ALMONDS WITH WILD AND BROWN RICE

Prep: 10 minutes   Cook: 49 to 56 minutes   Serves: 6

Here's a great way to stretch a pound of turkey breast. With all the textures and seasonings, tasters will be hard-pressed to guess this isn't veal or beef.

1 cup long-grain brown rice	½ cup sliced almonds
¼ cup wild rice	3 tablespoons tarragon vinegar
½ teaspoon ground ginger	
6 tablespoons peanut oil	1 tablespoon Dijon mustard
1 pound skinless, boneless turkey breast, cut into ½-inch cubes	1½ teaspoons minced fresh ginger
	½ teaspoon salt
4 scallions, chopped	¼ teaspoon pepper
½ cup red bell pepper, finely diced	

1. In a large saucepan, combine brown rice, wild rice, ground ginger, and 2½ cups cold water. Bring to a boil. Reduce heat to low, cover, and cook until water is absorbed and rice is tender, 40 to 45 minutes. (The rices can be cooked in advance.)

2. In a wok, heat 2 tablespoons oil over medium-high heat until hot, swirling to coat sides of pan. Add turkey ad stir-fry until meat is white throughout but still juicy, 4 to 5 minutes. Remove to a plate.

3. In same wok, heat 1 tablespoon oil over medium-high heat. Add scallions and bell pepper. Stir-fry until pepper is crisp-tender, 3 to 4 minutes. Add almonds. Cook 2 minutes. Return turkey to wok. Add cooked rice.

4. In a small bowl, whisk remaining 3 tablespoons peanut oil with vinegar, Dijon mustard, fresh ginger, salt, and pepper. Pour over turkey-rice mixture and toss to combine. Serve at room temperature.

264   HOISIN-SAUCED BRAISED TURKEY WITH ONION AND GREEN PEPPER

Prep: 10 minutes   Cook: 62 to 79 minutes   Serves: 4 to 6

I like the contrast of American turkey and the Asian flavors of hoisin sauce and ginger. If you've never used hoisin sauce, it is sold in jars in the Oriental foods sections of many groceries and in Chinese markets. It will keep almost forever in the refrigerator.

¼ **cup honey**
2 **tablespoons hoisin sauce**
2 **tablespoons pineapple or apricot preserves**
½ **teaspoon dried ginger**
1 **boneless turkey breast half (2 pounds), skin removed**

2 **tablespoons vegetable oil**
1 **large white onion, sliced**
1 **large green bell pepper, cut into thin strips**
1 **cup chicken broth**
½ **cup dry white wine**

1. In a small bowl, combine honey, hoisin, preserves, and ginger. Stir to mix well. Brush over turkey to coat lightly.

2. In a wok, heat oil over high heat. Add onion and bell pepper and stir-fry until vegetables are softened, 2 to 4 minutes. Set turkey on top of vegetables.

3. Add chicken broth and wine to wok. Bring to a boil; reduce heat to low. Cover and simmer, basting with pan juices several times, until turkey is tender and white throughout, 1 to 1¼ hours.

265   TURKEY GOULASH

Prep: 10 minutes   Cook: 15 to 17 minutes   Serves: 4

2 **tablespoons vegetable oil**
1 **pound ground turkey**
1 **large onion, chopped**
1 **medium green bell pepper, chopped**
½ **pound fresh mushrooms, sliced**
2 **garlic cloves, crushed through a press**

1 **(8-ounce) can tomato sauce**
1 **cup crushed tomatoes**
1 **cup beef broth**
½ **teaspoon dried basil**
½ **teaspoon oregano**
½ **teaspoon salt**
¼ **teaspoon pepper**
1 **cup spiral pasta**

1. In a wok, heat oil over medium-high heat, swirling to coat sides of pan. Add ground turkey, onion, bell pepper, mushrooms, and garlic and stir-fry until turkey is cooked through with no trace of pink, 5 to 7 minutes.

2. Add tomato sauce, tomatoes, beef broth, basil, oregano, salt, pepper, and 1 cup water. Bring to a boil. Add pasta. Reduce heat to medium and cook until pasta is just tender, about 10 minutes.

266 SMOKED TURKEY AND WILD RICE
Prep: 10 minutes   Cook: 47 to 55 minutes   Serves: 4

2 tablespoons butter
2 tablespoons vegetable oil
2 medium leeks (white part
    only), chopped
2 medium carrots, chopped
2 medium celery ribs,
    chopped
½ pound fresh mushrooms,
    sliced

1 cup wild rice
1 pound smoked turkey
    breast, cut into 1-inch
    cubes
2 (14½-ounce) cans chicken
    broth
½ cup dry white wine
2 tablespoons soy sauce
¼ teaspoon pepper

1. In a wok, heat butter and oil over medium-high heat until hot, swirling to coat sides of pan. Add leeks, carrots, and celery and cook until leeks and celery are softened, 4 to 6 minutes. Add mushrooms and cook, stirring, until mushrooms are soft, 3 to 4 minutes.

2. Add wild rice and stir to coat. Add smoked turkey, chicken broth, wine, soy sauce, and pepper. Heat to boiling; reduce heat to low. Cover and cook until rice is tender and most of liquid is absorbed, 40 to 45 minutes.

267 TURKEY MEATBALLS IN SWEET AND SOUR SAUCE
Prep: 15 minutes   Cook: 56 to 58 minutes   Serves: 6

3 tablespoons vegetable oil
4 scallions (white part only),
    minced
2 medium onions, chopped
2 celery ribs, chopped
1 medium carrot, grated
3 cups tomato puree
1 cup apple juice

½ cup packed brown sugar
¼ cup lemon juice
2 pounds ground turkey
¾ cup fresh bread crumbs
1 egg, beaten
1 teaspoon salt
¼ teaspoon pepper

1. In a wok, heat 1 tablespoon oil over medium-high heat until hot. Add scallions and cook until softened, 2 to 3 minutes. Transfer to a large bowl and let cool completely.

2. In same wok, heat remaining 2 tablespoons oil over medium-high heat. Add onions, celery, and carrot and cook until onions and celery are soft, 4 to 6 minutes. Add tomato puree, apple juice, brown sugar, and lemon juice and mix well. Simmer 5 minutes.

3. Meanwhile, add ground turkey, bread crumbs, egg, salt, and pepper to scallions in bowl. Thoroughly mix, preferably with your hands. Shape into balls 1 inch in diameter.

4. Place meatballs in sauce. Reduce heat to low. Cover and cook 45 minutes.

268   BEEF STROGANOFF
Prep: 10 minutes   Cook: 18 to 23 minutes   Serves: 4

1½ pounds boneless sirloin
    steak
3 tablespoons vegetable oil
1 medium onion, sliced and
    separated into rings
¼ pound fresh mushrooms,
    sliced
1 garlic clove, minced
½ cup dry red wine

2 tablespoons red wine
    vinegar
½ (6-ounce) can tomato paste
¼ cup chopped parsley
½ teaspoon salt
¼ teaspoon pepper
½ pound egg noodles, cooked
    and drained
1 cup sour cream

1. Cut steak across grain on a slight diagonal into thin strips. In a wok, heat 2 tablespoons oil over high heat until hot, swirling to coat sides of pan. Add beef and cook, stirring, until meat loses its red color, 2 to 3 minutes. With a slotted spoon, remove meat to a plate.

2. In same wok, heat remaining 1 tablespoon oil over medium-high heat. Add onion, mushrooms, and garlic and cook, stirring, until onion is softened and mushrooms are tender, about 4 minutes. Return beef to wok.

3. Add wine, vinegar, tomato paste, parsley, salt, pepper, and ⅔ cup water. Reduce heat to medium-low, cover, and cook until sauce reduces slightly, 10 to 12 minutes. Add noodles. Reduce heat to low.

4. Add sour cream and toss to coat. Cook until heated through, 2 to 3 minutes, but do not boil.

---

269   STOVE-TOP BARBECUED BEEF WITH POTATOES AND CARROTS
Prep: 10 minutes   Marinate: 3 hours   Cook: 3 hours   Serves: 6

2 tablespoons corn oil
2 garlic cloves, minced
¼ cup soy sauce
¼ cup dry red wine
1 cup beef broth
1 tablespoon chopped fresh
    rosemary or 1 teaspoon
    dried
2 pounds boneless beef
    chuck, cut into 1½-inch
    pieces

1 (16-ounce) bottle barbecue
    sauce
4 medium russet potatoes
    (about 1½ pounds),
    peeled and quartered
3 medium carrots, peeled and
    cut into 2-inch lengths
1 medium onion, coarsely
    chopped

1. Combine oil, garlic, soy sauce, wine, beef broth, and rosemary in a large bowl. Add meat, turning to coat all surfaces. Cover and marinate at room temperature 3 hours.

2. Drain meat, reserving marinade. Place meat, barbecue sauce, and 1 cup water in wok. Bring to a boil. Reduce heat to low, cover, and cook 2 hours.

3. Add potatoes, carrots, and onion. Pour in reserved marinade. Cook, covered, 1 hour, or until meat and vegetables are tender.

---

270   ALE-SAUCED CHILI
Prep: 10 minutes   Cook: 42 to 49 minutes   Serves: 6

Beer and molasses are the two secret ingredients in this tangy chili, which is easy to double for a party. Serve with an assortment of your favorite chili condiments: chopped onion, chopped olives, pickled jalapeños, sour cream, shredded Cheddar, and tortilla chips.

1 tablespoon vegetable oil	1 (12-ounce) bottle ale or
1½ pounds ground chuck	amber beer
(80% lean)	1 (16-ounce) can red kidney
1 medium onion, chopped	beans, undrained
2 garlic cloves, minced	1 (4-ounce) can chopped green
2 teaspoons chili powder	chiles, undrained
1 teaspoon ground cumin	1 tablespoon molasses
1 teaspoon salt	2 tablespoons red wine
¼ teaspoon crushed hot red	vinegar
pepper	
1 (28-ounce) can tomatoes,	
with their juices	

1. In a wok, heat oil over medium-high heat until hot, swirling to coat sides of pan. Add ground chuck, onion, and garlic and cook, stirring, until meat is brown and onions are soft, 5 to 7 minutes. Add chili powder, cumin, salt, and hot pepper. Cook, stirring, 2 minutes.

2. Add tomatoes with their juices and ale. Bring to a boil. Add kidney beans, chiles, molasses, and vinegar. Reduce heat to low, cover, and cook until chili is thickened, 35 to 40 minutes.

271   SWEET AND SOUR BEEF AND CABBAGE
Prep: 15 minutes   Cook: 50 minutes   Serves: 6

Reminiscent of the taste of stuffed cabbage, this recipe is a snap to prepare without sacrificing one bit of flavor. I like to serve this dish with egg noodles and green beans.

2 tablespoons vegetable oil	1½ pounds ground chuck (80%
1 small head of cabbage,	lean)
cored and shredded	1 small onion, grated
4 scallions, chopped	¼ cup chopped parsley
2 garlic cloves, minced	¼ cup dried bread crumbs
1 (28-ounce) can tomato puree	1 egg, beaten
1 (10-ounce) jar apricot	½ teaspoon salt
preserves	¼ teaspoon pepper
Juice of 1 lemon	

1. In a wok, heat oil over medium-high heat until hot, swirling to coat sides of pan. Add cabbage, scallions, and garlic. Stir-fry until softened, 5 to 6 minutes. Add tomato puree, apricot preserves, and lemon juice and mix well. Bring to a boil.

2. Meanwhile, in a large bowl, combine ground chuck, grated onion, parsley, bread crumbs, egg, salt, and pepper. Mix thoroughly and shape into balls 1 inch in diameter.

3. Place meatballs in cabbage-tomato sauce. Reduce heat to low. Cover and simmer 45 minutes.

272   MUSHROOM BEEF ROLL-UPS
Prep: 15 minutes   Cook: 52 to 60 minutes   Serves: 4

Cutting the beef into thin slices is a little tricky, so you may want to ask your butcher to do it for you.

1 pound round steak	½ teaspoon dried thyme leaves
3 tablespoons vegetable oil	½ teaspoon salt
1 small onion, minced	¼ teaspoon pepper
¼ pound fresh mushrooms,	1 (10-ounce) can brown gravy
minced	with mushrooms
1 cup dry bread crumbs	½ cup dry red wine
2 tablespoons chopped	1 teaspoon Worcestershire
parsley	sauce
½ cup beef broth	

1. Cut steak into 4 thin slices and pound to ⅛-inch thickness. Set aside.

2. In a wok, heat 1 tablespoon oil over high heat until hot. Add onion and mushrooms and cook, stirring, until mushrooms are lightly browned and onion is soft, 3 to 4 minutes. Remove to a medium bowl and let cool.

3. Add bread crumbs, parsley, beef broth, thyme, salt, and pepper to onion-mushroom mixture and mix well. Spread one-fourth of filling on one piece of round steak. Roll up, enclosing ends. Secure with toothpicks. Repeat with remaining 3 pieces of meat and filling.

4. Wipe out wok, add remaining 2 tablespoons oil, and place over high heat until hot, swirling to coat sides of pan. Add beef roll-ups and cook, turning, until browned all over, 4 to 6 minutes. Add gravy, wine, and Worcestershire sauce. Reduce heat to medium-low and simmer, covered, until meat is tender, 45 to 50 minutes.

273   GROUND BEEF WITH EGGPLANT AND CHEESE

Prep: 5 minutes   Cook: 17 to 20 minutes   Serves: 4 to 6

1 tablespoon vegetable oil	1½ tablespoons cornstarch
1 pound ground chuck (80% lean)	1 (8-ounce) can tomato sauce
1 small onion, chopped	1 large eggplant, peeled and cut into ½-inch slices
1 medium red bell pepper, chopped	½ teaspoon salt
1 teaspoon dried basil	¼ teaspoon pepper
1 teaspoon dried oregano	1 cup grated Monterey Jack cheese, about 4 ounces
1 teaspoon chili powder	

1. In a wok, heat oil over medium-high heat until hot, swirling to coat sides of pan. Add ground chuck, onion, and red bell pepper. Stir-fry until meat is brown and vegetables have softened, about 6 minutes. Add basil, oregano, and chili powder.

2. Dissolve cornstarch in ½ cup cold water and stir into wok. Pour in tomato sauce. Cook 2 minutes.

3. Arrange eggplant over mixture. Add salt and pepper. Reduce heat to low. Cover and cook until eggplant is tender, 8 to 10 minutes. Sprinkle with cheese. Cover and cook until cheese is melted, 1 to 2 minutes.

274   BEEF STEW WITH POTATOES AND OLIVES
Prep: 10 minutes   Cook: 2 to 2⅓ hours   Serves: 6

3   tablespoons olive oil
2½ pounds chuck roast, cut into
     1-inch cubes
2   onions, chopped
2   garlic cloves, minced
2   (14½-ounce) cans beef broth
3   tablespoons tomato paste
¾ cup pimiento-stuffed green
     olives

2   pounds red potatoes, peeled
     and quartered
1   teaspoon dried marjoram or
     thyme leaves
1   teaspoon salt
¼ teaspoon pepper

1. In a wok, heat 2 tablespoons olive oil over high heat until hot, swirling to coat sides of pan. Add chuck cubes and cook, turning, until browned all over, 6 to 8 minutes. Remove to a plate.

2. In same wok, heat remaining 1 tablespoon oil over medium-high heat. Add onions and garlic. Cook, stirring, until soft, 3 to 5 minutes. Return meat to wok.

3. Add beef broth, tomato paste, olives, and ½ cup water. Bring to a boil; reduce heat to medium-low. Cover and cook for 1½ hours. Add potatoes, marjoram, salt, and pepper. Cook, covered, until meat and potatoes are tender, 25 to 30 minutes.

275   RUSSIAN HAMBURGERS
Prep: 10 minutes   Cook: 29 to 32 minutes   Serves: 3 to 4

These special hamburgers taste great with potato and carrot chunks cooked right in the wok along with the meat during the last twenty minutes of cooking time.

1   pound ground chuck (80%
     lean)
1   small potato, peeled and
     finely grated
2   scallions, minced
1   garlic clove, minced
¼ cup dry bread crumbs

1   egg
¾ teaspoon salt
¼ teaspoon pepper
2   tablespoons vegetable oil
1   large onion, sliced
1   cup boiling water

1. In a medium bowl, combine ground chuck, potato, scallions, garlic, bread crumbs, egg, ½ teaspoon salt, and ⅛ teaspoon pepper. Mix until well blended. Shape into 6 patties.

2. In a wok, heat 1 tablespoon oil over medium-high heat until hot, swirling to coat sides of pan. Arrange hamburgers extending up sides of pan and cook, turning once until browned on both sides, 6 to 8 minutes. Remove to a plate. Drain off fat.

3. In same wok, heat remaining 1 tablespoon oil over medium-high heat. Add onion and cook, stirring, until softened, 3 to 4 minutes. Add boiling water and stir, scraping up browned bits from bottom of wok. Return hamburgers to wok. Add remaining salt and pepper. Reduce heat to medium-low, cover, and cook 20 minutes.

276   CHILI CHILE BRISKET
Prep: 10 minutes   Cook: 2¾ to 3 hours   Serves: 6

Brisket is a maligned and misunderstood cut of beef. Thought to be tough, here it slow-cooks to tenderness with little effort. Remember to keep the heat as low as possible.

1 **(1¾-ounce) package dry chili seasoning**	1 **garlic clove, crushed**
2 **pounds brisket of beef, first cut**	1 **(28-ounce) can crushed tomatoes, liquid reserved**
3 **tablespoons vegetable oil**	1 **(7-ounce) bottle beer**
1 **large onion, chopped**	¼ **cup canned diced green chiles**
1 **medium green bell pepper, chopped**	1 **(15-ounce) can red kidney beans, rinsed and drained**

1. Place chili seasoning in a shallow dish. Coat brisket with mix, pressing seasoning into meat, coating all surfaces.

2. In a wok, heat 2 tablespoons oil over medium-high heat until hot, swirling to coat sides of pan. Add brisket and cook, turning, until meat is browned on both sides, 8 to 10 minutes. Remove to a plate.

3. In same wok, heat remaining 1 tablespoon oil over medium-high heat. Add onion, bell pepper, and garlic and cook, stirring, until softened, 3 to 5 minutes. Return brisket to wok, along with any juices that have accumulated on plate.

4. Add tomatoes with their liquid, beer, and chiles. Reduce heat to low, cover, and cook 2 hours. Add kidney beans and cook, covered, until meat is very tender, 35 to 45 minutes longer. Remove brisket from wok and let cool to room temperature. Shred with a fork. Return brisket to wok and cook until heated through, 2 to 3 minutes.

277   ORANGE BEEF CURRY
Prep: 10 minutes   Cook: 2⅔ to 3 hours   Serves: 4 to 6

½ cup flour
1 tablespoon Madras curry powder
1 teaspoon grated orange zest
½ teaspoon ground cumin
½ teaspoon ground ginger
½ teaspoon salt
¼ teaspoon cayenne
2 pounds brisket of beef, first cut

¼ cup olive oil
2 medium onions, chopped
2 garlic cloves, minced
3 cups dry red wine
1 (8-ounce) can mandarin oranges, juice reserved
2 tablespoons red wine vinegar
1 tablespoon cornstarch

1. Combine flour, curry powder, orange zest, cumin, ginger, salt, and cayenne in a shallow dish. Dredge brisket in seasoned flour, patting flour into meat to coat all over; set aside.

2. In a wok, heat 2 tablespoons olive oil over medium-high heat until hot. Add onions and garlic and cook, stirring often, until softened, 3 to 4 minutes. Remove to a plate.

3. In same wok, heat remaining 2 tablespoons oil over medium-high heat, swirling to coat sides of pan. Add brisket and cook, turning once, until meat is nicely browned on both sides, 8 to 10 minutes. Return onions to wok.

4. Add wine, reserved mandarin orange juice, and vinegar. Reduce heat to low, cover, and cook until brisket is fork-tender, 2½ to 2¾ hours. Remove meat to a cutting board. Let rest 10 to 15 minutes before cutting into thin slices crosswise on a slight diagonal. Arrange meat on a deep platter.

5. Dissolve cornstarch in ¼ cup cold water and stir into wok. Add mandarin oranges. Cook over high heat, stirring, until sauce boils and thickens, 1 to 2 minutes. Pour sauce and oranges over meat and serve.

278   DELI-STYLE CORNED BEEF
Prep: 5 minutes   Cook: 2 to 2½ hours   Standing Time: 20 minutes
Serves: 6

3 pounds corned beef brisket
2 onions, quartered
2 carrots, quartered
2 celery ribs, quartered

2 tablespoons pickling spices
2 bay leaves
1½ teaspoons salt
¼ teaspoon pepper

1. Place brisket in a wok. Top with onions, carrots, celery, pickling spices, bay leaves, salt, and pepper. Add enough cold water to cover.

2. Bring to a boil. Reduce heat to low, cover, and cook until meat is very tender, 2 to 2½ hours. Remove meat from liquid; discard vegetables. Let brisket stand 20 minutes before cutting into thin slices.

279   BRISKET AND ONIONS

Prep: 10 minutes   Cook: 2⅔ to 3⅓ hours   Serves: 6

3 pounds beef brisket, first cut
2 garlic cloves, thinly slivered
3 tablespoons vegetable oil
3 medium onions, sliced
2 cups dry red wine
½ cup tomato sauce

3 tablespoons brown sugar
2 tablespoons Dijon mustard
2 tablespoons lemon juice
1 teaspoon salt
¼ teaspoon pepper

1. With tip of a paring knife, make incisions all over brisket 1 inch deep. Press slivered garlic into slits.

2. In a wok, heat 2 tablespoons oil over medium-high heat until hot. Add onions and cook, stirring, until soft and golden, 6 to 8 minutes. Remove to a bowl.

3. In same wok, heat remaining 1 tablespoon oil over medium-high heat, swirling to coat sides of pan. Add brisket and cook, turning once, until browned on both sides, 8 to 10 minutes. Return onions to wok.

4. Add wine, tomato sauce, brown sugar, mustard, lemon juice, salt, and pepper. Bring to a boil. Reduce heat to low, cover, and cook until meat is very tender, 2½ to 3 hours. Remove meat to a cutting board. Let rest 10 to 15 minutes before slicing, thinly, crosswise, on a slight diagonal.

280   ROAST PORK FRIED RICE

Prep: 10 minutes   Cook: 9 to 11 minutes   Serves: 4

3 tablespoons corn oil
1 egg, beaten
3 scallions, chopped
2 garlic cloves, minced
2 cups cooled cooked rice
½ pound roast pork, cut into
     ¼-inch slices

1 (8-ounce) can sliced water
     chestnuts, drained
¼ cup chicken broth
2 tablespoons soy sauce
¼ teaspoon pepper

1. In a wok, heat 1 tablespoon oil over medium-high heat until hot. Add egg and cook, stirring, until firm, 1 to 2 minutes. Remove to a plate. Cut into small pieces.

2. In same wok, heat remaining 2 tablespoons oil over medium-high heat, swirling to coat sides of pan. Add scallions and garlic and stir-fry until softened, 3 to 4 minutes. Add rice, roast pork, and water chestnuts. Stir-fry 3 minutes. Add egg and cook, stirring, 1 minute.

3. Add chicken broth, soy sauce, and pepper. Cook, stirring, 2 minutes.

281   VEAL STEW IN LEMON WINE SAUCE
Prep: 10 minutes   Cook: 1⅔ to 2¼ hours   Serves: 6

½ cup flour
1 teaspoon grated lemon zest
1 teaspoon dried thyme leaves
½ teaspoon salt
¼ teaspoon pepper
2½ pounds boneless veal
    shoulder, cut into 1-inch
    cubes
3½ tablespoons olive oil

1 medium onion, chopped
1 carrot, chopped
1 garlic clove, minced
½ pound fresh mushrooms,
    sliced
1 (16-ounce) can tomato puree
2 cups dry white wine
¼ cup lemon juice

1. In a shallow dish, combine flour, lemon zest, thyme, salt, and pepper. Lightly coat veal cubes with seasoned flour, shaking off excess.

2. In a wok, heat 2 tablespoons olive oil over medium-high heat until hot, swirling to coat sides of pan. Add veal and cook, turning, until browned on all sides, 8 to 10 minutes. Remove to a bowl.

3. In same wok, heat remaining 1½ tablespoons oil over medium-high heat. Add onion, carrot, garlic, and mushrooms and cook until onion is softened, 4 to 6 minutes. Return veal to wok.

4. Add tomato puree, wine, lemon juice, and 1 cup water. Bring to a boil. Reduce heat to low, cover, and simmer until tender, 1½ to 2 hours.

282   VEAL SHANKS IN MUSHROOM SAUCE
Prep: 15 minutes   Cook: 2 to 2⅓ hours   Serves: 4 to 6

½ cup flour
1 teaspoon dried oregano
½ teaspoon salt
¼ teaspoon pepper
6 medium veal shanks, cut
    into 1-inch pieces
3½ tablespoons olive oil
1 large onion, chopped

1 medium carrot, chopped
2 garlic cloves, minced
1 (14½-ounce) can crushed
    tomatoes
1 (10¾-ounce) can cream of
    mushroom soup
1 bay leaf

1. In a shallow dish, combine flour, oregano, salt, and pepper. Dredge veal in seasoned flour to lightly coat all over; shake off excess.

2. In a wok, heat 2 tablespoons olive oil over high heat until hot, swirling to coat sides of pan. Add veal shanks and cook, turning, until browned all over, 8 to 10 minutes. Remove to a plate.

3. In same wok, heat remaining 1½ tablespoons oil over medium-high heat. Add onion, carrot, and garlic and cook, stirring occasionally until softened, 4 to 6 minutes. Return meat to wok.

4. Stir in tomatoes, soup, bay leaf, and 1 cup water. Heat to boiling. Reduce heat to low, cover, and cook until veal is tender, 1¾ to 2 hours.

283 LAMB STEW
Prep: 10 minutes   Cook: 1½ to 1¾ hours   Serves: 4

Rosemary, red wine, and black olives raise this savory stew to the level of company fare. Serve with noodles or mashed potatoes.

½ cup flour
1 teaspoon dried rosemary
½ teaspoon salt
¼ teaspoon pepper
1½ pounds boneless lamb shoulder, trimmed of fat and cut into 1-inch cubes
2 tablespoons olive oil

1 garlic clove, crushed
1 (10-ounce) can beef broth
1 cup dry red wine
½ (16-ounce) package frozen potatoes and carrots
½ cup pitted black olives, preferably Kalamata, chopped

1. In a shallow dish, combine flour, rosemary, salt, and pepper. Lightly coat lamb cubes all over; shake off excess.

2. In a wok, heat olive oil over high heat until hot, swirling to coat sides of pan. Add lamb and cook, turning, until brown all over, 5 to 7 minutes. Add garlic and cook, stirring, 1 minute. Add beef broth and wine. Bring to a boil. Reduce heat to medium-low, cover, and simmer 1 hour.

3. Add potatoes and carrots and olives. Cook until lamb is very tender, 30 to 40 minutes.

284 BRAISED HAM AND RED CABBAGE
Prep: 10 minutes   Cook: 43 to 51 minutes   Serves: 4

2 tablespoons vegetable oil
1 pound cooked ham, cut into 2 x ¼-inch strips
2 tablespoons butter
1 medium red onion, chopped
1 apple, peeled and cut into ¼-inch slices
1 small head red cabbage, shredded

½ cup apricot preserves
½ cup apricot nectar
2 tablespoons red wine vinegar
1½ teaspoons cinnamon
¼ teaspoon ground cloves

1. In a wok, heat 1 tablespoon oil over medium-high heat until hot. Add ham and stir-fry until lightly browned, 3 to 4 minutes. Remove to a plate.

2. Add remaining 1 tablespoon oil to wok and heat over medium-high heat. Add red onion and apple. Cook until soft, 4 to 6 minutes. Add cabbage. Cook, stirring, 2 minutes.

3. Add apricot preserves, apricot nectar, vinegar, cinnamon, and cloves. Bring to a boil. Reduce heat to low. Cover and cook until cabbage is very tender, 35 to 40 minutes. Return ham to wok. Cook 1 minute to heat through.

285 BARBECUED PORK AND BABY LIMA BEANS

Prep: 10 minutes   Cook: 1 to 1⅓ hours   Serves: 4 to 6

3 tablespoons vegetable oil
2 pounds boneless pork
    shoulder, trimmed of fat
    and cut into 1-inch cubes
1 medium onion, chopped
1 medium carrot, chopped
¾ cup ketchup
¼ cup cider vinegar
3 tablespoons molasses

1 tablespoon Worcestershire
    sauce
1 teaspoon hot pepper sauce
1 teaspoon dry mustard
¼ teaspoon garlic powder
¼ teaspoon pepper
1 (10-ounce) package frozen
    baby lima beans,
    defrosted

1. In a wok, heat 2 tablespoons oil over high heat until hot, swirling to coat sides of pan. Add pork cubes and cook, stirring, until meat is browned all over, 4 to 6 minutes. Remove to a plate.

2. Add remaining 1 tablespoon oil to wok. Reduce heat to medium-high. Add onion and carrot and cook, stirring, until softened, 3 to 4 minutes. Return pork to wok. Reduce heat to medium-low.

3. Add ketchup, vinegar, molasses, Worcestershire sauce, hot sauce, mustard, garlic powder, pepper, and ¾ cup water. Stir to combine. Cover and cook until pork is fork-tender, 50 minutes to 1 hour. Add lima beans. Cook until beans are tender, 5 to 7 minutes. If sauce remains too thin, remove pork and lima beans to a serving bowl and boil until slightly thickened.

286 SWEET AND SOUR PORK WITH ONIONS AND RAISINS

Prep: 10 minutes   Cook: 57 to 64 minutes   Serves: 4

3½ tablespoons olive oil
1 pound boneless pork
    shoulder, trimmed of fat
    and cut into 1-inch cubes
1 (20-ounce) package frozen
    whole onions, thawed
    and patted dry
1 garlic clove, minced
1 cup dry red wine

1 cup unsweetened apple
    juice
¼ cup white wine vinegar
2 tablespoons tomato paste
½ teaspoon dried thyme leaves
½ teaspoon salt
¼ teaspoon pepper
2 tablespoons brown sugar
½ cup raisins

1. In a wok, heat 1½ tablespoons olive oil over high heat until hot, swirling to coat sides of pan. Add pork cubes and cook, stirring, until meat is browned all over, 4 to 6 minutes. Remove to a plate.

2. In same wok, heat remaining 2 tablespoons oil over medium-high heat. Add onions and garlic and cook, stirring, until softened, about 3 minutes. Remove to plate with pork.

3. Add wine, apple juice, vinegar, tomato paste, thyme, salt, and pepper to wok. Bring to a boil, scraping up browned bits from bottom of pan. Reduce heat to medium-low. Return pork and vegetables to wok, cover, and cook 30 minutes.

4. Stir in brown sugar and raisins. Cook until pork is tender, 20 to 25 minutes.

---

287 STEWED PORK IN CRANBERRY MAPLE SAUCE

Prep: 10 minutes   Cook: 1½ to 1¾ hours   Serves: 6

2 **to 3 tablespoons olive oil**	2 **cups fresh or frozen**
2½ **to 3 pounds boneless pork**	**cranberries**
shoulder, trimmed of fat	¾ **cup orange juice**
and cut into 1-inch cubes	¾ **cup maple syrup**
3 **shallots, chopped**	¾ **teaspoon cinnamon**
2 **carrots, thinly sliced**	½ **cup raisins**
1 **garlic clove, minced**	

1. In a wok, heat 2 tablespoons olive oil over high heat until hot, swirling to coat sides of pan. Add pork and stir-fry until nicely browned all over, 5 to 7 minutes. With a strainer or slotted spoon, remove pork to a plate.

2. If necessary to measure 2 tablespoons, add additional oil to wok. Reduce heat to medium-high. Add shallots, carrots, and garlic and cook, stirring, until softened, about 3 minutes. Return pork to wok.

3. Add cranberries, orange juice, maple syrup, cinnamon, and 1⅓ cups water. Reduce heat to medium-low, cover, and cook until pork is fork-tender, 1¼ to 1½ hours. Add raisins. Simmer 10 minutes.

288   SMOTHERED PORK
Prep: 10 minutes   Cook: 31 to 34 minutes   Serves: 4

½ cup yellow cornmeal
½ teaspoon salt
¼ teaspoon cayenne
1 pound boneless pork
    cutlets, ¼ inch thick
2 tablespoons olive oil
1 medium onion, chopped

1 garlic clove, crushed
1 (14-ounce) can crushed
    tomatoes
½ cup prepared salsa
¼ cup chopped cilantro
¼ cup chopped pitted green
    olives

1. In a shallow dish, combine cornmeal, salt, and cayenne. Dredge pork in mixture; shake off excess.

2. In a wok, heat 1 tablespoon olive oil over medium-high heat until hot, swirling to coat sides of pan. Arrange cutlets in wok and cook, turning once, until brown on both sides, 6 to 8 minutes. Remove to a plate.

3. In same wok, heat remaining 1 tablespoon oil over medium-high heat. Add onion and garlic and cook until soft, 3 to 4 minutes. Add tomatoes, salsa, cilantro, and olives. Cook, stirring, 2 minutes.

4. Return pork to wok. Spoon some of sauce over meat. Cook, covered, 20 minutes, or until tender.

289   ORANGE ROUGHY IN TOMATO-LEEK SAUCE
Prep: 10 minutes   Cook: 27 to 36 minutes   Serves: 4

Orange roughy is becoming a new favorite on the fish scene. Its mild flavor blends well with the tomatoes, leeks, and wine in this dish.

2 tablespoons olive oil
1 leek (white part only),
    chopped
1 small carrot, grated
1 garlic clove, minced
1 (14-ounce) can Italian peeled
    tomatoes, drained and
    coarsely chopped
½ cup dry white wine

¼ cup chopped Italian flat-leaf
    parsley
1 teaspoon sugar
½ teaspoon dried oregano
½ teaspoon salt
¼ teaspoon pepper
1½ pounds orange roughy
    fillets

1. In a wok, heat olive oil over medium-high heat until hot. Add leek, carrot, and garlic and cook, stirring, until softened, 4 to 6 minutes.

2. Add tomatoes, wine, parsley, sugar, oregano, salt, and pepper. Reduce heat to medium-low, cover, and cook until reduced slightly, 15 to 20 minutes.

3. Place fillets in wok. Spoon some of sauce over fish. Cook until fish is opaque and cooked through, 8 to 10 minutes.

290   BLUEFISH IN ZESTY HERBED TOMATO SAUCE

Prep: 10 minutes   Cook: 28 to 37 minutes   Serves: 4

Bluefish has an assertive flavor that can stand up to a highly seasoned sauce. I like to serve this dish with rice or orzo and buttered zucchini.

2 tablespoons olive oil	1 teaspoon dried basil
1 medium onion, chopped	½ teaspoon salt
1 garlic clove, crushed	¼ teaspoon black pepper
1 small carrot, grated	⅛ teaspoon crushed hot red
1 (14½-ounce) can crushed	pepper
tomatoes	4 bluefish fillets, about
1 (6-ounce) can tomato paste	6 ounces each
1 teaspoon dried oregano	

1. In a wok, heat olive oil over medium-high heat until hot. Add onion, garlic, and carrot and cook, stirring, until softened, 3 to 5 minutes.

2. Add tomatoes, tomato paste, oregano, basil, salt, black pepper, and hot pepper. Bring to a boil. Reduce heat to medium. Cook, partially covered, until sauce reduces slightly, 15 to 20 minutes.

3. Add bluefish. Cover and cook, turning once, until fish is opaque and cooked through, 10 to 12 minutes.

291   SHERRIED SALMON WITH POTATOES AND ONIONS

Prep: 10 minutes   Cook: 22 to 26 minutes   Serves: 4

2 tablespoons vegetable oil	4 salmon fillets (6 ounces
1 tablespoon butter	each), skin removed
2 medium red potatoes,	2 tablespoons chopped
peeled and thinly sliced	parsley
1 medium onion, sliced	1 teaspoon grated orange zest
1 garlic clove, crushed	½ teaspoon salt
1 cup dry sherry	¼ teaspoon pepper
½ cup orange juice	

1. In a wok, heat oil and butter over medium-high heat until hot, swirling to coat sides of pan. Add potatoes, onion, and garlic. Cook, stirring, until potatoes are translucent, 4 to 5 minutes. Add sherry and orange juice, cover, and cook 10 minutes.

2. Arrange salmon fillets on top of potatoes. Sprinkle with parsley, orange zest, salt, and pepper. Reduce heat to medium-low. Cover and cook until fish is opaque throughout and about half of liquid is evaporated, 8 to 10 minutes.

292   FILLET OF SOLE WITH BULGUR
Prep: 5 minutes   Cook: 13 to 16 minutes   Serves: 4

Bulgur, a form of cracked wheat, is used frequently as the main ingredient in the classic tabbouleh. Here it "steams" in clam juice and tomatoes and becomes a bed for the sole.

2 tablespoons olive oil	1 tablespoon white wine
1 medium onion, chopped	vinegar
2 celery ribs, sliced	½ teaspoon salt
1 (8-ounce) can stewed	¼ teaspoon pepper
tomatoes	1 cup bulgur
1 cup clam juice	1 pound fresh sole fillets

1. In a wok, heat olive oil over medium-high heat until hot. Add onion and celery and cook, stirring, until softened, 3 to 4 minutes.

2. Add stewed tomatoes, clam juice, vinegar, salt, and pepper. Bring to a boil. Reduce heat to low. Add bulgur. Stir briefly. Top with sole fillets. Cover and cook until fish is opaque and most of liquid is absorbed, 10 to 12 minutes.

293   SPEEDY SPICY FISH STEW
Prep: 10 minutes   Cook: 20 to 25 minutes   Serves: 6

3 tablespoons olive oil	1 (16-ounce) bottle cocktail
2 celery ribs, sliced	sauce
1 medium onion, chopped	1 pound haddock fillets, cut
1 (16-ounce) bag frozen	into 1-inch pieces
potatoes and carrots,	2 tablespoons lemon juice
thawed	¼ cup chopped parsley
2 cups canned crushed	1 teaspoon salt
tomatoes	¼ teaspoon pepper
1 cup dry white wine	

1. In a wok, heat olive oil over medium-high heat until hot. Add celery and onion and cook until crisp-tender, 4 to 5 minutes.

2. Add potatoes and carrots, tomatoes, wine, cocktail sauce, and 2 cups cold water. Cover and cook until potatoes are almost tender, 10 to 12 minutes.

3. Add fish. Reduce heat to low and simmer until fish is opaque throughout, 4 to 6 minutes. Add lemon juice, parsley, salt, and pepper. Cook 2 minutes longer and serve at once.

Chapter 10

Wok Sautéing and Pan-Frying

In this chapter, your wok turns into your favorite skillet—even more utilitarian because of its large surface area. Both the bottom and the sides of the wok are used to quickly brown foods or fry them in a small amount of oil. When a sauté is finished with a bit of wine, broth, or what-have-you to complete the cooking and produce a little sauce, the lid is added and the heat lowered. Still, all the recipes in this chapter take no more than half an hour, and many are completed in less than fifteen minutes.

Recipes like Pork Chops in Spinach-Flecked Sauce, Sweet and Sour Turkey, and Peppered Rib-Eye Steaks are quick, easy dishes to whip up after work for family or on short notice to feed your most demanding guests.

When sautéing in the wok, be sure to swirl the oil around with the stir-fry spatula, so that the sides are coated with the hot oil. Steaks, chops, chicken breasts, and the like are placed in a single layer around the sides of the wok—not just in the bottom—and turned and rotated for even cooking.

---

294 CHICKEN AND SHIITAKE RICE PILAF
Prep: 10 minutes   Cook: 25 to 29 minutes   Serves: 4

3½ tablespoons olive oil	1 celery rib, sliced
1¼ pounds skinless, boneless chicken breasts, cut into 1-inch pieces	1 garlic clove, crushed
	1 (14½-ounce) can beef broth
¼ pound shiitake mushrooms, stemmed and sliced	½ cup dry red wine
	½ teaspoon dried sage
1 medium onion, chopped	¼ teaspoon pepper
	1 cup long-grain white rice

1. In a wok, heat 1½ tablespoons olive oil over medium-high heat until hot, swirling to coat sides of pan. Add chicken and stir-fry until meat is white throughout but still juicy, 3 to 4 minutes. Remove to a plate.

2. In same wok, heat remaining 2 tablespoon oil over medium-high heat. Add mushrooms, onion, celery, and garlic and stir-fry until celery is crisp-tender, 4 to 5 minutes. Return chicken to wok.

3. Add beef broth, wine, sage, and pepper. Bring to a boil. Add rice. Reduce heat to low. Cover and cook until rice is tender and most of liquid is absorbed, 18 to 20 minutes.

295   SUN-BELT CHICKEN
Prep: 10 minutes   Cook: 12 to 16 minutes   Serves: 4

½ cup flour
1 teaspoon dried thyme leaves
1 teaspoon grated lemon zest
1 teaspoon grated orange zest
½ teaspoon salt
¼ teaspoon pepper
4 skinless, boneless chicken breast halves (4 to 5 ounces each), pounded to ¼-inch thickness

3 tablespoons vegetable oil
4 scallions, sliced
1 tablespoon butter
1 cup dry white wine
¼ cup orange juice
2 tablespoons lemon juice
1 seedless orange, peeled and sectioned

1. In a shallow dish, combine flour, thyme, lemon zest, orange zest, salt, and pepper. Dredge chicken in seasoned flour to coat both sides; shake off excess.

2. In a wok, heat 2 tablespoons oil over medium-high heat until hot. Add scallions and cook, stirring, until scallions are softened, 2 to 3 minutes. Remove to a plate.

3. In same wok, heat remaining 1 tablespoon oil and butter over medium-high heat until hot, swirling to coat sides of pan. Add chicken and cook, turning, until brown on both sides, 6 to 8 minutes. Return scallions to wok.

4. Add wine, orange juice, and lemon juice. Raise heat to high and cook until sauce is reduce slightly, 3 to 4 minutes. Add orange sections. Cook until heated through, about 1 minute.

296   CHICKEN WITH TOMATOES AND MUSHROOMS
Prep: 5 minutes   Cook: 50 to 59 minutes   Serves: 3

1 cup Italian-seasoned bread crumbs
6 medium chicken thighs (2 pounds total)
3 tablespoons olive oil
1 medium onion, chopped
¼ pound fresh mushrooms, sliced
1 garlic clove, chopped

1 (15-ounce) can tomato sauce with mushrooms
2 tablespoons chopped parsley
1 teaspoon dried basil
1 teaspoon dried oregano
½ teaspoon salt
¼ teaspoon pepper
¼ cup grated Parmesan cheese

1. Place bread crumbs in a shallow dish. Dredge chicken thighs in crumbs to coat all over, shaking off excess.

2. In a wok, heat 2 tablespoons olive oil over medium-high heat until hot, swirling to coat sides of pan. Add chicken and cook, turning, until brown all over, 5 to 7 minutes. Using tongs, remove to a plate. Pour off fat from wok.

3. In same wok, heat remaining 1 tablespoon oil over medium-high heat. Add onion, mushrooms, and garlic. Cook until onion is softened and mushrooms are tender, 3 to 5 minutes. Return chicken to wok.

4. Add tomato sauce, parsley, basil, oregano, salt, and pepper. Bring to a boil. Reduce heat to medium-low. Cook, covered, until chicken is tender, 40 to 45 minutes. Sprinkle with cheese. Cook 2 minutes and serve.

---

297 FRIED CHICKEN
Prep: 10 minutes   Cook: 20 to 25 minutes   Serves: 4

My mother used to prepare this dish by browning it on the stove and finishing it in the oven. The wok cooks the chicken crispy on the outside and juicy and tender inside, with no need for baking. Don't forget biscuits!

1 egg
½ cup milk
½ cup flour
½ teaspoon salt
½ teaspoon paprika
¼ teaspoon garlic powder

¼ teaspoon pepper
2 cups dry bread crumbs
4 chicken breast halves, bone in
1 cup vegetable oil

1. In a shallow dish, combine egg with milk, flour, salt, paprika, garlic powder, and pepper. Beat until batter is smooth. Place bread crumbs in a paper bag.

2. Dip chicken pieces in batter; shake off excess. Add chicken, 2 pieces at a time, to bag, and shake to coat evenly.

3. In a wok, heat oil over medium heat until it reaches 350° to 360°F on a deep-frying thermometer. Add chicken and fry, turning, until browned all over, about 10 minutes. Reduce heat to medium-low, cover, and cook until meat is cooked through but still juicy, 10 to 15 minutes, turning pieces after about 6 minutes. Drain on paper towels.

298   CORNMEAL-COATED CHICKEN WITH TOMATO-CREAM SAUCE

Prep: 10 minutes   Cook: 24 to 27 minutes   Serves: 4

2 eggs
1 (8½-ounce) package corn
   muffin mix
4 skinless, boneless chicken
   breast halves (4 to 5
   ounces each)
3 tablespoons olive oil

1 large onion, chopped
1 garlic clove, minced
1 (8-ounce) can tomato sauce
½ teaspoon dried basil
½ teaspoon dried oregano
½ cup heavy cream

1. In a shallow bowl, beat eggs until blended. Place corn muffin mix in a shallow pan. Dip chicken in beaten eggs, then dredge in cornmeal to coat; shake off excess.

2. In a wok, heat 2 tablespoons olive oil over medium-high heat until hot, swirling to coat sides of pan. Arrange coated chicken breasts in pan, and fry until golden on bottom, 3 to 4 minutes. Turn and cook until brown on other side, about 4 minutes. Remove to a serving plate and tent with aluminum foil to keep warm.

3. In same wok, heat remaining 1 tablespoon oil over medium-high heat. Add onion and garlic. Cook, stirring, until soft, 4 to 5 minutes. Add tomato sauce, basil, and oregano. Cook 10 minutes. Add cream and cook until slightly thickened, about 3 minutes. Spoon sauce over chicken and serve.

299   CHICKEN DIJON

Prep: 10 minutes   Cook: 6 to 8 minutes   Serves: 4

Everyone loves chicken flavored with the zesty bite of Dijon mustard. This version, cut into bite-size pieces, is particularly popular with children. Serve with rice and steamed broccoli doused with lemon juice and a little melted butter.

½ cup mayonnaise
2 tablespoons Dijon mustard
1 garlic clove, crushed
1½ cups dried bread crumbs
1 teaspoon onion salt
¼ teaspoon pepper

1¼ pounds boneless, skinless
   chicken breasts, cut into
   1-inch pieces
2 tablespoons olive oil
1 tablespoon butter

1. In a bowl, combine mayonnaise, Dijon mustard, and garlic. In a shallow dish, combine bread crumbs, onion salt, and pepper. Brush chicken with mayonnaise mixture, then dredge in bread crumbs to coat; shake off excess.

2. In a wok, heat olive oil and butter over medium-high heat until hot, swirling to coat sides of pan. Add chicken and cook, turning once, until golden brown on both sides and white throughout but still juicy, 6 to 8 minutes.

300 CASHEW CHICKEN WITH MUSHROOM SAUCE

Prep: 10 minutes   Cook: 15 to 19 minutes   Serves: 6

4 ounces cashews, finely
 ground (about ¾ cup)
¾ cup fresh bread crumbs
½ teaspoon salt
⅛ teaspoon cayenne
1 egg
6 skinless, boneless chicken
 breast halves (4 to 5
 ounces each), pounded to
 ¼-inch thickness

¼ cup vegetable oil
¾ cup cream of mushroom
 soup
¼ cup milk
1 tablespoon lemon juice
2 teaspoons Worcestershire
 sauce

1. In a shallow dish, mix ground cashews, bread crumbs, salt, and cayenne. In another dish, beat egg with 2 tablespoons cold water until blended. Dip chicken pieces in egg; then dredge in cashew crumbs to coat.

2. In a wok, heat 2 tablespoons oil over medium-high heat until hot, swirling to coat sides of pan. Add half of chicken breasts, arranging them up sides of pan as necessary without overlapping. Cook, turning once, until golden brown on both sides, 6 to 8 minutes. Remove to a serving platter. Repeat with remaining oil and chicken.

3. Add mushroom soup, milk, lemon juice, and Worcestershire sauce to wok. Cook, stirring and scraping up browned bits from bottom of pan, 3 minutes. Pour sauce over chicken and serve.

301 PEPPERED RIB-EYE STEAKS

Prep: 10 minutes   Cook: 6 to 8 minutes   Serves: 4

These seasoned steaks taste terrific and cook up quickly. Take note, if you have an exhaust fan: Turn it on before the meat hits the wok.

½ teaspoon paprika
¼ teaspoon salt
¼ teaspoon black pepper
¼ teaspoon garlic powder
¼ teaspoon lemon pepper
 seasoning
⅛ teaspoon cayenne

⅛ teaspoon crushed hot red
 pepper
⅛ teaspoon dried oregano
⅛ teaspoon ground cumin
2 tablespoons vegetable oil
4 boneless rib-eye steaks
 (6 ounces each)

1. In a small bowl, mix paprika, salt, black pepper, garlic powder, lemon pepper seasoning, cayenne, hot pepper, oregano, cumin, and oil. Brush seasoned oil evenly over both sides of steaks.

2. Heat wok over high heat until very hot. Add steaks in one layer and cook until brown on bottom, 3 to 4 minutes. Turn and cook until brown on other side and pink inside, 3 to 4 minutes. Serve at once.

302   SWEET AND SOUR TURKEY
Prep: 10 minutes   Cook: 17 to 24 minutes   Serves: 4

3 tablespoons vegetable oil	1 (16-ounce) can tomato puree
1½ pounds boneless, skinless turkey breast, cut into 2 x ½-inch strips	1 (10-ounce) jar pineapple preserves
1 medium onion, chopped	1 (8-ounce) can unsweetened crushed pineapple
1 celery rib, chopped	2 tablespoons apple cider vinegar
1 medium red bell pepper, cut into ¼-inch-wide strips	

1. In a wok, heat 1½ tablespoons oil over medium-high heat until hot, swirling to coat sides of pan. Add turkey and cook, stirring, until meat is white throughout but still juicy, 4 to 5 minutes. Remove to a plate.

2. In same wok, heat remaining 1½ tablespoons oil over medium-high heat. Add onion, celery, and bell pepper and cook, stirring, until softened, 3 to 4 minutes. Return turkey to wok.

3. Add tomato puree, pineapple preserves, crushed pineapple, and vinegar. Stir to combine. Reduce heat to medium-low. Cover and cook 15 minutes.

303   ONION BURGERS IN TOMATO-MUSHROOM SAUCE
Prep: 5 minutes   Cook: 18 to 22 minutes   Serves: 6

2 pounds ground chuck (80% lean)	1 tablespoon vegetable oil
1 envelope (½ box) dry onion soup mix	1 (8-ounce) can tomato sauce
1 garlic clove, minced	1 (10¾-ounce) can cream of mushroom soup
½ cup fresh bread crumbs	½ teaspoon dried thyme leaves
1 egg	¼ teaspoon pepper

1. In a large bowl, combine ground chuck, onion soup mix, garlic, bread crumbs, and egg. Mix until well blended. Shape into patties about ¾ inch thick.

2. In a wok, heat oil over medium-high heat until hot, swirling to coat sides of pan. Add patties, arranging them up sides of pan. Cook, turning once, until browned on both sides, 8 to 10 minutes. Drain off fat.

3. In a medium bowl, whisk together tomato sauce, mushroom soup, thyme, pepper, and ½ cup water. Pour into wok. Bring to a boil, scraping up any browned bits from bottom of pan. Reduce heat to medium-low. Partially cover and cook until sauce is reduced by about one-third, 10 to 12 minutes.

304   SALISBURY STEAK

Prep: 5 minutes   Cook: 15 to 18 minutes   Serves: 4

This recipe is based on a favorite dish served at a now long-gone restaurant. We always ate salisbury steak with mashed potatoes and gravy—we still do!

1½ pounds ground chuck (80% lean)	1 tablespoon vegetable oil
¼ cup regular or quick-cooking oats	1 (10¾-ounce) can beef broth
¼ cup dried bread crumbs	¼ cup ketchup
1 egg, beaten	1 tablespoon Dijon mustard
½ teaspoon salt	1 teaspoon Worcestershire sauce
¼ teaspoon pepper	1 tablespoon cornstarch

1. In a large bowl, combine ground chuck, oats, bread crumbs, egg, salt, and pepper. Mix until well blended. Shape into 6 patties about ½ inch thick.

2. In a wok, heat oil over high heat until hot, swirling to coat sides of pan. Add patties, arranging them up sides of wok, and cook, turning once, until browned on the outside, 4 to 6 minutes. Drain off fat.

3. In a medium bowl, whisk together beef broth, ketchup, mustard, and Worcestershire sauce. Pour into wok over patties. Stir carefully so as not to break up patties, scraping up any browned bits from bottom of pan. Reduce heat to medium-low, cover, and cook for 10 minutes.

4. Dissolve cornstarch in ¼ cup cold water and stir into wok. Cook over high heat, stirring, until sauce boils and thickens, 1 to 2 minutes.

305   LAMB CHOPS IN CITRUS SAUCE

Prep: 5 minutes   Cook: 15 to 17 minutes   Serves: 6

2 tablespoons vegetable oil	¼ cup packed brown sugar
6 shoulder lamb chops, cut ¾ inch thick	1 teaspoon minced fresh ginger
¼ cup bottled steak sauce	1 teaspoon grated orange zest
¼ cup orange juice	

1. In a wok, heat oil over high heat until hot, swirling to coat sides of pan. Add lamb chops, arranging them up sides of wok without overlapping. Cook, turning once, until brown on both sides, 5 to 7 minutes. Remove to a plate. Drain off fat.

2. Reduce heat to medium. Combine steak sauce, orange juice, brown sugar, ginger, and orange zest in wok. Cook 5 minutes. Return lamb to wok. Simmer, covered, 5 minutes.

306 VEAL WITH CAPERS IN LEMON-BUTTER SAUCE

Prep: 10 minutes   Cook: 11 to 17 minutes   Serves: 4

½ cup flour
½ teaspoon dried thyme leaves
½ teaspoon salt
¼ teaspoon pepper
1 pound veal scaloppine (tenders), pounded to ¼-inch thickness

2 tablespoons olive oil
2 tablespoons butter
1 medium onion, chopped
¾ cup chicken broth
3 tablespoons lemon juice
2 tablespoons capers, drained

1. In a shallow dish, combine flour, thyme, salt, and pepper. Dredge veal in seasoned flour mixture; shake off excess.

2. In a wok, heat 1 tablespoon olive oil and 1 tablespoon butter over medium-high heat until hot, swirling to coat sides of pan. Add coated veal, arranging pieces up sides of wok without overlapping. Cook until golden on bottom, 2 to 3 minutes. Turn and brown on other side, about 2 minutes. Remove to a plate.

3. In same wok, heat remaining 1 tablespoon oil and 1 tablespoon butter over medium-high heat. Add onion and cook, stirring, until softened, 3 to 5 minutes. Add chicken broth and lemon juice. Boil over high heat, scraping up browned bits from bottom of pan, until reduced by half, 3 to 5 minutes. Return veal to pan and add capers. Cook just until heated through, 1 to 2 minutes.

307 VEAL WITH TOMATOES, CHIVES, AND TARRAGON

Prep: 10 minutes   Cook: 5 to 8 minutes   Serves: 4

1 egg
½ cup flour
½ teaspoon salt
¼ teaspoon pepper
1 pound veal scaloppine (tenders), pounded to ¼-inch thickness
2 tablespoons butter
2 tablespoons vegetable oil

1 pint cherry tomatoes, halved
2 tablespoons minced chives
1½ tablespoons minced fresh tarragon, or 1 teaspoon dried
¾ cup dry white wine
1 tablespoon Dijon mustard
1 tablespoon capers, drained

1. Break the egg into a shallow bowl and beat well. In a shallow dish, combine flour, salt, and pepper. Dip veal in beaten egg, then dredge in seasoned flour to coat; shake off excess.

2. In a wok, melt 1 tablespoon butter in 1 tablespoon oil over high heat until hot, swirling to coat sides of pan. Arrange veal in wok, extending up sides of pan, and cook, turning, until brown on both sides, 3 to 4 minutes. Remove to a plate.

3. In same wok, melt remaining 1 tablespoon butter and remaining 1 tablespoon oil over medium-high heat. Add tomatoes, chives, and tarragon and stir-fry until tomatoes just begin to soften, 1 to 2 minutes. Remove to plate with veal.

4. Add wine and Dijon mustard to wok. Bring to a boil, scraping up browned bits from bottom of pan. Return veal, tomatoes, and chives to wok. Add capers. Cook until heated through, 1 to 2 minutes.

---

308 PORK CHOPS IN SPINACH-FLECKED SAUCE

Prep: 10 minutes   Cook: 13 to 18 minutes   Serves: 4

1 tablespoon vegetable oil	¼ cup dry white wine
4 boneless loin pork chops, cut ½ inch thick (6 ounces each)	¼ cup chicken broth
	1 cup heavy cream
	½ teaspoon grated nutmeg
2 tablespoons butter	½ teaspoon salt
1 medium onion, finely chopped	¼ teaspoon pepper
½ (10-ounce) package frozen spinach, thawed and well drained	1 tablespoon lemon juice

1. In a wok, heat oil over medium-high heat until hot, swirling to coat sides of pan. Add pork and cook, turning, until brown on both sides and cooked through with no trace of pink, 5 to 7 minutes. Remove to a serving platter. Cover with foil to keep warm. Pour off fat from wok.

2. In same wok, heat butter over medium-high heat. Add onion and spinach. Cook, stirring, until onion is softened, 3 to 4 minutes. Add wine and chicken broth. Cook until most of liquid is absorbed, 3 to 4 minutes.

3. Add cream, nutmeg, salt, and pepper. Cook, stirring, until sauce is slightly thickened, 3 to 4 minutes. Add lemon juice. Cook, stirring, 2 minutes. Spoon sauce over meat.

309   PORK WITH SAUTÉED APPLES
Prep: 10 minutes   Cook: 11 to 14 minutes   Serves: 4

1 pound boneless pork loin, trimmed of excess fat	½ cup apple juice
3½ tablespoons peanut oil	¼ cup dry white wine
1 tablespoon minced fresh ginger	2 tablespoons soy sauce
1 garlic clove, minced	1 tablespoon brown sugar
2 Golden Delicious apples, peeled, cored, and sliced	1 tablespoon cornstarch
	½ cup chopped walnuts

1. Cut pork into 2 x ½-inch strips. In a wok, heat 2 tablespoons oil over high heat until hot, swirling to coat sides of pan. Add pork, ginger, and garlic and stir-fry until meat is cooked through and white to the center, 3 to 5 minutes. Remove to a plate. Drain off fat.

2. In same wok, heat remaining 1½ tablespoons oil over medium-high heat. Add apples and cook, stirring, until just tender, about 5 minutes. Add apple juice, wine, soy sauce, and brown sugar. Cook, stirring, 2 minutes.

3. Dissolve cornstarch in ¼ cup cold water and stir into wok. Cook over high heat, stirring, until sauce boils and thickens, 1 to 2 minutes. Return pork to wok. Add walnuts and serve.

310   LAMB CHOPS IN RED WINE SAUCE
Prep: 10 minutes   Cook: 11 to 15 minutes   Serves: 4 to 6

8 loin lamb chops, cut 1 inch thick	2 tablespoons butter
1 teaspoon dried thyme	1 medium carrot, finely diced
¾ teaspoon salt	1 medium leek (white part only), finely diced
¼ teaspoon pepper	1 medium tomato, diced
2 tablespoons olive oil	⅔ cup dry red wine

1. Season lamb chops on both sides with ¾ teaspoon thyme, salt, and pepper. In a wok, heat 1½ tablespoons olive oil over high heat until hot, swirling to coat sides of pan. Add chops, arranging them up sides of wok without overlapping. Cook, turning once, until browned outside but still pink inside (medium rare), 5 to 7 minutes. Remove to a platter. Cover with foil to keep warm. Pour out fat from wok.

2. In wok, melt butter in remaining ½ tablespoon oil over medium-high heat. Add carrot and leek and cook, stirring, until just softened, 3 to 4 minutes. Add tomato and cook 1 minute longer. Pour wine into wok and add remaining ¼ teaspoon thyme. Bring to a boil over high heat, scraping up browned bits from bottom of pan. Boil until reduced by half, 2 to 3 minutes. Pour sauce with vegetables over chops and serve.

311 LEMONY HERBED LAMB CHOPS IN MADEIRA SAUCE
Prep: 5 minutes   Cook: 17 to 20 minutes   Serves: 4

1½ tablespoons herbes de
    Provence
1 teaspoon grated lemon zest
4 shoulder blade lamb chops
    (1¾ pounds)
3 tablespoons olive oil
1 small onion, minced

1 garlic clove, minced
¼ cup dry Madeira
1 (10¼-ounce) can brown
    gravy
2 teaspoons lemon juice
¼ teaspoon pepper

1. Place herbes de Provence and lemon zest in a shallow dish. Coat lamb with mixture, pressing seasoning into meat.

2. In a wok, heat 2 tablespoons olive oil over high heat until hot, swirling to coat sides of pan. Add lamb, arranging chops up sides without overlapping. Cook, turning, until chops are browned on both sides, 4 to 6 minutes. Remove to a plate. Pour off fat.

3. In same wok, heat remaining 1 tablespoon oil over medium-high heat. Add onion and garlic and cook, stirring, until soft, 3 to 4 minutes. Add Madeira and boil until reduced by half, about 2 minutes. Add gravy, lemon juice, and pepper.

4. Return lamb to wok. Bring sauce to a boil. Reduce heat to medium-low and simmer, uncovered, 10 minutes, or until meat is tender.

312 BLUEFISH WITH HONEY-MUSTARD SAUCE
Prep: 10 minutes   Cook: 14 to 19 minutes   Serves: 4

3 tablespoons olive oil
4 bluefish fillets (6 ounces
    each), skin removed
2 leeks (white part only),
    chopped
½ cup dry white wine

¼ cup chicken broth
2 tablespoons honey mustard
½ teaspoon salt
¼ teaspoon pepper
½ cup heavy cream

1. In a wok, heat 1 tablespoon olive oil over medium-high heat until hot, swirling to coat sides of pan. Arrange fillets up sides of wok without overlapping and cook, turning, until opaque in center and cooked through, 6 to 8 minutes. Remove to a platter and cover to keep warm.

2. In same wok, heat remaining 2 tablespoons oil over medium-high heat. Add leeks and cook, stirring, until softened, 3 to 5 minutes.

3. Add wine, chicken broth, mustard, salt, and pepper. Boil, scraping up browned bits from bottom of wok, 3 minutes. Add cream. Cook, stirring, until reduced by half, 2 to 3 minutes. Pour sauce over fish and serve.

313   BLUEFISH IN CLAM SAUCE WITH CAPERS
Prep: 10 minutes   Cook: 11 to 15 minutes   Serves: 4

½ cup flour
½ teaspoon dried oregano
½ teaspoon salt
¼ teaspoon pepper
4 bluefish fillets (6 ounces each)
¼ cup olive oil
1 medium onion, chopped
1 garlic clove, minced

1 medium tomato, chopped
¼ cup pitted black olives, chopped
1 cup dry white wine
½ cup clam juice
1 (6½-ounce) can chopped clams, drained
2 tablespoons capers, drained

1. In a shallow dish, combine flour, oregano, salt, and pepper. Dredge bluefish in seasoned flour to coat lightly on both sides; shake off excess.

2. In a wok, heat 2 tablespoons olive oil over medium-high heat, swirling oil with spatula to coat sides of pan. Add fish, arranging fillets up sides of wok without overlapping. Cook, turning once and rotating as necessary for even cooking, until golden outside and opaque throughout, 6 to 8 minutes. Remove fillets to a platter and cover to keep warm. Remove wok from heat and carefully wipe dry with paper towels.

3. Heat remaining 2 tablespoons oil in wok over high heat. Add onion and garlic and stir-fry until softened, 2 to 3 minutes. Add tomato and olives. Cook, stirring, 1 minute longer.

4. Add wine and clam juice. Bring to a boil and cook over high heat until liquid reduces by one-third, 2 to 3 minutes. Stir in clams and capers. Pour sauce over fish and serve at once.

314   SOUTHERN FRIED CATFISH
Prep: 10 minutes   Cook: 4 to 6 minutes   Serves: 4

¾ cup buttermilk
⅛ teaspoon hot pepper sauce
1 cup yellow cornmeal
½ teaspoon salt
¼ teaspoon cayenne

¼ teaspoon garlic powder
¼ teaspoon celery salt
4 catfish fillets (6 ounces each)
1 cup vegetable oil

1. In a shallow bowl, combine buttermilk and hot sauce. In a shallow dish, combine cornmeal, salt, cayenne, garlic powder, and celery salt. Stir to mix well. Dip catfish into buttermilk and then dredge in seasoned cornmeal to coat both sides; shake off excess.

2. In a wok, heat oil over medium-high heat until temperature measures 350°F on a deep-frying thermometer. Fry catfish, turning once, until golden brown and cooked through, 4 to 6 minutes. Drain on paper towels.

315   CORNMEAL CATFISH WITH MUSTARD WINE SAUCE

Prep: 10 minutes   Cook: 15 to 17 minutes   Serves: 4

2 eggs	3 tablespoons butter
½ cup milk	3 tablespoons vegetable oil
1½ cups yellow cornmeal	1 medium onion, chopped
½ teaspoon salt	¼ cup Dijon mustard
¼ teaspoon pepper	½ cup dry white wine
4 catfish fillets (about 6 ounces each)	½ cup heavy cream

1. In a shallow bowl, mix eggs and milk until blended. In a shallow pan, combine cornmeal, salt, and pepper. Dip fish fillets in egg, then dredge in seasoned cornmeal, shaking off excess.

2. In a wok, melt 2 tablespoons butter in 2 tablespoons oil over medium-high heat, swirling to coat sides of pan. Arrange fillets in pan without overlapping, and cook until golden on bottom, 3 to 4 minutes. Turn and cook until fish is brown on other side, and opaque throughout, 3 to 4 minutes longer. Remove fish to a serving plate and tent with aluminum foil to keep warm.

3. In same wok, heat remaining 1 tablespoon each oil and butter over medium-high heat. Add onion and cook until softened, about 6 minutes. Stir in mustard. Add wine and cream. Bring to a boil, scraping up browned bits from bottom of wok. Cook, stirring, until sauce is slightly thickened, about 3 minutes. Spoon sauce over fish and serve.

316   COD OLÉ

Prep: 5 minutes   Cook: 10 to 13 minutes   Serves: 4

2 tablespoons olive oil	1 (12-ounce) jar salsa
1 medium onion, chopped	1 tablespoon lemon juice
2 celery ribs, sliced	¼ teaspoon black pepper
1 medium green bell pepper, chopped	2 pounds cod fillets, ½ inch thick
¼ cup pitted black olives, sliced	¼ cup chopped cilantro

1. In a wok, heat olive oil over medium-high heat until hot. Add onion, celery, and bell pepper. Cook until softened, 3 to 5 minutes. Stir in olives, salsa, lemon juice, and black pepper. Simmer 3 minutes.

2. Place fish in sauce. Spoon some of sauce over fillets. Reduce heat to medium. Cover and cook until fish is opaque throughout, 4 to 5 minutes. Sprinkle with cilantro and serve.

317 ORANGE-FLAVORED COD WITH MUSHROOMS AND SNOW PEAS

Prep: 10 minutes   Cook: 10 to 13 minutes   Serves: 4

½ cup cornstarch
1 teaspoon grated orange zest
½ teaspoon salt
¼ teaspoon pepper
1 egg
1½ pounds cod fillets
4½ tablespoons olive oil
¼ pound snow peas, stemmed
    and stringed

½ pound mushrooms, sliced
2 scallions, sliced
1 garlic clove, minced
⅓ cup fresh orange juice
1 tablespoon soy sauce
1 teaspoon Asian sesame oil

1. In a shallow dish, combine cornstarch, orange zest, salt, and pepper. In another dish, beat egg until blended. Dip cod fillets in egg, then dredge in seasoned cornstarch to coat both sides; shake off excess.

2. In a wok, heat 1 tablespoon olive oil over high heat until hot. Add snow peas and stir-fry until bright green and crisp-tender, 1 to 2 minutes. Remove to a plate.

3. Add 1½ tablespoons oil to wok and heat over high heat. Add mushrooms, scallions, and garlic and stir-fry until mushrooms are lightly browned, about 3 minutes. Remove to plate with snow peas.

4. Heat remaining 2 tablespoons oil in wok over medium-high heat, swirling to coat sides of pan. Add coated fish fillets, arranging them up sides of wok without overlapping. Fry, turning once, until golden brown on both sides and opaque throughout, 5 to 7 minutes.

5. Return vegetables to wok. Add orange juice, soy sauce, and sesame oil. Cook 1 minute and serve.

318 TUNA FRITTERS WITH TARTAR SAUCE

Prep: 10 minutes   Cook: 8 to 12 minutes   Serves: 4

1¼ cups mayonnaise
¼ cup chopped cilantro or
    parsley
2 tablespoons India relish
1 tablespoon capers, drained
1 (14-ounce) can tuna, drained
    and flaked
¼ cup dried bread crumbs

3 tablespoons sour cream
1 egg, beaten
1 tablespoon Old Bay
    seasoning
½ teaspoon garlic powder
½ teaspoon Chinese hot oil
4 tablespoons butter
¼ cup vegetable oil

1. In a bowl, combine 1 cup mayonnaise, 2 tablespoons cilantro, relish, and capers. Stir until well blended. Set tartar sauce aside.

2. In a large bowl, combine tuna, bread crumbs, remaining ¼ cup mayonnaise, sour cream, egg, remaining 2 tablespoons cilantro, Old Bay seasoning, garlic powder, and hot oil. Blend well.

3. In a wok, heat 2 tablespoons butter and 2 tablespoons oil over medium-high heat until hot, swirling to coat sides of pan. Using half of tuna mixture, drop fritters in by heaping tablespoons and fry, turning once, until golden, 4 to 6 minutes. Drain on paper towels. Repeat procedure with remaining tuna mixture, butter, and oil. Serve with tartar sauce on the side.

319 TUNA BURGERS WITH HORSERADISH-MUSTARD SAUCE

Prep: 10 minutes   Chill: 30 minutes   Cook: 8 to 10 minutes
Serves: 3

These make a great last-minute family supper. To please youngsters, serve with potato chips or French fries and coleslaw, on buns if you like.

1 **(14-ounce) can tuna, drained and flaked**	¼ **teaspoon pepper**
¼ **cup regular or quick oats**	2 **cups dried bread crumbs**
1 **egg**	½ **cup mayonnaise**
1 **small onion, minced**	2 **tablespoons Dijon mustard**
1 **celery rib, minced**	1 **tablespoon prepared white horseradish**
1 **teaspoon dried dill**	3 **tablespoons vegetable oil**
½ **teaspoon salt**	

1. In a medium bowl, combine tuna, oats, egg, onion, celery, dill, salt, and pepper. Mix well. Divide into 6 patties about ½ inch thick. Dredge in bread crumbs to coat and refrigerate 30 minutes.

2. In a small bowl, combine mayonnaise, mustard, and horseradish. Stir to blend well.Set sauce aside.

3. In a wok, heat oil over medium-high heat until hot, swirling to coat sides of pan. Add tuna burgers, extending them up sides of wok, and cook until golden brown on bottom, 4 to 6 minutes. Turn and brown on other side, 4 minutes. Serve with horseradish-mustard sauce on the side.

320   SALMON CAKES

Prep: 10 minutes   Chill: 30 minutes   Cook: 8 to 11 minutes
Serves: 4

Savory salmon croquettes by another name. I like to serve these with baked potatoes and peas and lots of lemon wedges to squeeze onto the salmon cakes.

1 cup flour	1 egg, beaten
1 cup milk	½ cup mayonnaise
2½ cups seasoned dried bread crumbs	2 tablespoons Old Bay seasoning
1½ tablespoons butter	2 tablespoons chopped parsley
1 small onion, minced	2 cups vegetable oil
½ celery rib, minced	
2 (14¾-ounce) cans sockeye salmon, drained and broken into chunks	

1. Place flour in a shallow dish. Pour milk into a bowl. In another shallow dish, place 2 cups seasoned bread crumbs.

2. In a wok, melt butter over medium-high heat. Add onion and celery and cook, stirring, until soft, 4 to 5 minutes. Remove to large bowl and let cool slightly. Wipe out wok.

3. Combine salmon, egg, mayonnaise, remaining ½ cup seasoned bread crumbs, Old Bay seasoning, and parsley with sautéed vegetables in bowl. Mix well. Form salmon mixture into 8 patties about ½ inch thick.

4. Dip each salmon cake into flour, then in milk, and finally in bread crumbs, turning to coat evenly; shake off excess. Place on a wax paper–lined cookie sheet and refrigerate 30 minutes.

5. In a wok, heat oil over medium-high heat until temperature measures 350°F on a deep-frying thermometer. Fry salmon cakes in batches without crowding, until golden on bottom, 3 to 4 minutes. Turn and cook until golden brown on other side, 1 to 2 minutes. Drain on paper towels. Serve hot.

321 SAUTÉED SALMON WITH MUSHROOMS AND GINGER

Prep: 10 minutes   Cook: 15 to 20 minutes   Serves: 4

3 tablespoons vegetable oil
4 salmon fillets, skin removed
   (6 to 8 ounces each)
½ cup dry white wine
¼ pound fresh mushrooms,
   sliced

3 scallions, chopped
2 teaspoons minced fresh
   ginger
2 tablespoons soy sauce,
   preferably mushroom soy
¼ teaspoon pepper

1. In a wok, heat 2 tablespoons oil over medium-high heat until hot, swirling to coat sides of pan. Arrange salmon fillets extending up sides of pan without overlapping. Cook until light brown on bottom, 3 to 5 minutes. Turn and cook until brown on other side, about 3 minutes. Add wine, cover, and cook until fish is opaque in center, about 2 minutes. Remove salmon and liquid to a bowl. Wipe wok dry.

2. In same wok, heat remaining 1 tablespoon oil over medium-high heat. Add mushrooms, scallions, and ginger and cook until mushrooms are tender, 3 to 5 minutes.

3. Add soy sauce, pepper, and liquid from salmon. Scrape up any browned bits from bottom of wok. Cook, stirring, 3 minutes. Return salmon to wok. Cook until heated through, 1 to 2 minutes.

322 SALMON AND POTATOES SIMMERED IN CHAMPAGNE

Prep: 10 minutes   Cook: 24 to 28 minutes   Serves: 4

2 tablespoons vegetable oil
2 tablespoons butter
2 large russet potatoes, peeled
   and thinly sliced
3 shallots, chopped
1 cup champagne or sparkling
   wine

1 cup chicken broth
4 salmon fillets (6 ounces
   each), skin removed
2 tablespoons chopped fresh
   dill or 1½ teaspoons dried
½ teaspoon salt
¼ teaspoon pepper

1. In a wok, heat oil and butter over medium-high heat until hot. Add potatoes and shallots and cook, stirring, until potatoes are translucent, 4 to 6 minutes.

2. Add champagne and chicken broth. Bring to a boil. Reduce heat to medium-low, cover, and cook 10 minutes.

3. Arrange salmon fillets on top of potatoes. Season with dill, salt, and pepper. Cook, covered, until fish is opaque throughout, 10 to 12 minutes.

323   SHARK WITH TEQUILA AND PEPPERS
Prep: 10 minutes   Cook: 16 to 20 minutes   Serves: 4

3½ tablespoons olive oil
4 shark steaks (8 ounces each)
1 small red bell pepper, finely diced
1 small onion, chopped
1 jalapeño pepper, seeded and minced
1 garlic clove, minced

1 large tomato, seeded and diced
¼ cup tomato juice
¼ cup tequila
½ teaspoon salt
¼ teaspoon pepper
¼ cup chopped cilantro

1. In a wok, heat 2 tablespoons olive oil over medium-high heat until hot, swirling to coat sides of pan. Add shark steaks, arranging them up sides of wok so they do not overlap. Cook, turning once, until browned outside and opaque throughout, 10 to 12 minutes. Remove to a serving platter and cover to keep warm.

2. In same wok, heat remaining 1½ tablespoons oil over medium-high heat. Add bell pepper, onion, jalapeño, garlic, and tomato. Cook, stirring, until bell pepper is crisp-tender, 3 to 4 minutes.

3. Add tomato juice, tequila, salt, and pepper. Cook until vegetables are soft, 3 to 4 minutes. Add cilantro and spoon sauce over fish.

324   SHARK FILLETS WITH CITRUS-VERMOUTH SAUCE
Prep: 15 minutes   Cook: 8 to 12 minutes   Serves: 4

¼ cup cornstarch
½ cup sweet vermouth
1 garlic clove, minced
½ teaspoon salt
¼ teaspoon pepper
1½ pounds shark fillets, skin removed, cut into 1-inch chunks
3 tablespoons vegetable oil

⅓ cup orange juice
1 teaspoon grated lime zest
1 teaspoon grated orange zest
Juice of 1 lime
¼ cup chopped flat-leaf parsley
1 seedless orange, peeled and sectioned

1. In a medium bowl, combine cornstarch, ¼ cup vermouth, garlic, salt, and pepper. Stir to blend. Add fish and toss to coat.

2. In a wok, heat oil over high heat until hot, swirling to coat sides of pan. Add shark fillets and cook, turning, until golden outside and just opaque throughout, 4 to 6 minutes. Remove to a serving plate. Tent with foil to keep warm.

3. Add remaining ¼ cup vermouth, orange juice, lime and orange zests, and lime juice to wok. Boil until syrupy, 2 to 3 minutes. Add parsley and orange wedges. Pour sauce over fish and serve.

325   MARYANNE'S CRAB CAKES
Prep: 15 minutes   Chill: 1½ hours   Cook: 6 to 9 minutes   Serves: 6

Maryanne, of Martino Seafood in Philadelphia, offers this fabulous recipe for crab cakes. She stresses the importance of chilling the cakes very well before frying so they will hold together.

2 tablespoons butter
1 small onion, minced
½ small green bell pepper, minced
6 slices of firm-textured white bread, broken into pieces
1 (12-ounce) can evaporated milk
1½ tablespoons mayonnaise

1 pound lump crabmeat, picked over to remove bits of shell and cartilage
Salt and freshly ground pepper
2 cups fine cracker crumbs
2 eggs
2 cups bread crumbs
2½ cups vegetable oil, for frying

1. In a wok, heat butter over medium-high heat until hot. Add onion and bell pepper and cook, stirring, until onion is translucent, 3 to 4 minutes. Remove to a bowl and let cool slightly. Wipe out wok.

2. In a large bowl, combine bread, evaporated milk, and mayonnaise. Blend well to form a paste. Stir in crabmeat, sautéed vegetables, salt, and pepper. Mixture will be soft.

3. Place cracker crumbs in a shallow dish. In a shallow bowl, beat eggs until blended. Place bread crumbs in another shallow dish.

4. Form crab mixture into 6 patties about ¾ inch thick. Dip each cake into cracker crumbs and then in beaten eggs. Dredge in bread crumbs, turning to coat evenly; shake off excess. Place on a wax paper–lined cookie sheet and refrigerate until well chilled, 1½ hours.

5. In a wok, heat oil over medium-high heat until temperature measures 350°F on a deep-frying thermometer. Fry cakes, in batches without crowding, until golden on bottom, 2 to 3 minutes. Turn and cook until golden brown on other side, 1 to 2 minutes. Drain on paper towels. Serve hot.

326   CURRIED COD WITH RAISINS AND CASHEWS

Prep: 10 minutes   Marinate: 1 hour   Cook: 14 to 16 minutes
Serves: 4

¼ cup bottled clam juice
¼ cup lemon juice
2 garlic cloves, minced
1 teaspoon ground cumin
½ teaspoon chili powder
4 cod fillets (6 ounces each)
3 tablespoons vegetable oil

2 onions, thinly sliced
1 tablespoon Madras curry powder
1 cup dry white wine
⅓ cup golden raisins
⅓ cup chopped cashews

1. In a shallow dish, combine clam juice, lemon juice, garlic, cumin, and chili powder. Add cod fillets and turn to coat. Marinate at room temperature 1 hour.

2. In a wok, heat oil over medium-high heat until hot. Add onions and cook, stirring until softened, 3 to 4 minutes. Add curry powder and cook, stirring 1 to 2 minutes.

3. Add wine. Bring to a boil; reduce heat to medium-low. Add marinated fish with liquid and raisins. Cover and cook 10 minutes. Add nuts and serve.

327   MONKFISH WITH SNOW PEAS AND FETA

Prep: 10 minutes   Cook: 7 to 11 minutes   Serves: 6

2 tablespoons olive oil
2 tablespoons butter
3 scallions, chopped
¼ pound snow peas, stemmed and stringed
2 garlic cloves, minced
1½ pounds monkfish, skin removed, cut into 1-inch cubes

1 medium tomato, seeded and chopped
1 cup dry white wine
1½ teaspoons minced fresh oregano or ½ teaspoon dried
¼ teaspoon pepper
1 cup feta cheese, finely crumbled (4 ounces)

1. In a wok, heat 1 tablespoon olive oil and 1 tablespoon butter over medium-high heat until hot. Add scallions, snow peas, and garlic and cook, stirring, until snow peas are bright green and crisp-tender, 1 to 2 minutes. Remove to a plate.

2. In same wok, heat remaining 1 tablespoon oil and 1 tablespoon butter over medium-high heat until hot. Add monkfish and cook, turning, until opaque and cooked through, 6 to 8 minutes. Remove to plate with vegetables.

3. Add tomato, wine, oregano, and pepper to wok and cook, scraping up browned bits from bottom of pan, until liquid is reduced by half, 3 to 4 minutes. Return monkfish and vegetables to wok. Add feta cheese. Cover and cook until cheese melts, 1 to 2 minutes. Serve at once.

328 SAUTÉED FLOUNDER WITH TOMATO AND WHITE WINE

Prep: 7 minutes   Cook: 9 to 13 minutes   Serves: 4

The simple sauce for this dish is light, pleasingly tart, and quite colorful with its flecks of red tomato and green parsley. Serve with steamed rice and buttered asparagus.

½ cup flour
½ teaspoon salt
¼ teaspoon pepper
4 flounder fillets (5 to 6 ounces each)
2 tablespoons olive oil
2 tablespoons butter
2 shallots or 1 small onion, minced

1 small tomato, seeded and finely diced
½ cup dry white wine
1 tablespoon lemon juice
2 tablespoons chopped parsley

1. In a shallow dish, combine flour, salt, and pepper. Dredge fish in seasoned flour to coat both sides; shake off excess.

2. In a wok, heat 1 tablespoon olive oil and 1 tablespoon butter over medium-high heat until hot, swirling to coat sides of pan. Add flounder, arranging fillets up sides of wok without overlapping. Cook, turning once, until golden brown on the outside and opaque throughout, 5 to 7 minutes. Remove to a platter. Cover with foil to keep warm.

3. In same wok, heat remaining 1 tablespoon each oil and butter. Add shallots and cook until softened and fragrant, 1 to 2 minutes (or slightly longer for onion). Add tomato, stirring 1 minute longer.

4. Pour wine and lemon juice into wok. Raise heat to high and boil until sauce is reduced slightly, 2 to 3 minutes. Add parsley, pour over fish, and serve at once.

Chapter 11

Slim Wok Steaming and Poaching

Cooking in a wok does not necessarily require oil, as this chapter proves. Its even heating and high-domed lid make it a perfect steamer, and the large bowl is excellent for poaching. With this light kind of cooking, moisture is sealed in naturally, along with the vitamins and fresh flavors of the food.

A wide variety of seafood, meats, and vegetables can be steamed successfully. Citrus-Steamed Salmon and Snow Peas, Steamed Flounder with Black Beans and Ginger, Steamed Asparagus and Bell Pepper with Ginger Soy Sauce, and Bluefish Steamed with Summer Vegetables and Dill Dressing are just some of the light, flavorful recipes you'll find here.

The technique is to place the food in a heatproof glass baking dish atop a round wire or bamboo rack in the wok. Enough water is added to reach to about 1 inch below the dish. When the water is brought to a boil, the food steams quickly inside the covered wok.

Basic tastes can be enhanced with the addition of cut-up vegetables, such as scallions, leeks, celery, carrots, and mushrooms. When they are available (and affordable), fresh herbs are a lovely touch. A small amount of broth, wine, or citrus or tomato juice added to the baking dish can be spooned over the steamed food as a light sauce.

329 STEAMED CHICKEN BREASTS WITH SCALLIONS AND GINGER

Prep: 10 minutes   Cook: 12 to 15 minutes   Serves: 4

Chicken steamed in a wok emerges moist, juicy, and delicious.

3 scallions, chopped
1 teaspoon minced fresh
    ginger
1 garlic clove, crushed
2 teaspoons dry sherry
2 tablespoons "lite" soy sauce
2 tablespoons orange juice

2 tablespoons apricot nectar
1 teaspoon grated orange zest
¼ teaspoon pepper
4 skinless, boneless chicken
    breast halves (4 to 5
    ounces each)

1. In a small bowl, combine scallions, ginger, garlic, sherry, soy sauce, orange juice, apricot nectar, orange zest, and pepper.

2. Arrange chicken in a single layer in an 8-inch square glass baking dish or a glass pie plate. Pour scallion mixture over chicken. Place dish on a small wire or bamboo rack inside wok. Pour enough water into wok to come to 1 inch below dish. Bring to a boil. Cover and steam over high heat until chicken is tender and white throughout, 12 to 15 minutes.

330 TURKEY STEAMED IN A WOK

Prep: 15 minutes   Cook: 3½ to 4¼ hours   Serves: 8

1 small turkey, preferably
    fresh (about 8 pounds)
1 onion, quartered
1 carrot, quartered
¼ cup honey
2 garlic cloves, crushed

2 tablespoons lime juice
1 teaspoon dried oregano
½ teaspoon salt
¼ teaspoon pepper
1 cup dry white wine
    About 1 quart chicken broth

1. Rinse and dry turkey. Place onion and carrot inside cavity.

2. In small bowl, combine honey, garlic, lime juice, oregano, salt, and pepper. Brush mixture over turkey skin. Tie legs together. Place turkey, breast side up, on a wire rack small enough to fit in wok.

3. Pour wine and 2 cups chicken broth into wok. Over high heat, bring to a boil. Reduce heat to medium-low. Cover and cook, basting every 30 minutes with pan liquids, 3½ to 4¼ hours, until juices run clear when thigh is pricked near bone. Add more chicken broth as necessary to keep liquid at same level.

4. Remove turkey to a cutting board. Let rest 10 to 15 minutes before carving. Strain cooking liquid. Spoon over sliced turkey.

331 DILLED POACHED CHICKEN WITH WINE, CARROTS, AND LEEKS

Prep: 7 minutes   Cook: 41 minutes   Serves: 4

3 medium carrots, peeled and cut into 1-inch pieces
2 medium leeks (white part only), coarsely chopped
4 chicken breast halves bone in (6 to 8 ounces each), skin removed
1½ teaspoons salt
½ teaspoon white pepper
2¼ cups dry white wine
2 tablespoons chopped fresh dill or 2 teaspoons dried
2 tablespoons chopped parsley
1 tablespoon cornstarch

1. Place carrots and leeks in a wok. Arrange chicken breasts on top of vegetables. Season with salt and pepper. Add 2 cups wine and 4 cups cold water. Bring to a boil.

2. Add dill and parsley. Reduce heat to low, partially cover, and simmer until chicken is tender, about 40 minutes. With a flat strainer or slotted spoon, remove chicken and vegetables to a serving platter.

3. Skim off any fat on surface of broth in wok. Dissolve cornstarch in remaining ¼ cup wine. Stir into wok. Bring to a boil over high heat and cook, stirring, until sauce boils and thickens, 1 to 2 minutes. Pour over chicken and serve.

332 BLUEFISH STEAMED WITH SUMMER VEGETABLES AND DILL DRESSING

Prep: 10 minutes   Cook: 8 to 10 minutes   Serves: 4

2 tablespoons lemon juice
2 shallots, minced
2 garlic cloves, crushed
1 tablespoon Dijon mustard
1 tablespoon chopped fresh dill
¼ cup olive oil
4 bluefish fillets (6 ounces each)
1 large ripe tomato, seeded and chopped
1 medium green bell pepper, chopped
1 medium red onion, chopped

1. In a small bowl, combine lemon juice, shallots, garlic, mustard, and dill. Whisk in olive oil until well blended. Set dill dressing aside.

2. Arrange bluefish fillets in a 9-inch square glass baking dish or a glass pie plate. Top with tomato, bell pepper, and onion. Pour dill dressing over fish. Place dish on a small wire or bamboo rack inside wok. Pour enough water into wok to come to 1 inch below rack. Bring to a boil. Cover and continue boiling until bluefish is opaque and cooked through, 8 to 10 minutes.

333 BARBARA'S BLUEFISH WITH AVOCADO MAYONNAISE

Prep: 10 minutes   Cook: 10 to 12 minutes   Serves: 4

My sister Barbara often picks up a take-out dinner on her way home from work in New York. When she does want to cook, the choice is usually simple and fish. This is her recipe adapted for the wok.

1 cup orange juice	1 teaspoon grated orange zest
¼ cup Italian dressing	½ teaspoon garlic powder
2 tablespoons light soy sauce	½ teaspoon onion salt
1 small ripe avocado	Freshly ground pepper
½ cup mayonnaise	4 bluefish fillets (6 ounces
¼ cup grated Parmesan cheese	each), skin removed
1 tablespoon Dijon mustard	

1. In a small bowl, combine orange juice, Italian dressing, and soy sauce; set aside.

2. Split avocado in half lengthwise; remove pit. Scoop out avocado from skin and place in another bowl. Mash with a fork. Add mayonnaise, Parmesan cheese, Dijon mustard, orange zest, garlic powder, onion salt, and pepper to avocado. Blend to form a paste.

3. Place bluefish in a 9-inch square glass baking dish or a glass pie plate. Spread avocado mixture over fish. Place dish on a round wire or bamboo rack inside wok. Pour orange juice mixture around fish in dish. Pour enough water into wok to reach to 1 inch below dish. Bring to a boil, cover, and steam over high heat until bluefish is opaque throughout, 10 to 12 minutes.

334 STEAMED COD WITH ZUCCHINI, PARSLEY, AND LEMON

Prep: 10 minutes   Cook: 6 to 8 minutes   Serves: 4

¼ cup chopped flat-leaf parsley	½ teaspoon salt
4 shallots, finely chopped	¼ teaspoon pepper
1 garlic clove, minced	3 tablespoons olive oil
1 tablespoon lemon juice	4 cod fillets (6 ounces each)
1 teaspoon grated lemon zest	1 medium zucchini, thinly sliced

1. In a medium bowl, combine parsley, shallots, garlic, lemon juice, lemon zest, salt, and pepper. Whisk in olive oil until blended.

2. Arrange fish in a 9-inch square glass baking dish or a glass pie plate. Top with zucchini slices. Spoon parsley mixture over fillets.

3. Place baking dish on a small wire or bamboo rack inside wok. Pour water into wok to come to 1 inch below dish. Bring to a boil. Cover wok and steam until fish is opaque in center and cooked through, 6 to 8 minutes.

335 STEAMED COD WITH HORSERADISH MAYONNAISE

Prep: 5 minutes   Cook: 10 to 12 minutes   Serves: 4

Horseradish flavored mayonnaise adds a piquancy to the mild-mannered cod. To keep calories and fat way down, use no-cholesterol mayonnaise and nonfat yogurt.

¼ **cup mayonnaise**
3 **tablespoons plain yogurt**
1½ **tablespoons prepared white horseradish**
1½ **tablespoons Dijon mustard**
¼ **teaspoon Worcestershire sauce**

3 **scallions, minced**
½ **teaspoon salt**
¼ **teaspoon pepper**
1½ **pounds cod fillets, cut into 4 equal pieces**

1. In a small bowl, combine mayonnaise, yogurt, horseradish, Dijon mustard, Worcestershire sauce, scallions, salt, and pepper. Mix to blend well.

2. Place cod in a 9-inch square glass baking dish or a glass pie plate. Spread horseradish mayonnaise over fish. Place dish on a round wire or bamboo rack inside wok. Pour enough water into wok to reach to 1 inch below rack. Bring to a boil, cover, and steam over high heat until cod is opaque throughout, 10 to 12 minutes.

336 STEAMED FLOUNDER WITH BLACK BEANS AND GINGER

Prep: 10 minutes   Cook: 8 to 10 minutes   Serves: 4

4 **flounder fillets (8 ounces each)**
3 **scallions, chopped**
2 **tablespoons Chinese fermented black beans, rinsed and drained**
1 **garlic clove, minced**

1 **teaspoon minced fresh ginger**
¼ **cup chicken broth**
1½ **tablespoons soy sauce**
2 **teaspoons Asian sesame oil**
¼ **teaspoon crushed hot red pepper**

1. Place fillets in an 8-inch square glass baking dish or a glass pie plate. Scatter scallions, black beans, garlic, and ginger over fish.

2. In a small bowl, combine chicken broth, soy sauce, sesame oil, and hot pepper. Pour over fish.

3. Place baking dish on a small wire or bamboo rack inside wok. Pour enough water into wok to come to 1 inch below dish. Bring to a boil. Cover and steam over high heat until fish is opaque and cooked through, 8 to 10 minutes.

337   CITRUS-STEAMED SALMON AND SNOW PEAS

Prep: 10 minutes   Cook: 8 to 10 minutes   Serves: 4

4 salmon fillets, skin removed
  (about 6 ounces each)
¼ pound fresh snow peas,
  stemmed and stringed
2 shallots, minced
¼ cup orange juice

¼ cup lemon juice
1 tablespoon chopped fresh
  dill or 1 teaspoon dried
1 teaspoon grated lemon zest
½ teaspoon salt
¼ teaspoon white pepper

1. Place salmon fillets in an 8-inch square glass baking dish or a glass pie plate. Scatter snow peas and shallots on top.

2. In a small bowl, combine orange juice, lemon juice, dill, lemon zest, salt, and white pepper. Pour over fish.

3. Place baking dish on a small wire or bamboo rack inside wok. Pour enough water into wok to come to 1 inch below dish. Bring to a boil. Cover and steam over high heat until fish is opaque and cooked through, 8 to 10 minutes.

338   STEAMED SWORDFISH WITH HONEY-MUSTARD SAUCE

Prep: 10 minutes   Cook: 16 to 21 minutes   Serves: 4

2 swordfish steaks, cut ¾ inch
  thick (about 12 ounces
  each), divided in half
3 scallions, sliced
¼ cup chopped parsley
½ cup dry white wine
1 tablespoon butter
1 tablespoon vegetable oil

1 leek (white part only),
  cleaned well, chopped
½ cup heavy cream
¼ cup chicken broth
¼ cup honey mustard
2 tablespoons capers, drained
½ teaspoon salt
¼ teaspoon pepper

1. Place steaks in an 8-inch square glass baking dish or a glass pie plate. Top with scallions and parsley. Pour wine over fish.

2. Place baking dish on a small wire or bamboo rack in wok. Pour enough water into wok to come to 1 inch below dish. Bring to a boil. Cover and simmer over high heat until fish is opaque and cooked through, 10 to 12 minutes. Remove swordfish and baking dish from heat. Reserve fish liquid in dish. Pour out water from wok and wipe dry.

3. In same wok, heat butter and oil over medium-high heat until hot. Add leek and cook, stirring, until soft, 3 to 5 minutes. Add cream, chicken broth, mustard, and reserved fish liquid from baking dish. Bring to a boil and cook, stirring, until reduced by half, 2 to 3 minutes. Add capers, salt, and pepper. Cook 1 minute. Place swordfish on a serving platter. Pour sauce over fish and serve.

339 STEAMED ASPARAGUS AND BELL PEPPER WITH GINGER SOY SAUCE

Prep: 10 minutes   Cook: 4 to 6 minutes   Serves: 4

¼ cup orange juice
2 tablespoons soy sauce
1 garlic clove, minced
1 teaspoon minced fresh ginger
½ teaspoon Asian sesame oil

¼ teaspoon pepper
½ pound asparagus, preferably thin, tough ends removed
1 medium red bell pepper, cut into ¼-inch-wide strips

1. In a small bowl, combine orange juice, soy sauce, garlic, ginger, sesame oil, and pepper; set aside.

2. Arrange asparagus and bell pepper in an 8-inch square glass baking dish or a glass pie plate. Place dish on a small wire or bamboo rack inside wok. Pour enough water into wok to reach to 1 inch below rack. Bring to a boil, cover and steam over high heat until vegetables are tender, 4 to 6 minutes. Serve sauce on the side for dipping.

340 STEAMED POTATOES WITH LEMON BUTTER

Prep: 5 minutes   Cook: 15 to 20 minutes   Serves: 4

1 pound small red potatoes, scrubbed
3 tablespoons butter
1 tablespoon lemon juice

2 teaspoons minced fresh dill or ¾ teaspoon dried
¼ teaspoon salt
⅛ teaspoon pepper

1. Place potatoes in an 8- or 9-inch square glass baking dish or a glass pie plate. Place dish on a round wire or bamboo rack inside wok. Pour enough water into wok to reach to 1 inch below rack. Bring to a boil, cover, and steam over high heat until potatoes are tender, 15 to 20 minutes.

2. About 5 minutes before potatoes are done, melt butter in a small glass bowl in a microwave oven or in a butter melter or small saucepan on top of stove over medium-low heat. Stir in lemon juice, dill, salt, and pepper.

3. When potatoes are done, turn them into a serving bowl. Pour lemon-dill butter over hot potatoes, toss, and serve.

Chapter 12

Wok Desserts

You wouldn't think twice about whipping up a dessert in a saucepan or skillet, so why not in the all-purpose wok? Here are poached fruits, fried pastries, steamed, sautéed, and stewed desserts—all guaranteed to garner the sweetest praise.

Carrot Cake and old-fashioned Chocolate and Vanilla Custard, which are ordinarily baked in the oven, are set in a pan on a rack inside the wok and steamed over boiling water. A luscious assortment of fruits is prepared every which way. There are Pear Mascarpone Pancakes, Peaches with Brandied Custard Sauce, Sautéed Apples in Butterscotch Sauce, and Poached Ruby Apples and Raspberries, to name just a few. And whatever you do, don't miss Cocoa Fudge Pudding Cake—one of those kids-of-all-ages crowd pleasers.

For fried pastries, the wok turns into the perfect deep fryer, with plenty of room for uncrowded, nongreasy frying. One of my favorite easy recipes transforms store-bought refrigerated biscuits into Easy Jelly Donuts.

A lot of people think dessert is the best part of the meal. After trying these recipes in the wok, I hope you will feel they are just about the easiest part as well.

---

341 CRUNCHY CANDIED ALMONDS
Prep: 10 minutes   Cook: 7 to 10 minutes   Serves: 4

2 tablespoons unsalted butter	1 teaspoon almond extract
2 tablespoons peanut oil	1 teaspoon cinnamon
½ cup packed brown sugar	½ teaspoon grated nutmeg
2 tablespoons light corn syrup	2 teaspoons grated orange zest
¼ cup amaretto liqueur	2 cups shelled whole almonds

1. In a wok, melt butter in oil over medium-high heat. Add brown sugar and corn syrup and cook until sugar is smooth and syrupy in consistency, 3 to 5 minutes.

2. Add amaretto, almond extract, cinnamon, nutmeg, and orange zest. Cook, stirring, 2 minutes.

3. Add almonds and cook, stirring, 2 minutes longer.

342   SAUTÉED APPLES IN BUTTERSCOTCH SAUCE

Prep: 10 minutes   Cook: 9 to 12 minutes   Serves: 6

Serve these flavorful apples warm in their sauce, or let cool and spoon over vanilla ice cream.

5 tablespoons unsalted butter	1 teaspoon cinnamon
½ cup packed brown sugar	½ teaspoon grated nutmeg
3 medium apples, peeled, cored, and sliced	¾ cup heavy cream
	1 teaspoon vanilla extract

1. In a wok, combine 3 tablespoons butter and 3 tablespoons brown sugar, cook over medium-low heat, stirring until sugar dissolves. Add apples, cinnamon, and nutmeg. Cook, stirring, until apples are just tender, 5 to 6 minutes. Remove to a plate.

2. In same wok, combine remaining 2 tablespoons butter and 5 tablespoons brown sugar. Cook over medium-low heat, stirring, until sugar dissolves, 2 to 3 minutes.

3. Add cream and vanilla. Raise heat to medium-high. Bring to a boil. Cook, stirring, until slightly thickened, 2 to 3 minutes. Remove to a bowl and let sauce cool to room temperature.

4. To serve, place sautéed apples in dessert bowls. Top with some of butterscotch sauce.

343   GINGER APPLE PEAR SAUCE

Prep: 10 minutes   Cook: 13 to 15 minutes   Serves: 4

3 medium Bartlett pears, peeled, cored, and cut into ½-inch cubes	¼ cup apple juice
	¼ cup honey
	¼ cup sugar
3 medium McIntosh apples, peeled, cored, and cut into ½-inch cubes	2 teaspoons minced fresh ginger
	½ teaspoon grated nutmeg
½ cup pear nectar	

1. In a wok, combine pears, apples, pear nectar, and apple juice. Cover and cook over medium heat until fruit is just tender, 8 to 10 minutes.

2. Add honey, sugar, ginger, and nutmeg. Cook, stirring, 5 minutes. Remove from heat, spoon into a serving dish, cool, and refrigerate.

344   CHUNKY THREE-APPLE APPLESAUCE
Prep: 10 minutes   Cook: 15 to 17 minutes   Serves: 4

2 medium Granny Smith
   apples, peeled, cored,
   and cut into ½-inch cubes
2 medium Red Delicious
   apples, peeled, cored,
   and cut into ½-inch cubes
2 medium Golden Delicious
   apples, peeled, cored,
   and cut into ½-inch cubes

⅔ cup apple juice
2 teaspoons cinnamon
1 teaspoon grated orange zest
½ cup packed brown sugar

1. In a wok, combine all three kinds of apples with apple juice, cinnamon, orange zest, and ½ cup water. Simmer, stirring, 5 minutes.

2. Add brown sugar, cover, and continue to simmer until apples are tender, 10 to 12 minutes. Remove to a bowl, let cool, and refrigerate.

345   APPLE FRITTERS
Prep: 10 minutes   Cook: 2 to 4 minutes per batch   Serves: 4 to 6

1⅓ cups flour
3   tablespoons sugar
1½ teaspoons baking powder
1   teaspoon cinnamon
½   cup apple cider
2   eggs, lightly beaten
2   tablespoons butter, melted

1   tablespoon apple cider
    vinegar
4   medium apples, peeled,
    cored, and cut into ¼-inch
    slices
2½ cups vegetable oil, for frying

1. In a large bowl, combine flour, sugar, baking powder, cinnamon, apple cider, eggs, melted butter, and vinegar. Mix well to form a smooth batter.

2. In a wok, heat oil over medium-high heat until temperature measures 350°F on a deep-frying thermometer. Working in batches, dip apple slices into batter, coating well, and lower carefully into wok. Fry until golden on bottom, 1 to 2 minutes. Turn and cook until light brown on other side, 1 to 2 minutes. Remove with a slotted spoon and drain on paper towels. Repeat with remaining apples and batter, adding more oil, if necessary, to maintain level.

346   SWEET SPICED STEWED APPLES
Prep: 10 minutes   Cook: 12 to 16 minutes   Serves: 4

2 tablespoons unsalted butter
2 pounds (5 medium) apples,
     peeled, cored, and cut
     into ½-inch chunks
⅓ cup packed brown sugar
1 tablespoon lemon juice

1 teaspoon grated lemon zest
1 teaspoon cinnamon
½ teaspoon grated nutmeg
½ teaspoon ground cloves
½ teaspoon mace

1. In a wok, melt butter over medium heat. Cook apples, stirring frequently, until softened, 6 to 8 minutes.

2. Add brown sugar, lemon juice, lemon zest, cinnamon, nutmeg, cloves, and mace. Cook over medium-high heat, stirring, until brown sugar is syrupy in consistency, 6 to 8 minutes.

347   CANDIED BRANDIED APPLES
Prep: 5 minutes   Stand: 30 minutes   Cook: 10 to 12 minutes
Serves: 4

½ cup golden raisins
¼ cup Calvados or apple
     brandy
¼ cup orange juice
4 tablespoons unsalted butter
3 medium Golden Delicious
     apples, peeled, cored,
     and sliced

⅓ cup packed brown sugar
1 teaspoon cinnamon
½ teaspoon grated nutmeg

1. In a small bowl, combine raisins with Calvados and orange juice. Let stand for 30 minutes.

2. In a wok, heat butter over medium heat until hot. Add apples and cook, stirring, until crisp-tender, 4 to 5 minutes.

3. Add brown sugar, cinnamon, and nutmeg. Cook, stirring, until sauce is syrupy in consistency, 4 to 5 minutes. Add raisin-Calvados mixture. Cook 2 minutes and serve.

348 POACHED RUBY APPLES AND RASPBERRIES

Prep: 10 minutes   Cook: 18 to 20 minutes   Serves: 4

End the meal with this elegant light dessert.

1 **cup dry red wine**
¼ **cup orange juice**
¼ **cup Chambord liqueur**
¼ **cup sugar**
1 **teaspoon cinnamon**
1 **teaspoon grated orange zest**

4 **medium Golden Delicious apples, peeled, cored, and sliced**
½ **cup fresh or frozen raspberries**

1. In a wok, combine wine, orange juice, Chambord, sugar, cinnamon, orange zest, and 1 cup water. Bring to a boil.

2. Add apples and return to a boil. Reduce heat to low; cover and cook until apples are tender, about 10 minutes. With a slotted spoon, remove apples to a bowl.

3. Raise heat to high. Boil until liquid is slightly thickened and syrupy, 6 to 8 minutes. Return apples to wok. Add raspberries. Cook 2 minutes. Remove from heat and cool. Serve at room temperature or cold.

349 BANANAS AND ALMONDS IN RUM-CREAM SAUCE

Prep: 5 minutes   Cook: 7 to 9 minutes   Serves: 6

3 **tablespoons granulated sugar**
5 **tablespoons unsalted butter**
3 **bananas, cut into ½-inch slices**
2 **tablespoons slivered almonds**

¼ **cup packed brown sugar**
2 **tablespoons dark rum**
2 **tablespoons banana liqueur**
½ **teaspoon almond extract**
⅓ **cup heavy cream**

1. In a wok, cook granulated sugar and 3 tablespoons butter over medium-low heat, stirring until sugar dissolves. Add bananas and cook, stirring gently, until just tender but still firm, 2 to 3 minutes. Add almonds. Cook 1 minute. Remove to a plate.

2. In same wok, combine remaining 2 tablespoons butter and brown sugar. Cook over medium-low heat, stirring, until brown sugar dissolves, 2 to 3 minutes.

3. Add rum, banana liqueur, and almond extract. Raise heat to medium. Cook 2 minutes. Whisk in cream.

4. To serve, place bananas in dessert bowls. Top with some of rum-cream sauce. Serve warm or chilled.

350 WALNUT BUTTERMILK BLINI WITH ORANGE BUTTER

Prep: 5 minutes   Cook: 12 to 15 minutes   Serves: 4

2 eggs	¼ cup regular or quick oats
⅓ cup sugar	2 teaspoons baking powder
1 stick (4 ounces) unsalted butter, melted	½ cup chopped toasted walnuts
1¼ cups buttermilk	About ½ cup vegetable oil
¼ cup orange juice	⅓ cup orange marmalade
1 teaspoon vanilla extract	1 teaspoon grated orange zest
1½ cups flour	

1. In a medium bowl, combine eggs and sugar. Whisk until well blended. Beat in 3 tablespoons melted butter, buttermilk, orange juice, and vanilla.

2. Add flour, oats, and baking powder. Mix until just combined. Stir in walnuts.

3. In a wok, heat 3 tablespoons oil over medium-high heat until hot, swirling to coat sides of pan. Drop in about one-third of batter by heaping tablespoons without crowding. Cook until blini are golden on bottom, 2 to 3 minutes. Turn and brown on other side, about 2 minutes. Remove from wok and place on warmed serving plate. Repeat procedure 2 times with remaining batter and oil.

4. In a small bowl, combine remaining 5 tablespoons melted butter with orange marmalade and orange zest. Whisk until sauce is well blended. Serve with warm blini.

351 PEACH ORANGE ALMOND SAUCE

Prep: 10 minutes   Cook: 15 to 18 minutes   Serves: 4

Dried peaches add thickness as well as flavor to this delicious double-duty sauce. Warm, it is ideal with fresh fruit or berries. Cold, it's fabulous over ice cream.

1½ cups dried peaches, chopped	¼ cup amaretto liqueur
1 seedless orange, peeled and chopped	½ cup sugar
	½ cup heavy cream
½ cup peach nectar	½ cup slivered almonds

1. In a wok, combine dried peaches, chopped orange, peach nectar, amaretto, and sugar. Cook over medium heat until thick, 12 to 15 minutes.

2. Add cream and cook, stirring, until reduced slightly, about 3 minutes. Add nuts. Serve warm or transfer to a bowl and let cool, then cover and refrigerate until chilled.

352   STEAMED CARROT CAKE

Prep: 10 minutes   Cook: 65 to 70 minutes   Serves: 6 to 8

2 eggs
½ cup granulated sugar
½ cup vegetable oil
½ pound carrots, grated (about
    1½ cups)
1 cup flour
1 teaspoon baking powder
½ teaspoon baking soda

1 teaspoon cinnamon
¼ teaspoon grated nutmeg
¼ teaspoon mace
½ (8-ounce) can unsweetened
    crushed pineapple,
    drained
Powdered sugar, for dusting

1. In an electric mixer, beat eggs, sugar, and oil on medium speed, until light, 2 to 3 minutes. Add carrots and mix 1 minute.

2. Add flour, baking powder, baking soda, cinnamon, nutmeg, and mace. Mix until just combined. Stir in pineapple. Spread batter into a greased 8-inch round cake pan.

3. Place a round wire or bamboo rack in a wok. Put filled cake pan on rack. Pour boiling water into wok to reach halfway up sides of baking pan. Over low heat, steam, covered, until cake is cooked through but still moist, 65 to 70 minutes. A toothpick inserted in center will not be completely dry and top should look shiny and feel slightly sticky. Remove baking dish from rack. Let cool to room temperature. Sprinkle with powdered sugar.

353   CHILLED RASPBERRY PLUM SOUP

Prep: 10 minutes   Cook: 15 minutes   Serves: 4

If you've never savored cold fruit soup, try this one. The fresh fruit flavor really comes through. If raspberries are unavailable, substitute strawberries and strawberry vinegar.

1½ pounds small purple plums,
    halved and pitted
1 pint fresh or frozen
    raspberries
½ cup fruity red wine, such as
    Beaujolais
⅓ cup honey

½ teaspoon cinnamon
¼ teaspoon ground ginger
2 cups buttermilk
1 tablespoon raspberry
    vinegar
2 tablespoons lime juice

1. In a wok, cook plums and raspberries over low heat, covered, for 5 minutes. Add wine, honey, cinnamon, and ginger. Cook 10 minutes. Remove from heat and pour fruit and liquid into a bowl; let cool slightly.

2. Blend or process mixture. Strain into a large bowl through a fine sieve to remove seeds and skins.

3. Whisk in buttermilk, vinegar, and lime juice. Cover and refrigerate several hours, or until chilled, before serving.

354 COCOA FUDGE PUDDING CAKE
Prep: 10 minutes   Cook: 20 to 25 minutes   Serves: 6 to 8

This cake is pure magic. While cooking, two layers form; the top is cake-like, and the bottom becomes a gooey fudge sauce. Make sure to spoon some of the sauce over each portion of cake.

1 cup strong brewed coffee
¾ cup granulated sugar
¼ cup plus 3 tablespoons unsweetened cocoa powder
1 egg
½ cup packed brown sugar

4 tablespoons unsalted butter, melted
⅓ cup heavy cream
1 teaspoon vanilla extract
¾ cup flour
1½ teaspoons baking powder

1. Grease bottom and sides of an 8-inch square baking pan.

2. In a medium bowl, combine coffee, granulated sugar, and ¼ cup cocoa. Whisk until well blended.

3. In a large bowl, combine egg, brown sugar, melted butter, cream, and vanilla. Blend well. Add flour, remaining 3 tablespoons cocoa, and baking powder. Pour into prepared pan. Top with coffee mixture.

4. Place a round wire or bamboo rack in a wok. Put filled baking pan on rack. Pour boiling water into wok to reach halfway up sides of baking pan. Cover and cook over low heat until toothpick inserted in top half of cake comes out clean, 20 to 25 minutes. Remove baking dish from rack. Serve warm, spooning fudge sauce over cake.

355 EASY JELLY DONUTS
Prep: 5 minutes   Cook: 6 to 8 minutes   Serves: 5

1 (7½-ounce) can refrigerator biscuits
½ (10-ounce) jar cherry preserves

2½ cups vegetable oil, for frying
Powdered sugar, for dusting

1. Separate biscuits. Make a deep slit in the side of each biscuit with a paring knife. Place preserves in a pastry bag fitted with a ½-inch round tip. Insert tip into opening and squeeze to fill lightly. If pastry tip is unavailable, insert preserves with a teaspoon. Pinch to seal opening.

2. In a wok, heat 4 inches of oil over medium-high heat until temperature reaches 350°F on a deep-frying thermometer. Carefully lower half of donuts into hot oil and cook until golden on one side, 2 to 3 minutes. Turn donuts over and cook until brown on other side, about 1 minute. Remove from wok with slotted spoon or skimmer and drain on paper towels; let cool. Repeat with remaining donuts. Sprinkle powdered sugar over donuts before serving.

356   FILLED STRAWBERRY PUFFS
Prep: 10 minutes   Cook: 6 to 8 minutes   Serves: 5

½ cup sugar
2 teaspoons cinnamon
1 (7½-ounce) can refrigerator
   biscuits

½ cup strawberry preserves
2½ cups vegetable oil, for frying

1. In a small bowl, combine sugar and cinnamon; set aside.

2. Roll out biscuits into 3-inch circles. Place 2 teaspoons strawberry preserves on bottom half of each circle. Fold top over to enclose filling and form half circles. Pinch edges to seal.

3. In a wok, heat 4 inches oil over medium-high heat until temperature reaches 350°F on a deep-frying thermometer. Carefully lower half of filled biscuits into hot oil and cook until golden on bottom, 2 to 3 minutes. Turn and cook until brown on other side, about 1 minute. Remove from wok with a slotted spoon or skimmer and drain on paper towels. Repeat with remaining biscuits. Sprinkle puffs with cinnamon-sugar and serve while still warm.

357   PINEAPPLE FRITTERS WITH RASPBERRY SAUCE
Prep: 10 minutes   Cook: 6 to 8 minutes   Serves: 5

1 (10-ounce) package frozen
   raspberries with juice
¼ cup raspberry preserves
2 tablespoons framboise or
   Chambord
2 tablespoons orange juice

1 (7½-ounce) can refrigerator
   biscuits
½ cup unsweetened crushed
   pineapple, drained
2½ cups vegetable oil, for frying
   Powdered sugar, for dusting

1. In a blender or food processor, puree raspberries, raspberry preserves, framboise, and orange juice until smooth. If desired, strain through a sieve into a medium bowl to remove seeds. Set the sauce aside.

2. Roll out biscuits into 3-inch circles. Place 2 teaspoons crushed pineapple on bottom half of each circle. Fold top over to enclose filling and form half circles. Pinch edges to seal.

3. In a wok, heat oil over medium-high heat until temperature reaches 350°F on a deep-frying thermometer. Carefully lower half of filled biscuits into hot oil and cook until golden on bottom, 2 to 3 minutes. Turn and cook until brown on other side, about 1 minute. Remove from wok with slotted spoon or skimmer and drain on paper towels. Repeat with remaining biscuits. Sprinkle with powdered sugar.

4. To serve, place 2 warm fritters on each dessert plate. Drizzle on some of raspberry sauce. Pass remainder on the side.

358   BRANDIED STEWED FRESH AND DRIED FRUIT

Prep: 5 minutes   Cook: 14 to 17 minutes   Serves: 4

1 (18-ounce) jar brandied
  cherries, liquid reserved
½ cup orange juice
⅓ cup packed brown sugar
1 teaspoon cinnamon
1 teaspoon grated orange zest
1 seedless orange, peeled and
  cut into ¼-inch slices

1 apple, peeled, cored, and cut
  into ¼-inch slices
1 cup pitted prunes
1 cup dried apricots
½ cup raisins

1. In a wok, combine reserved brandied cherry liquid, orange juice, brown sugar, cinnamon, and orange zest. Bring to a boil.

2. Add sliced orange, apple, prunes, apricots, and raisins. Reduce heat to medium-low. Cook until fruit is tender and liquid has reduced slightly, 12 to 15 minutes. Add cherries. Cook 2 minutes.

3. Transfer to a bowl or container and let cool, then cover and refrigerate. Serve chilled.

359   FIVE-FRUIT SAUCE

Prep: 10 minutes   Cook: 12 to 14 minutes   Serves: 6

Cranberry, orange, apple, pear, and lemon team up in this zippy confection. I like to serve it over pure rich vanilla ice cream. It's great as a side dish for pork and poultry as well.

¾ cup sugar
⅓ cup orange marmalade
1 teaspoon cinnamon
½ teaspoon ground ginger
¼ teaspoon mace
3 cups fresh or frozen
  cranberries
1 seedless orange, peeled and
  coarsely chopped

1 medium tart-sweet apple,
  peeled, cored, and
  coarsely chopped
1 medium pear, peeled,
  cored, and coarsely
  chopped
1 teaspoon grated lemon zest
1 lemon, peeled, seeded, and
  coarsely chopped

1. In a wok, combine sugar, marmalade, cinnamon, ginger, mace, and 2 cups water. Bring to a boil over high heat. Cook 2 minutes.

2. Add cranberries, orange, apple, pear, lemon zest, and chopped lemon. Reduce heat to medium-low, cover, and cook until cranberry skins pop and fruit is tender, 10 to 12 minutes. Serve at room temperature or chilled.

360 PEAR MASCARPONE PANCAKES

Prep: 10 minutes   Cook: 15 to 18 minutes   Serves: 4

Mascarpone cheese is a rich Italian cream cheese whose consistency is a cross between cream cheese and sour cream. It is available at Italian markets and some specialty food stores. Ripe Bosc or Bartletts would be excellent choices for the pear in this recipe.

4 ounces mascarpone cheese
    or cream cheese, softened
½ cup sour cream
2 tablespoons sugar
2 eggs
2 tablespoons unsalted butter,
    melted and cooled
1 teaspoon vanilla extract

1 pear, peeled, cored, and
    finely chopped
½ cup flour
1 teaspoon baking powder
½ teaspoon cinnamon
½ cup plus 1 tablespoon
    vegetable oil

1. In a large bowl, combine mascarpone cheese, sour cream, sugar, eggs, butter, and vanilla. Whisk until well blended and smooth. Mix in pear. Stir in flour, baking powder, and cinnamon until just combined.

2. In a wok, heat 3 tablespoons oil over medium-high heat until hot, swirling to coat sides of pan. Drop in about one-third of batter by tablespoons. Fry until golden on bottom, 3 to 4 minutes. Turn and cook until brown on other side, about 2 minutes. Remove from wok with a slotted spatula and drain on paper towels. Repeat procedure 2 times with remaining cheese mixture and oil. Serve pancakes hot.

361 BLUEBERRY CORNMEAL PANCAKES

Prep: 10 minutes   Cook: 15 to 18 minutes   Serves: 6

1¼ cups flour
¾ cup yellow cornmeal
2 teaspoons baking powder
½ teaspoon baking soda
⅓ cup sugar
1 teaspoon grated lemon zest
1½ cups buttermilk

3 tablespoons butter, melted
    and cooled
2 eggs, lightly beaten
1 cup fresh or frozen
    blueberries
Corn oil, for frying

1. In a large bowl, combine flour, cornmeal, baking powder, baking soda, sugar, and lemon zest.

2. In a medium bowl, mix together buttermilk, cooled melted butter, and eggs. Add liquid mixture to dry ingredients. Stir just until combined. Fold in blueberries.

3. In a wok, heat 3 tablespoons oil over medium-high heat until hot, swirling to coat sides of pan. Drop in about one-fourth of batter by tablespoons, without crowding. Fry until golden on bottom, 3 to 4 minutes. Turn and cook until brown on other side, about 2 minutes. Remove from wok and drain on paper towels. Repeat procedure 3 times with remaining batter.

362   CRANBERRY APPLE TOPPING
Prep: 10 minutes   Cook: 13 to 15 minutes   Serves: 4

Serve this sweet-tart fruit topping over ice cream or pound cake for dessert. It can double as a relish for Thanksgiving dinner as well.

½ cup apple juice
¼ cup spiced cranberry jelly
½ cup packed brown sugar
1 tablespoon minced fresh
    ginger
1 tablespoon lemon juice
1 teaspoon grated lemon zest

½ teaspoon cinnamon
½ teaspoon grated nutmeg
¼ teaspoon ground cloves
2 green apples, peeled and
    coarsely chopped
1 (12-ounce) bag fresh
    cranberries

1. In a wok, combine apple juice, cranberry jelly, brown sugar, ginger, lemon juice, lemon zest, cinnamon, nutmeg, and cloves. Bring to a boil, reduce heat to medium-low, and cook 5 minutes.

2. Add apples and cook until crisp-tender, 3 to 4 minutes. Add cranberries, cover, and cook until soft and skins begin to pop, 5 to 6 minutes. Remove to a bowl. Let cool to room temperature, then refrigerate until chilled before serving.

363   PEACHES WITH BRANDIED CUSTARD SAUCE
Prep: 10 minutes   Cook: 7 to 9 minutes   Serves: 4

1 (16-ounce) jar brandied
    peaches, juice reserved
1 cup milk
1 cup heavy cream
3 whole eggs

3 egg yolks
½ cup sugar
2 tablespoons lemon juice
1 teaspoon grated lemon zest
2 tablespoons cornstarch

1. Divide peaches among 4 dessert bowls. Set aside while you prepare sauce.

2. In a wok, combine reserved peach juice, milk, and cream. Cook over medium heat until hot, about 2 minutes. Remove to a measuring glass or heatproof bowl.

3. In a medium bowl, combine whole eggs, egg yolks, sugar, lemon juice, lemon zest, and cornstarch. Beat with portable electric mixer or whisk until light and thick, 3 to 5 minutes. Gradually whisk in warm peach cream and blend well. Return mixture to wok and cook over medium heat, stirring, until sauce just begins to boil, about 2 minutes. Pour sauce into a bowl. Place a sheet of plastic wrap directly on surface of sauce and refrigerate until cool. Ladle sauce over peaches and serve.

364   POACHED PEACH SAUCE
Prep: 10 minutes   Cook: 6 to 8 minutes   Serves: 4 to 6

This is a great way to use peaches when you're tired of eating them out of hand—or when you pick up a large basket of ripe fruit from your local farmer's market. This sauce is especially good over ice cream, pound cake, or fresh fruit.

⅔ cup granulated sugar
1 tablespoon lemon juice
1 teaspoon vanilla extract
1 teaspoon grated lemon zest

1 pound ripe peaches (about 4), peeled, halved, and pitted
¼ cup powdered sugar

1. In a wok, combine granulated sugar, lemon juice, vanilla, and lemon zest with 2 cups water. Bring to a boil over medium-high heat, stirring to dissolve sugar.

2. Add peaches. Reduce heat to medium-low and cook until fruit is tender, 6 to 8 minutes.

3. In a food processor or blender, puree peaches with ½ cup poaching liquid. Add more poaching liquid, if necessary, to achieve desired sauce consistency. Add powdered sugar and whisk to combine. Cover and refrigerate.

365   VANILLA CUSTARD
Prep: 10 minutes   Cook: 45 to 50 minutes   Serves: 4

2 cups scalded milk
½ teaspoon vanilla extract
3 eggs

⅓ cup sugar
1 tablespoon cornstarch

1. Grease 4 custard cups. In a medium bowl, combine hot milk and vanilla extract.

2. In a large bowl, lightly whisk eggs, sugar, and cornstarch. Gradually add hot milk to eggs, whisking constantly. Pour into custard cups.

3. Place a round wire (cake) rack in a wok. Put filled custard cups on rack. Pour boiling water into wok to reach halfway up sides of custard cups. Cover and cook over low heat until custard is firm and a knife inserted between center and rim comes out clean, 40 to 45 minutes. Remove filled cups from rack. Let cool before serving.

Index

Acknowledgments

This book is dedicated to Frank for helping me understand how much I have grown and to Leigh and David for their patience throughout. I thank my parents, Ben and Fran Letofsky, my sister Dr. Barbara Janoff, and all my friends, especially Polly Schnepf, Pat Tabibian, Dwayne Robinson, and W. Michael Boyer who shared their favorite recipes with me, for their support and enthusiasm. Special thanks to Susan Wyler, who gave me the opportunity for this project and encouraged me once again from inception to completion.

About the Author

Food writer, recipe developer, and culinary consultant Linda Drachman, whose articles have appeared in *Redbook* and *Food & Wine* magazines, is co-author of *Great Grains*.

To order any of the
365 Ways Cookbooks
visit your local bookseller or call 1-800-321-6890

Our bestselling **365 Ways Cookbooks** are wire-bound to lie flat and have colorful, wipe-clean Kivar® covers.

Each **365 Ways Cookbook** is $16.95 plus $3.50 per copy shipping and handling. Applicable sales tax will be billed to your account. No CODs. Please allow 4-6 weeks for delivery.

Please have your VISA, MASTERCARD or AMERICAN EXPRESS card at hand when calling.

• 365 •

Easy Italian Recipes 0-06-016310-0

Easy Low-Calorie Recipes 0-06-016309-7

Easy One-Dish Meals 0-06-016311-9

Great Barbecue & Grilling Recipes 0-06-016224-4

Great Chocolate Desserts 0-06-016537-5

Quick & Easy Microwave Recipes 0-06-016026-8

Snacks, Hors D'Oeuvres & Appetizers 0-06-016536-7

Ways to Cook Chicken 0-06-015539-6

Ways to Cook Fish and Shellfish 0-06-016841-2

Ways to Cook Hamburger & Other Ground Meats 0-06-016535-9

Ways to Cook Pasta 0-06-015865-4

Ways to Wok 0-06-016643-6

FORTHCOMING TITLES

Easy Chinese Recipes 0-06-016961-3

Great Cookies and Brownies 0-06-016840-4

Great Dessert Recipes 0-06-016959-1

Mexican Recipes 0-06-016963-X

Meatless Recipes 0-06-016958-3

20 Minute Menus 0-06-016962-1

Soups and Stews 0-06-016960-5

Ways to Prepare for Christmas 0-06-017048-4

Also available in a wire-bound format are:

The Bartender's Bible 0-06-016722-X $12.95
The Best Bread Machine Cookbook Ever 0-06-016927-3 $15.95